MODELS OF REALITY:

SHAPING THOUGHT AND ACTION

Jacques Richardson, Editor

Lomond Books
1984

Library of Congress Catalog Number: 83-80819

ISBN: 0-912338-35-0 (Clothbound)
      0-912338-36-9 (Microfiche)

More than half the chapters comprising the present volume appeared originally in Vol. 31, No. 4, of *impact of science on society*; Chapter 7, by J.N.R. Jeffers, is taken from *Nature and Resources*, Vol. XVII, No. 2; both © by the United Nations Educational, Scientific and Cultural Organization, 1981. This material is reproduced with the authorization of Unesco. Other chapters, copyright as indicated.

Composition by B. McGiffin and J. Moran.

Manufactured by Automated Graphic Systems, Inc.,
    White Plains, Maryland.

Published by Lomond
Publications, Inc., P.O. Box 88,
Mt. Airy, MD 21771

Published in cooperation
with Unesco, 7 place de
Fontenoy, 75700 Paris

Publisher's Foreword

This volume is the second in a series being published cooperatively by Lomond Publications and the United Nations Educational Scientific and Cultural Organization. It is based in part on an issue of the quarterly journal, *impact of science on society* (published by Unesco), which dealt with the theme, "Models, Tools for Shaping Reality." Here, the editor has added new material to the original effort, from both specially prepared and reprinted sources.

Models surround us, from the language we learn as infants to that of the computer; from our myths of conjecture on how the future might be; from the coins, banknotes, and chits and tokens we carry on our persons to the religious icons and monumental statuary occupying our places of culture; from the genetic code borne in the tiniest of cells to the diaries and ships' logs that man has filled since he learned to count and write. Model building and model use has proceeded beyond the simple prototypes of basic speech, icons and genetic code to the representation of many variables in a complex environment, rendered possible by the availability of contemporary mathematical science and electronic information technology.

The special contribution of this book is to bridge, for both amateur and expert, awareness of the nature of models and their use for a better understanding of the complex world in which we live. It is a remarkable set of papers assembled to explain and illustrate models of reality—physical, biological, social, economic, managerial, and political.

The publisher is pleased to have undertaken this significant joint project with Unesco. We consider *Models of Reality: Shaping Thought and Action* an important addition to our list of publications, and are grateful to Unesco and to the editor for the opportunity to produce this book.

We also extend our appreciation to the authors of the 21 chapters, and to original publishers for permission to include several papers as indicated in the text.

Lowell H. Hattery
Publisher

CONTENTS

PUBLISHER'S FOREWORD iii
LIST OF FIGURES xi
LIST OF TABLES xiii

PART 1. CONCEPT 1

Chapter 1   A Primer of Model Systems

by Jacques Richardson, Unesco 3

Defines, classifies, describes and explains models and their applications.

Chapter 2   The Earth as a System

by James Grier Miller and Jessie L. Miller, Center for Study of Democratic Institutions, USA 19

Presents a general theory of systems within the context of our planet as a "mixed living and nonliving system"; discusses its relationship to man and ecology and to policy making for the global system.

Chapter 3   The Determination of Form

by Hin Bredendieck, Georgia Institute of Technology, USA 51

Discusses "structure, form and position" from the perspective of designer and architect; proposes bilateral holism by attending to both "inside-out" and "outside-in" approaches.

Chapter 4   Some Principles of Mathematical Modeling
               by Blagovest Sendov, Kliment Ohridski
               University, Bulgaria 65

                   *A theoretical note on models, predictions, laws,
                   uncertainty and plausibility.*

Chapter 5   On Logic, Axioms, Theorems, Paradoxes
               and Proofs
               by Edward Jacobsen, Unesco 71

                   *Notes on the nature of mathematical models and
                   the problem of consistency.*

Chapter 6   An Interactive Modeling System as a Tool for
               Analyzing Complex Socio-economic Problems
               by Viktor A. Gelovani, Scientific Institute of
               Systems Research, USSR 75

                   *Cites the need for a "rational combination of
                   substantive methods with the formal modeling
                   of those aspects of development in which the
                   laws of change are sufficiently well known."
                   Describes the modeling methods at his institute.*

Chapter 7   The Development of Models in Urban and
               Regional Planning
               by J.N.R. Jeffers, Institute of Terrestrial
               Ecology, UK 87

                   *Suggests kinds of models and criteria for the
                   selection of models useful for decision-making
                   in Unesco's Man and the Biosphere Program,
                   with special attention to developing regions.*

Chapter 8   Social Models: Blueprints or Processes?
               by Graham R. Little, New Zealand 101

                   *Postulates a "process approach" to social
                   goal-setting.*

PART 2. APPLICATION 113

Chapter 9   Global Modeling in the 1980s
              by John M. Richardson, Jr., American
              University, USA 115

                  Outlines characteristics of global models and
                  several "widely discussed" models; offers an
                  agenda for global modeling during the decade.

Chapter 10   The Politics of Model Implementation
              by Kenneth L. Kraemer, University of
              California, Irvine, USA 131

                  A case study of the political environment of a
                  computerized fiscal-impact model for urban
                  planning.

Chapter 11   On Modeling, Limits and Understanding
              by Dennis Meadows, Dartmouth College, USA,
              interviewed by Geoffrey S. Holister, The
              Open University, UK 161

                  Comments on the validity and usefulness of
                  large economic models.

Chapter 12   Information Sources for Modeling the
              National Economy
              by Jay W. Forrester, Massachusetts Institute of
              Technology, USA 167

                  Describes the System Dynamics National Model,
                  which "draws on all classes of information for its
                  structure and policies," and its usefulness in
                  learning more about economic dynamics.

Chapter 13   Societal Use of Scientific and Technical
               Research: Existing and Alternative Models

               by Veronica Stolte-Heiskanen, University of
               Tampere, Finland 185

               *Speculates about the use of models in directing
               scientific and technical research to the solution of
               social/scientific problems (population challenge,
               energy challenge, environment challenge,
               nuclear challenge).*

Chapter 14   Simulating a Small Nation's International
               Scientific Contacts: An Evaluative Analysis

               by Pál Tamás, Institute of Sociology,
               Hungary 209

               *Explores the possible advantages and short-
               comings for a nation's scientific community in
               terms of access to study and training abroad,
               using as a model Hungary in the post-war years.*

Chapter 15   Uses and Limitations of Models in Policy
               Planning and Evaluation

               by Rahat Nabi Khan, Consultant, India 231

               *Defines and gives examples of the application
               of "system models" and "process models" to
               economics, demographics and other areas.*

Chapter 16   Micro-operational Research: A Simple
               Modeling Tool for Managers

               by James Clayson, The American College in
               Paris, France 247

               *Designing and applying "simple, heuristic"
               models, not necessarily expressed mathematically,
               for use by managers. Case example: location of
               warehouses by a French firm.*

Chapter 17   Models in Science Education

by George Marx, Eötvös University, and
Esther Tóth, Jószef Attila Grammar School,
Hungary 265

*Delineates the use of physical models and
games in the teaching of science in elementary
and secondary schools.*

Chapter 18   The Brain Builders

by Alissa Swerdloff, Writer, USA 277

*Creation and use of a computerized model to
further the understanding of the brain and its
workings.*

Chapter 19   Quantum Physics: The Power and Mystery of
the Subatomic World

by the Editors of *The Economist,* UK 285

*Explication of the quantum theory, one of
the most important hypothetical models
in modern science.*

Chapter 20   A New Model of Time, A New View of Physics

by Ilya Prigogine, Nobel Prize winner in
physics, and Isabelle Stengers, University
of Brussels, Belgium 303

*Analyzes the transition to new models
(of interrogation rather than certainties) in
physics and appraises the impacts of these
new models.*

Chapter 21   Models of Reality

by Geoffrey S. Holister, The Open
University,UK 317

*A concluding note on the nature and
validity of the simulation of reality.*

LIST OF FIGURES

Figure   3:1   Gruen Wrist-watch 54

         2   Samson Tandem Toaster .55

         3   Capitol Building, Washington, DC 56

         4   Early Radio 56

         5   Pendulum Clock 57

         6   Werkbund Building, Cologne 58

         7   Volkswagen 58

Figure   6:1   Functional Block Diagram of an Interactive
                  Modeling System 81

Figure 10:1   Implementation Guide to the Irvine
                  Economic Model 134

Figure 12:1   Mental Data Base and Decreasing Content
                  of Written and Numerical Data Bases 169

         2   Content of the Mental Data Base 170

         3   Three Prior Background Developments from
                  Which System Dynamics Emerges 176

         4   Creating a System Dynamics Model 177

Figure 13:1   Identification of Emerging Issues or Problems . . .193

Figure 15:1   Simplified Systems Model 232

         2   A Communications Process Model 233

         3   Web of Complexity in the Conversion of
                  Tropical Forest to Cattle Pasture 234

4   Population Pyramids for India and Sweden 240

5   Logistic Curve of Growth 241

6   A Model of the British Educational System 244

Figure 16:1   Sales Data for France by Department 256

2   Computer Map of France 256

3   Quartile Map 1 257

4   Quartile Map 2 258

5   Quartile Map 3 259

6   Unmodified Distribution Patterns 260

7   Pattern Showing Where Delivery Costs are
           Above National Average 261

Figure 19:1   A Simple Josephson Switch 299

Figure 20:1   Understanding the Three Laws of
           Thermodynamics 306

2   The Divergence or Bifurcation Parameter 312

LIST OF TABLES

Table 1:1   Some of the Features Characterizing a Dozen
              Different Model Systems 4

       2   Examples of Forecasts or Scenarios of a
              New Life in Years to Come 8

       3   Modeling a Problem-solving, Dynamic Model 13

Table 2:1   The 19 Critical Subsystems of a Living System ...27

       2   Examples of Variables and Indicators of the
              Living Systems in the Earth System 41

Table 8:1   Two Opposing Points of View 109

Table 10:1   Summary of Irvine General Plan Options 136

       2   Population Density by Options 142

Table 14:1   Scientific Experience Abroad, by Type of
              Research Institution 214

       2   Scientific Experience Abroad, by Social
              Background of Respondents 216

       3   Knowledge of Foreign Langusges by
              Level and Respondents' Type of Research
              Institution (percent) 219

       4   Scientific Experience Abroad, by Age of
              Respondents 220

       5   Scientific Experience Abroad, by Sexes of
              Respondents 222

       6   Scientific Experience Abroad, According to
              Academic Degree 223

7   International Cooperation, Scientific Experience
           According to Academic Degree 224

8   Typology of Scientific Trips, According
           to Purpose 225

9   International Cooperation, Scientific Experience
           According to Respondent's Experience Abroad . .227

10   Typologies of International Cooperation, by
           Types of Research 228

Table 15:1 Three Numerical Models of Indian
           Development 236

2   Matrices of Gross Flows 242

PART 1. CONCEPT

The models we use in daily life and professional activity are grouped into a dozen varieties, from small-scale replicas to highly complex global depictions which must be developed by interdisciplinary research teams having access to large computer systems. We use models to simplify the complex, to understand otherwise elusive processes or systems, to plan business, teaching, environmental control, broad-based strategy, and especially to help us solve problems of every kind.

Chapter 1

A PRIMER OF MODEL SYSTEMS

Jacques G. Richardson

Samples and Symbols

Why a book on models and simulations? What does an examination of the modeling process add to our appreciation of the reality of an object or system transformed into a simile of itself? And how does one avoid distraction by the model from the reasons leading us to seek and build a model as the means better to understand a structure or process and how it functions? There seem to be several answers to these questions. This chapter and the one following use different approaches, but each response helps to shed light on the mind's endeavor to translate a complex shape or mechanism into another, simpler form in order better to appreciate the genuine original, the purpose it serves, or how it works. Table 1 is a summary of these responses, a typology of the dozen kinds of model, with a comparative evaluation of their various

The author has served since 1972 as editor of the Unesco quarterly journal, *impact of science on society*, currently published in Arabic, Chinese, English, French, Russian and Spanish editions. His address is Unesco SC, 7 place de Fontenoy, 75700 Paris, France.

characteristics. The types of model proffered are: analogy, caricature, computer, design, forecast, holism, life, paradigm perfection, sample, scale, simplification and symbolism.[1] Let us examine each of the dozen models shown.

Table 1. Some of the features characterizing a dozen different model systems.

Type \ Feature	Detail	Completeness	Comprehensibility	General Appropriateness	Objectivity	Subjectivity	Complexity	Reliability
Analogy	Medium	Medium	Medium	Medium	Medium	High	Medium	Medium
Caricature	Low	Low	Medium	Medium	Medium	High	Low	Medium
Computer	High	High	High	High	High	Low	High	High
Design	Medium	High	High	High	Medium	Medium	High	High
Forecast	Low	Low	Medium	Low	Medium	Medium	High	Low
Holism	High	High	?	High	High	?	High	High
Life	High	Medium	High	Medium	High	Low	High	Medium
Paradigm Perfection	High	High	Medium	High	High	Low	High	Medium
Sample	Medium	Low	High	Medium	Medium	High	Low	Medium
Scale	Medium	–	High	Medium	High	Low	–	High
Simplification	Low	Medium	High	Medium	High	Medium	Low	High
Symbolism	Medium	Low	High	High	High	Low	Low	High

The model by *sample* extends from the tasting of a grape or the probing of a vegetable at market to the checking of a manufactured item emerging from an industrial batch process or to a public opinion poll ("polls, those maddening instruments of democracy"[2]) intended to sound popular reactions to the stability or mobility of a political situation. A referendum or plebiscite is a much larger scale sampling of the same variety. The reader will readily think of other kinds of samples directly related to his or her vocational interests, whether in economic theory, experimental research, energy calculation, or the selection of paints for bridge protection or street markings.

A second type of modeling, recognized by anyone needing to resolve an enigma, is the *symbolism* to be found mainly in mathematics—

arithmetic, algebra, geometry, trigonometry and calculus—as well as in studies of logic and decision. As young students we learned to express the Pythagorean theorem as $a^2 + b^2 = c^2$, a tidy specimen of the model of a model. The conventional signs used by cartographers and the makers of highway and street markers, and the plimsoll lines to mark loading limits for cargo ships, in addition to the devices used by sports referees and the blazes cut by foresters and planters, are further species of this simulation process. The pieces or "men" associated with chess and other board games are still another example of symbolism, each having its own mathematical value in terms of playing force; in this case, one model is surmounted on another. Codes, ciphers and other cryptography are further illustrations of symbolistic models of reality; these generate, in turn, new models meant to solve the problems they pose—the complex logico-mathematical field of cryptanalysis. Symbols put to work to solve other complexities have enabled René Thom to elaborate his catastrophe theory and, more recently, other researchers to formulate the new theory of chaos—which helps remove the randomness long ascribed to processes such as the formation of smoke or changes in the weather.

An elusive symbolic representation of reality is found in the recent probable solution of the classic "simplex algorithm" used in agricultural, other biological, engineering and some sociological problemsolving. This algorithm is a computing method to solve linear programming problems often involving thousands of inequalities (e.g. selecting purchasing sources in order to minimize costs of product distribution, or maximizing the availability throughout a regional hospital system of whole blood for transfusion). These problems can be translated geometrically into a search for vertices of multidimensional polygons, the boundaries of which are established by the constraints bearing on the problems to be solved.[3] The simplex method is intended to find the probable optimal vertex. Operational research and system analysis use such algorithms extensively, the general methodology deriving largely from the analysis required in military systems and similar large operating complexes which require highly detailed planning and programming.[4]

In non-mathematical symbolism, the plastic arts, photography, radiography, television, and imagery by satellite are means whereby objects and their movement can be analogized by manual or by chemico- or electromechanical means.

Simplification, Analogy and Design

Simulation also takes the form of *simplification*, such as schemas of the construction and dynamics of the atom and its particles, the molecule and other structures at the sub-cellular level, as well as of the cosmos as a whole. Simplification helps us better to visualize the microscopic and to reduce the macroscopic—for example city plans, regional topography shown in colors, or underground mineral deposits marked by simple signs—to manageable proportions. Other forms of simplification include diagrams of radio circuits, or instructions for the use of a household device, machine tool or private automobile. The printed instructions for a board or electronic game are, indeed, excellent examples of a simplified model of a more complex counterpart. A highly detailed form of simplification (if these terms are not mutually contradictory) is found in current work on artificial intelligence, the literature of which is already abundant: see the comments, further on, dealing with computer simulation.[5]

When simplification is undesirable or possibly misleading (such as the modeling of the lunar surface preparatory to a manned or unmanned landing[6]), *analogy* is another type of simulation. Most familiar in this category are electronic circuit diagrams, telephone networks,[7] highway and other maps[8] and those depicting municipal transport or sewage systems; clocks, odometers, tachometers, balances, strain gauges, thermometers and virtually every other metrological device; directional compasses, gyroscopes and surveying instruments; and certain mathematical and computer models. Also included are musical scores, mechanical recordings and electronic transcriptions.

Another kind of analogic model is the familiar vocal puzzle, frequently larded with simple humor: What is black and white, and re[a]d all over? Response: a newspaper. . . Strategic games—whether for purposes of national economic planning,[9] management of natural resources, military exercises, or just for fun—also fit into this category of rigorously organized make-believe. The measurement devices previously mentioned can also be incorporated within this classification. A very recent type of analogy is Benoit Mandelbrot's fractals, which are interpreted Koch curves used to depict schematically coastlines, expressions in linguistics, mathematics and aerodynamics.[10] Statistical analogy as used in econometrics is a painstaking reduction to numbers of a vastly complicated field—economics and its myriad applications.[11]

Yet another sort of modeling concentrates on *design*: how a process, product, conceptional schema, or service should be constructed so as to best serve its intended purpose. Examples include national health insurance systems, blueprints for a building or other forms of civil engineering,[12] manufacturing processes, personnel management and career development plans, budgeting in its many variants, tax programs, demographic patterns, census-taking and voting operations, patents, the exploitation/conservation of natural resources,[13] the development of national power and other energy grids, the conception and formulation of research projects, and many others.

An improved case or housing for a familiar implement, such as a steam iron, insulated pincers or power saw, also fits this category, as does the associated field of ergonomics. Ergonomics is the combined esthetic-pragmatic approach to the designing of tools and instruments so that they conform to the shape and function of the human body; ergonomics finds, in turn, application to robotics, the technique of tool-wielding machines which themselves are modeled on man and his use of simple or complex tool arrays.[14] A final specimen of design is, alas, the war plan: a complex of putative strategies dependent on interacting contingencies applying to "our" side as well as the adversary.

Scale, Forecast and Paradigm Perfection

One of the most familiar kinds of model emulates the scalar aspect of reality, or simply, *scale*. As infants and children, we have all been treated by our elders to toys which, often in a colorful and cunning fashion, model the reality of the everyday world. Their smallness and maneuverability intrigue the developing mind, and they invite the child to recreate real-life situations in play—as in the case of dolls, amulets, small tools and miniature household artifacts. Later, beginning approximately at the age of reason, the child reproduces in play situations similar to those found in the family, at school, in places of worship or other cultural heritage, even in play itself (as in the case of very young children copying the play of youths). Scale assumes increasingly complex proportions as children are introduced to mechanical toys and play ensembles requiring equipment which can be made by themselves or their parents or else bought in shops.

Scale is also expressed in the familiar table models used by architects and town and regional planners, by designers of automobiles and chemical engineering facilities, and by planners of museum, gallery and world's fair exhibits. These are compact, economical, and absorbed in a sweep of the eye.[15]

Forecasts and scenarios are models which have existed, in one form or other, since antiquity (see Table 2). Today, they include the weather predicted for the next few days,[16] actuarial tables used by life insurance groups, health and retirement schemes, manpower requirements and business plans, analyses of anticipated economic development,[17] predicted results of horse races and other sporting events, seismological

Table 2. Examples of forecasts or scenarios of a new life in years to come. Some of the first known prophesies are Plato's *Republic* (4th century B.C.), a legend set in an idealized community, Euphemerus' *Sacred History* (300 B.C.) and Plutarch's *Life of Lycurgus* (about 100 A.D.), an essay on a new Sparta. More's work of fourteen centuries later was followed quickly by Doni's *I Mondi* (1552), Patrizi's *La Città Felice* (a year later), and Campanella's *La Città del Sole* (1602). The past century has been especially rich in utopian prognostics of the kind, including the Russian poetry of Khlebnikov (early 20th century), and the initiatives remain largely in the European cultures.

Enterprise	Source	Date	Main Feature	Strong Point	Weak Point	Comprehensiveness	Locus
Brothers of Common Life	Groot	c.1380	Christian community	Crafts and labor for common good	Seemed contermovement to mendicancy	Limited appeal	Utrecht
Utopia	More	1516	Christian communism	Incentives, restraints, return to nature	Fantasy	Appeal to reason	Great Britain
New Atlantis	Bacon	1627	Scientific program			Speculative of religion, philosophy	Great Britain
Communitarian colonies	Mennonites	1663	Religious cooperatives	Faith and zeal	Few in number		Holland, Germany, USA
Gulliver's Travels	Swift	1726	Satire	"Practical solutions"	Ridicule	World travel depicted	Great Britain
L'An 2440	Mercier	1770	Speculation			Anticipated Revolution	France
Communes	Fournier, Cabet	1840 -60	"Utopian socialism"	Exposed the limitations of economic planning		Limited appeal	France
Oneida communities	Noyes	1848	"Bible communism"	"Complex marriage"	"Complex marriage"	Limited appeal	USA
Das Kapital	Marx	1867	"Scientific socialism"	Foundation on reason	Disregarded individual motivation	Near-thorough	Germany, Great Britain, Russia
The Coming Race	Bulwer-Lytton	1871	Satire	Total elimination of economics		Ridicule of existing conditions	Great Britain
Bruderhof	Christian Protestant beginnings	19th century	Social association	Communal religion			Germany, Paraguay, Great Britain, USA

Jewish Nation	Herzl	End of century	State socialism	Jewish orthodoxy	Non-Jews cannot govern	Struggle v. anti-semitism	Austro-Hungary, Palestine
Essays	K'ang Yuwei	1858-1927	Philosophy of world unity	Peace; no social distinctions			China
Looking Backward	Bellamy	1887	Futuristic novel	Forecast of technological modernism	Author without technical background	Present confirms prophesy	USA
Freiland; A Visit to Freeland	Hertzka	1890; 1891	Novel of "social anticipation"				Austro-Hungary
Foma Gordeyev; Mother	Gorky	1900; 1907	Proletarian novels	Portrayals of the bitterness of poverty lent a certain monotony		Reflections of broad social consciousness	Russia
The Iron Heel; My; We	London; Zamyatin	1907; 1924; 1925	Novels of ridicule				USA, Soviet Union
Futurism	Marinetti	1909	Art movement	Constructive new ideas in art	Glorification of war; total rejection of the past	Limited appeal	Paris, New York
Kibbutzim	Origins in Zionism	1909	Collective settlements	Security and defense	Starkness of environment	Limited to a single nation	Palestine
Brave New World	Huxley	1932	Satire	Dystopian analysis	Exaggerated irony		Mainly Europe
Nazi architecture[a]	Speer	1930s	Invocation of 1000-year state	Created employment	Served a warped autocrat	Sustained a national effort only	Germany
Nineteen Eighty-Four[b]	Orwell	1949	Ironical satire of tyranny	Related closely to technological evolution	Depicted ghastly future through social engineering	Thorough, and utterly frightening	World
A Clockwork Orange	Burgess	1962; 1970	Novel and film of brutal satire	Related closely to biomedical evolution	Ascribed negative motives to youth	Limited	Great Britain
Limits to Growth[c]	Forester, Meadows, Meadows	1972	Computer-based accounting	Imperative for resource conservation	Incomplete data	Global in sweep	World
The Fate of the World	Schell	1982	Portrayal of nuclear holocaust is credible	Scenario depicting destruction of New York	Lack of balancing preventive actions	Overlooked role and function of UN	USA; World

a. See Albert Speer's memoirs and esp. Bernhard Leitner, Albert Speer, the Architect (trans. Sophie Wilkins), October, No. 20, Spring 1982.

b. For a "re-visit" in advance to the year 1984, see Impact of Science on Society, vol. 33, no. 2 (entire issue), April-June 1983.

c. A considerably revised perspective in the context of the analyses undertaken by the Club of Rome, of which Limits to Growth was the first, is to be found in John M. Richardson, Jr., Making It Happen, 1982.

precautions and various preventive measures intended to combat or attenuate the effects of both natural and artificial disasters. Technological forecasting, embracing what is called social audit or risk (impact) assessment, is another kind of analytical prevision—this variety dating from about fifteen years ago.[18] Even clairvoyant science fiction (including the daily horoscope) belongs to this group.

In man's quest for perfectibility, he has long sought to idealize his social environment by developing sets of rules to be observed by him and his neighbors. Rules frequently become generalized and codified as laws—the ultimate expression of *perfection of the paradigm* of societal behavior. As in the case of many an ethic, however, rules and laws are assumed by man ultimately to be bent or broken, or not observed at all. Paradigm perfection, whether expressed by Lao-tse, Plato, St. Augustine, Rousseau, Adam Smith, Condorcet, Thoreau, Hitler, Guevara, and similar historical figures, is the search for a model to which (its author believes) every man aspires: of which he dreams, for which he may be willing to die or kill, but on which he himself is sometimes the first to infringe.

Laws, like other categories of model, are thus optimal constructions. They are intended to dissuade thievery, murder, war crimes and the full panoply of evil of which man is otherwise capable, individually or collectively. "A lock on the door," a colleague is fond of saying, "is intended to keep an honest person honest." The locked door (safe, bank, armory, nuclear power plant, mint, prime minister's cabinet, or an entire national territory) is consequently a dissuasive example meant to adduce restraint or inertia on the part of strangers to the site who might tend to break the rules if left to their own devices.[19] Paradigm perfection extends, as well, to social concepts such as etiquette (models of common courtesy between both friends and strangers), codes for the comportment of members of the liberal professions (Hippocrates' oath and the more transcultural medical practitioners' oath developed recently by the World Health Organization), national codifications of both civil and criminal law, the prototypes for a codex of war crimes set forth at Nurenberg and Tokyo in the late 1940s, codes of action on the part of transnational enterprises ("multinational" corporations), and the Law of the Sea elaborated during the 1970s and early 1980s.[20]

Life Models, Caricature, Computerization

Because the human body and its vital constituents do not lend themselves for ethical reasons to laboratory testing and experimentation, alternative *life models* have been devised.[21] These are common in psychology, pathology and pharmacology, running the gamut from tests on alternative cell and organ systems to macro-scale testing of group reactions to measurable conditions. Experiments done on the brains of white mice or chimpanzees and the heart or skin of a pig, or the pancreas of the dog, are among the most commonly used in etiology and pathology, because of the similarity in the reactions of the bestial organs to those in the human being. Testing in clinical pharmacology and cosmetic manufacture is almost never done on humans; instead, a variety of rodents, fowl and other animals serve as, literally, guinea pigs—living models subjected to destructive testing.

On the group scale, experiments are designed around subjects such as rats, cats and monkeys: these serve as man's surrogates too. The efficacy, economy and morality of using models of this nature are variable. Common ethics, however, makes their use customary if not mandatory.[22] In some cases, on the other hand, man himself is the model in testing group reactions (to prisoner status, "brain washing," life in professional isolation, e.g. living in the Antarctic or working on petroleum exploration platforms); here man is the model *sine qua non*.

In an entirely different embodiment, models fall into a type we can call *caricature*. This comprises the metaphors and similes of everyday speech, comic strips and political cartoons, effigies (and their burning), history, biography and a variety of dramatic creations (whether allegory, satire, parody or serious comedy), buffoonery and low comedy, sound-and-light spectacles and other material replication of history. All of these are studied depictions of the human condition and its course through the ages.

As the present volume was being assembled, several colleagues commented that surely the book would deal exclusively with *computer models*. ("What other models are there today?" a friend asked). We have chosen, however, to leave detailed discussion of simulations by digital or analog computer to specialists in informatics—of whom there are increasingly more, as there is of their output, each year. We have also been guided by the experience and wisdom of such specialists as C.S. Holling (a Canadian ecologist), director of the International Institute of Applied Systems Analysis (IIASA) at Laxenburg, Austria, and István Kiss, a Hungarian who directs the Bureau for Systems Analysis of the State Office for Technical Development in Budapest; they are among those who believe that we are still far from perfecting models, that new approaches to simulation remain to be developed, and that these must be far more holistic than ever before.[23] (For the present, suffice it to say that computers cannot yet model the infinitely large—just as they cannot yet model the infinitely small.)

From Reductionism to Holism

Indeed, many species of models evolved thus far have been characterized by an almost unfailing application of reductionism: a systematic, Cartesian disassembly of the real thing into its organizational elements. This has applied to such complex positivist processes as global problems and the corresponding models to "solve" them, yet many of us are aware that simply identifying problems by systematic typology of their constituents still leaves us far from coherent synthesis of the responses to such problems. A more holistic approach is indeed required, for "There is no reliable, complete information about the degree to which the earth's physical environment can absorb and meet the needs of further growth in population and capital. There is a great deal of partial information, which optimists read optimistically and pessimists read pessimistically."[24]

Which forms should a "more holistic" method assume? Some of the chapters which follow furnish useful clues and, in their aggregate, provide a synergetic lead as to what holism, in the future, might well include. Edward Jacobsen's brief essay hyperbolizes, as it were, symbolism and its flaws, while Hin Bredendieck's approach reflects a more classical view of design seen through reductionism. Ilya Prigogine and Isabelle Stengers, as well as Alissa Swerdloff express the novelty which radical departures from received ideas can bring to our reasoning. Prigogine and Stengers, for example, interpret some aspects of physics (i.e., statistical mechanics and thermodynamics) as a social science, with the randomness and flexibility that sociology implies. Swerdloff recounts some of the complexity confronted by Rudolfo Llinás and his colleagues in simulating the architecture and decision-making associated with the human brain.

In a somewhat different domain, Veronica Stolte-Heiskanen brings managerial rationale to the planning and execution of systematic research and development—another case of a model's model.[25] John Richardson, Geoffrey Holister, Viktor Gelovani, R.N. Khan and other authors emphasize the interdisciplinary and global considerations required in the pondering of contemporary and future problem-solving models.

Dynamic models (or systems, as they are usually called) seem therefore to be in the midst of shift of paradigm. In elaborating a model, we often ask key questions meant to help construct the coherence required (a model of the so-called *problématique*); see Table 3.

The images we have conjured in the past in order to answer such interrogation have been, as we have seen, essentially Cartesian in their historical scientific development. Their very formulation helped develop our powers of analytical thinking (indeed, René Descartes' analytical geometry was among the first such paradigms), but this concentration on analysis tended to inhibit a process of holistic thinking.[26]

Table 3. Modeling a problem-solving, dynamic model.

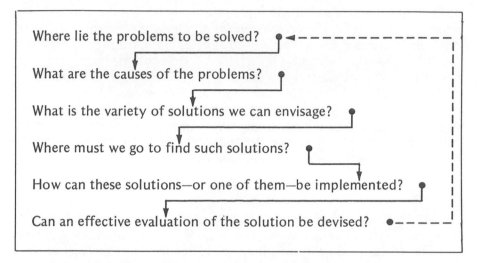

Where lie the problems to be solved?

What are the causes of the problems?

What is the variety of solutions we can envisage?

Where must we go to find such solutions?

How can these solutions—or one of them—be implemented?

Can an effective evaluation of the solution be devised?

Leading the Right Brain to Complement the Left Half

Roger Sperry, who won a Nobel Prize for his investigations on the working of the brain's halves, contends that society seems to be founded on the functioning of the left cerebral hemisphere (attention to detail, critical analysis). But Sperry also believes that novel solutions to both old and new problems will be based on the more abstractive operations of the brain's right hemisphere. These may, in turn, present the brain with not only a better choice of possibilities of action—selecting the solution most appropriate to the problem—but also an entirist, optimal perspective in choosing the option (the model) corresponding to the requirements as defined by the *problématique*.

As a consequence of such paradigm shifts, projections of what new simulations might resemble comprise what has been called the general equilibrium model. As applied to agriculture, for instance, Kirit Parikh of IIASA explains that this model is in equilibrium "because physical quantities of commodities are in balance. It is in 'general' equilibrium because. . .monetary valuations of countries and of individual producers and consumers are in balance. The important thing. . .is that since all countries are included, there are no infinite sources or sinks of goods and currency. Therefore the true effects of feedback from policy decisions cannot be masked."[27]

There has been an effort in recent years to approach a general equilibrium in the political, economic and other social previsional modeling which deals with the world as a whole. A good example of the approach is found in *Forecasting in International Relations*,[28] an interdisciplinary reader whose specialized authors come from East and West, North and South; a second is illustrated by Unesco's Medium-Term Plan for the period January 1984-December 1989;[29] a third, necessarily colored exemplar in this line of endeavor is *Science and Future Choice*, a view of evolving science, technology and society as seen in the politico-military outlook of the North Atlantic Treaty Organization.[30] The Warsaw Pact powers have undoubtedly prepared analogous material, but this is not available to the uninitiated.

* * * * *

These, then, are some of the ways by which the human mind is likely to continue adjusting the simulations and other models it creates in order to (a) give form to reality, (b) concentrate on analysis in order to identify and measure certain problems to be solved, and (c) proceed to make the solutions become reality.

FOOTNOTES

[1] Because most of these varieties of model use mathematics in their exposition, the "mathematical model" is not classified separately. See "symbolism."

[2] Quoted from Richard Reeves, writing on Alexis de Tocqueville.

[3] A good description of the problem and its solution, written by Gina Kolata, is found in *Science*, Vol. 217, 2 July 1982. Peter Atkins, the physical chemist, has commented that "the universe can be described mathematically: mathematics is a system of logic. . . .In a sense, mathematics mimics the ultimate structure. A formula written on a page is an expression of a particular group of relationships embedded in the structure of spacetime." P.W. Atkins, *The Creation*, San Francisco: W.H. Freeman, 1981, p. 108.

[4] See Hugh J. Miser, "Operations Research and Systems Analysis," *Science*, Vol. 209, 4 July 1980.

[5] For a good description of work being done in artificial intelligence, see John Haugeland

(ed.), *Mind Design*, Montgomery, Vermont, Bradford Books, 1981. See also Tom Alexander, "Computers on the Road to Self-Improvement," *Fortune*, 14 June 1982, p. 148, and Andrew Pollack, "The Selling of 'Artificial Intelligence,'" *International Herald-Tribune* (New York Times Service), 23 September 1982.

[6] It is worth noting, however, that the cosmological model used to plan and calculate both manned flights to the moon and unmanned exploration of the planets is that of Newtonian mechanics (a model now more than three centuries old) rather than that of the more highly perfected relativist physics of Einstein, from our century.

[7] Probably the best semi-popularization published to date on telephonic communication is John R. Pierce, *Signals, The Telephone and Beyond*, San Francisco: W.H. Freeman, 1981.

[8] An enjoyable study of mapping from antiquity to the age of extraterrestrial exploration is John Noble Wilford, *The Mapmakers*, New York: Random House, 1981.

[9] Current application is found, for example, within President François Mitterrand's government of Jacques Attali's *La Nouvelle Economie Française*, Paris: Flammarion, 1978.

[10] See Benoit Mandelbrot, *Les objets fractals, forme, hasard et dimension*, Paris: Flammairon, 1975; *The Fractal Geometry of Nature*, San Francisco: W.H. Freeman, 1982; and Bruce Schecter, "A New Geography of Nature," *Discover*, June 1982.

[11] A classical example of detailed econometric analysis is Wassily Leonticf, *et al.*, *The Future of the World Economy, A United Nations Study*, New York: Oxford University Press, 1977.

[12] Manfred Wehdorn, *Die Bautechnik der Wiener Ringstrasse*, Wiesbaden: Franz Steiner Verlag, 1979, is an informative text supported by 230 excellent illustrations dealing with the systematic reconstruction of central Vienna during the 19th century.

[13] For example, Rory Thompson, "A Tidal Pump to Raise Water from the Ocean's Depths," *Speculations in Science and Technology*, Vol. 5, No. 3, 1982.

[14] For a thorough exposition of this relatively new field, see *Scientific American*, September 1982 (entire issue, on the theme of The Mechanization of Work).

[15] For a critical analysis of scale surpassing that of man, see Kirkpatrick Sale, *Human Scale*, London: Secker & Warburg, 1980.

[16] See Andrei S. Monin, *Weather Forecasting As A Problem in Physics* (trans. Paul Superak), Cambridge, Mass.: MIT Press, 1972, published originally as *Prognoz Pogody Kak Zadachu Fiziki*, Moscow, Nauka, 1969; Konrad Cehak, "A Markov-Chain Model for Winter-strength in the Upper Danube Region," *Climatic Change*, Vol. 4, No. 3, 1982.

[17] For example, Thomas E. Jones, *Options for the Future*, New York, Praeger, 1980; Willis W. Harman, *An Incomplete Guide to the Future*, San Francisco: San Francisco Book Co. (The Portable Stanford Series), 1976; and *Global Models, World Futures and Public Policy: A Critique* (ref. OTA R-165), Washington: Office of Technology Assessment, 1982.

[18] Consult Clark C. Abt, *The Social Audit for Management*, New York: American Management Associations, 1977.

[19] *Cf.* Robert Nisbet, *History of the Idea of Progress*, New York: Basic Books, 1980; London: Heinemann Education Books, 1981. It was Henry David Thoreau (1817-1862) who ironically described the model of urban life as "millions of people being lonesome together." For an interesting disquisition concerning "philosophical thoughts on social action," see Martin Hollis, *Models of Man*, Cambridge, Cambridge University Press, 1977. A work which links "the pursuits of science and the overall ethical and moral concerns of society" is Valentin F. Turchin, *The Phenomenon of Science* (trans. Brand Frentz), New York: Columbia University Press, 1977. Another work of the same class is Loren R. Graham, *Between Science and Values*, New York: Columbia University Press, 1981.

[20] The Law of the Sea, which remains to be ratified by all the States taking part in its formulation, has been reported in detail by the mass media during its long years of negotiation. One of the Law's lesser known aspects deals with national navies and the power which they

represent. A useful appreciation of the new ocean order in regard to navies and their missions is found in Mark W. Janis, *Sea Power and the Law of the Sea*, Lexington, Mass.: D.C. Heath and Co., 1976.

[21] These are not to be confused with the familiar living model in the artist's studio.

[22] A discussion of the problem appears in Joanne Linnerooth, "The Value of Human Life: A Review of the Models," a research report issued by the International Institute of Applied Systems Analysis in June 1980 (doc. RR-80-25), reprinted from *Economic Inquiry*, Vol. 17, 1979. See also Michael Bliss, *The Discovery of Insulin*, Toronto: McClelland & Stewart, 1982.

[23] See, in this respect, Gerald I. Susman and Roger D. Evered, "An Assessment of the Scientific Merits of Action Research," *Administrative Science Quarterly*, Vol. 23, December 1978, and Peter Checkland, *Systems Thinking, Systems Practice*, Chichester: John Wiley & Sons Ltd., 1981. In both works, analytical criticism is made of the positivist, reductionist approaches used to arrive at complete understanding of natural and behavioral phenomena and of the systemic modeling of these.

[24] A thorough dissection of global modeling seen from the overall perspective is found in Donella Meadows, John Richardson and Gerhart Bruckmann, *Groping in the Dark, The First Decade of Global Modelling*, Chichester: John Wiley & Sons Ltd., 1981. The quotation is taken from p. xviii. Another, comparative, analysis is Magda C. McHale, *Ominous Trends and Valid Hopes*, Minneapolis: University of Minnesota, and Houston: American Leadership Forum, 1981.

[25] Models and systems related to the planning of research and development can be found in *R&D Management* (a periodical published by Basil Blackwell). For another specific approach to the modeling of research, see T. Higgins, *Research Training and Innovation*, Dublin: Stationery Office, 1977.

[26] No less a contemporary thinker than François Mitterrand has indicated that "I like those who ask themselves questions, I am wary of those who find answers," as he has written in *The Wheat and the Chaff*, New York: Seaver/Lattès, 1982 (a compendium of two earlier works published by Flammarion: Paris).

[27] K. Parikh, "Searching for Ways to A Hunger-Free World" (interview with Bradley Hitchings), *Options*, Winter 1982; K. Parikh, Ferenc Rabár (eds.), *Food for All in A Sustainable World: the IIASA Food and Agriculture Program*, Laxemburg: IIASA, 1981.

[28] Nazli Choucri, Thomas W. Robinson (eds.), *Forecasting in International Relations: Theory, Methods, Problems, Prospects*, San Francisco, W.H. Freeman, 1978.

[29] *Medium-Term Plan (Approved)* (doc. 22C/4), Paris: Unesco, 1983.

[30] Philip W. Hemily, M.N. Özdas (eds.), *Science and Future Choice* (2 vols.), Oxford: Clarendon Press, 1979.

To delve more deeply into the universe of models

AZOUVI, F. "Woman as a Model of Pathology in the Eighteenth Century," *Diogenes*, No. 115, Fall, 1981.

BERLEKAMP, E.; J. CONWAY and R. GUY. *Winning Ways* (2 vols.), London, Academic Press, 1982.

"Beware the Pitfalls, A Short Guide to Avoiding Common Errors in System Analysis" (Executive Report 2) (pamphlet), Laxenburg, IIASA, May 1980.

BISWAS, A.K., "World Models, Resources, and Environment," *Environmental Conservation*, Vol. 6, No. 1., 1979.

BRAUDEL, F. *La Méditerranée et le monde méditerranéen à l'époque de Philippe II* (rev.), Paris, Armand Colin, 1966; *The Mediterranean and the Mediterranean World in the Age of Philip II*, London, William Collins Sons & Co., 1972.

CHAUVIN, R.; B. CHAUVIN. *Le modèle animal*, Paris, Hachette, 1982.

DeJULIO, S.; A. RUBERTI. *Systems Sciences and Modeling* (Trends in Scientific Research series, Unesco monographs), Oxford, Pergamon, 1982.

EIGEN, M.; R. WINKLER. *The Laws of the Game*, London, Allen Lane, 1982.

FISCHER, R. "Matter's Mastermind: the Model-Making Brain," *Diogenes*, No. 116, Winter 1981.

GEIGER, M. "Game Simulation for the Resolution of Conflicts in Planning Policy," *International Social Science Journal*, No. 3, 1975.

HACKETT, J. *The Third World War, A Future History*, London, Sidgwick and Jackson, 1978.

HAPGOOD, F. "Seekers of the Golden Form," *Science Digest*, May 1982.

HOLLING, C. "Predicting the Unpredictable," *The Unesco Courier*, August-September 1982.

International Conference on Modelling and Simulation, 1-3 July 1982. For details, contact Association for the Advancement of Modelling and Simulation Techniques in Enterprises, 16 avenue de Grange Blanche, 69160 Tassin la Demi Lune, France.

LERNER, E. "Programming for Nonprogrammers," *IEEE Spectrum*, August 1982.

LEVIEN, R. "Systems Analysis in an International Setting: Recent Progress and Future Prospects," *Behavioral Science*, Vol. 25, 1980.

MAYOR, F. (ed). *Scientific Research and Social Goals, Towards a New Development Model*, Oxford, Pergammon, 1982.

MILLER, G. *Living Systems*, New York, McGraw-Hill Books, 1978.

PELIKAN, J. "The Two Cities: The Decline and Fall of Rome as Historical Paradigm," *Daedalus*, Summer 1982.

NALIMOV, V. *In the Labyrinths of Language: A Mathematician's Journey*, (trans. R. Colodny), Philadelphia, ISI Press, 1981; published originally as *Veroyatnostnaya Modelyazyka*, Moscow, VAP, 1974.

PFAFF, W. "Reflections, The Shape We See in Our Minds," *The New Yorker*, 24 August 1981.

POPPER, K. "On Theories as Nets," *New Scientist*, 29 July 1982.

QUADE, E. and H. MISER. *Handbook of Systems Analysis: Volume 1, Overview*, Chichester, John Wiley & Sons Ltd., 1983.

RICHE, P. "Le Pape de l'An Mille," *L'histoire*, No. 41, January 1982.

ROGNER, H. "A Long-term Macroeconomic Equilibrium for the European Community" (pamphlet) (doc. RR-82-13), Laxenburg, IIASA, April 1982.

ROHATGI, P.K. and P. ROHATGI. "Technological Forecasting of Education in India towards 2000 AD," *Journal of Scientific and Industrial Research*, Vol. 39, August 1980.

RUCKER, R. *Geometry, Relativity and the Fourth Dimension*, New York, Dover, 1977.

Science and Technology Policy for the 1980s, Paris, Organisation for Economic Co-operation and Development, 1981.

The Future Works!, Stockholm, The Secretariat for Future Studies, The Swedish
    Institute, 1982.
WILSON, A. *War Gaming* (Pelican), Harmondsworth, Penguin Books, 1970.

The planet Earth is a mixed living and nonliving system. It is the suprasystem of all supranational systems as well as the total ecological system, with all its living and nonliving components. The Earth is studied in this article in terms of a general theory of all concrete systems, with special attention to the important subset of living systems. The Earth is an open system, interacting with its atmosphere and with matter and energy in space. Its systemwide processes and the processes of its various components, as well as their variables and indicators, are discussed. In the light of known facts about the Earth as a system, consideration is given to future worldwide problems which must be dealt with by human planners and statesmen.

Chapter 2

THE EARTH AS A SYSTEM

James Grier Miller and Jessie L. Miller

The planet Earth, from its center to the outer limits of its atmosphere, including everything in and on it, is a mixed living and nonliving system within the solar system, the Milky Way galaxy, and ultimately, the universe.

When we say that something is a *system*, we are saying that it has a set of characteristics that are common to all systems and lacking in

James Grier Miller, a pioneer of systems science, is on the faculty of the University of California at Los Angeles and at Santa Barbara. He received A.B., A.M., M.D. and Ph.D. degrees from Harvard University. He has served on the faculties of several universities, including the University of Louisville, where he was president from 1973-1980. (Cont'd)

Note: Reprinted from *Behavioral Science*, Volume 27 (1982), pp. 303-320.

things that are not systems. A system necessarily has parts (or units, or components); these parts have some common properties, are interdependent, and interact within the system.

The parts of this system are aggregations of matter and energy that differ greatly in size, in other aspects of physical structure, in behavior, and in duration of existence. These parts are observed to interact in exceedingly complex ways. The pervasiveness of the interdependence among all parts of the Earth system is becoming increasingly apparent as the widespread effects of changes in variables are traced.

A General Theory of Systems

Concrete Systems

The world is a *concrete* system, which we define as a *nonrandom accumulation of matter and energy in a region in physical space-time organized into interacting, interrelated subsystems and components.* The word "system" also refers to systems of actions abstracted from the behavior of organisms (*abstracted systems*) and to systems of ideas expressed in symbolic form (*conceptual systems*); but the first meaning will be intended here unless we specify one of the others.

Concrete systems are phenomena of the physical world. They include atoms, molecules, planets, solar systems, star systems, galaxies, and, ultimately, the entire universe. Living systems of all sorts are also concrete systems, as are ecological systems with biotic and abiotic components. The various machines people make and use as well as man-machine and animal-machine systems are concrete systems also.

At the University of Chicago he was chairman of the Committee on Behavioral Sciences as well as the Department of Psychology. At the University of Michigan he founded and directed the multidisciplinary Mental Health Research Institute. He was a founder and the first head of EDUCOM (the Interuniversity Communications Council). He has been a fellow of the International Institute for Applied Systems Analysis in Laxenburg, Austria.

For 29 years Dr. Miller has been editor of the journal *Behavioral Science*. He has written or coauthored eight books and published more than 100 scientific and scholarly articles.

Jessie L. Miller received her A.B. at Radcliffe College and her M.S. in social work at Simmons College. She did graduate work in the Committee on Human Development at the University of Chicago. For years she has worked as a colleague of her husband in research and scientific writing.

Systems Hierarchy

An orderly progression in complexity is evident from subatomic particles to the total universe. Atoms make up molecules, molecules combine into all the substances of the physical world, planets make up the planetary systems that revolve around suns, and so on—to the as yet unfathomed totality of the universe.

The *components* of concrete systems are systems at the level of complexity immediately below them in this hierarchy of concrete systems except that the smallest systems, which may be atoms, have components which are not themselves systems. Below atoms are electrons, protons, neutrons, and other subatomic particles.

The concept of *level* is of major importance. Systems at any given level are more like each other in many ways than like systems at other levels. They are the same sorts of things and have similar components. Although systems at a given level may vary greatly in size, their median is usually larger than that of systems at the level below and smaller than the median of the level above. One sort of molecule, for example, is like all the others in being composed of atoms. The median molecule is larger than the median atom.

Structure and Process

At any time, the parts of a concrete system, living or nonliving, are arranged in space in a specific pattern. This spatial arrangement is the system's structure. As the parts of the system move in relation to one another, structure changes. System change can be continuous or episodic, or may remain relatively fixed over long time spans.

All change in a system over time is *process*. Some processes are essentially reversible, as when a car moves forward and then slips back into the same rut. Others are difficult or impossible to reverse. A cat can withdraw the paw it has stretched out toward its toy, but a diver cannot rise feet first from the water and ascend to the diving board, as he appears to do when a film is run backwards.

Process includes both the system's *function*, the often reversible actions that succeed each other from moment to moment, and its *history*, the less reversible or irreversible changes that alter both the structure and the function of the system. The succession of reversible structural changes in a typist as she works at her machine are functional processes. Aging of organisms, decay of mountain ranges, and cooling of suns are historical processes. The regular beating of a heart is functional. The scars that result from a coronary occlusion make a permanent historical change in the heart muscle.

The structure, function, and history of a system interact. Structure changes as the system functions from moment to moment. When a change is great enough to be essentially irreversible, a historical process has occurred.

Living Systems

Living systems are multimolecular aggregates like the nonliving objects in the environment. Life, however, requires a degree of molecular complexity beyond that of nonliving substances. All living systems are composed of organic molecules. Most importantly, they all contain nucleic acids and a score of amino acids organized into proteins. These nucleic acids and proteins are produced in nature only in living systems. All living systems have a remarkable molecular similarity that makes it reasonable to assume that they arose from the same primodrial genes, diversified by evolutionary change. The overall evolutionary progression has been toward increasingly complex systems.

The increase in complexity came about by an evolutionary process which we call shred-out. It is as if each strand of a many-stranded rope had unraveled progressively into more and more pieces, as more and increasingly complicated units were needed to perform each life process.

Levels

Living systems exist at seven levels, each with characteristic structure and processes. The seven levels are:

(a) *Cells*. These systems occur as freeliving or colonial forms and as specialized components of the tissues or organisms. Although cells are exceedingly complicated systems, they are the least complex organization of matter and energy that can carry out essential life processes. Their components are nonliving molecules and multimolecular complexes. Viruses are not living systems, but they occupy the borderland between living and nonliving systems. They are very large protein molecules which have genes and can reproduce inside cells by gaining control of the cell's protein-synthesizing process but are otherwise inert.

(b) *Organs*. These are the specialized structures which carry out organism processes. Their components are cells aggregated into tissues.

(c) *Organisms*. This level includes multicellular plant and animal life forms. The components of organisms are organs.

(d) *Groups*. Two or more organisms interacting as systems form groups. No social system at a higher level than this is found among animals. Although the complex "societies" of social insects have many similarities to human societies, their structures and processes are more similar to those of human groups than to those of either organizations or societies.

(e) *Organizations*. These systems are distinguished from groups not by their size but by the presence of two or more echelons in their decider structures.[1] Their components are groups and smaller organizations. This level includes a diversity of types of systems, some of which are: governmental units like cities, states, provinces, and legislatures; manufacturing and business concerns; religious organizations; charitable organizations; and universities.

(f) *Societies*. *Society* has been defined as ". . .the type of social system which contains within itself all the essential prerequisites for its maintenance as a self-subsistent system.[2] In our terminology, such a system is *totipotential*. The modern form of society is the nation. Nations claim and defend specific geographical territories, have some form of central government, and ordinarily have distinct cultural characteristics. The components of societies are organizations of diverse types and functions.

(g) *Supranational systems*. These systems are composed of two or more societies which undertake cooperative decision making and, to a greater or lesser extent, submit to the control of a decider superordinate to themselves. The level includes alliances, coalitions, and blocs as well as single-purpose and multipurpose intergovernmental organizations. Societies are represented in the meetings of these organizations by delegates. Examples of multipurpose intergovernmental organizations are the United Nations, the Warsaw Pact, and the European Economic Community. The European Organization for Nuclear Research (CERN) and the Food and Agriculture Organization (FAO) are single-purpose intergovernmental organizations.

Emergents

Each higher level of living system, as it evolved, developed capacities for behavior qualitatively different from that of lower-level systems. As a result, the more complex, higher-level systems have characteristics that cannot be described only in terms used for systems below them in the hierarchy without neglecting significant aspects of the higher-level systems. Such characteristics are *emergents*. Life emerged with the first primitive cells. The ability to adjust to more and severer stresses by pooling resources among the cells of a multicellular structure emerged with organs. Many aspects of adaptive behavior emerged at the organism level as increasingly complex nervous systems provided for learning and other higher mental processes. Groups have the emergent ability to perform motor activities and to make artifacts beyond the capacity of a single organism. The use of symbolic language in communication also emerged at the group level, in human groups. There is no evidence that apes in the wild use symbols in interspecific communication, although certain research suggests that they may have the ability to learn to use them.[3] New forms of social organization emerged with the appearance of larger social systems.

Most people readily agree that cells, organs, and organisms are alive. Some may question whether systems at levels above the organism can be considered alive in a comparable sense. Their system characteristics are evident enough, but there is no physical connection among the components as there is among the cells and organs of lower level systems. Components can move from one system to another. In addition, such systems, particularly those at levels above the group, include a great many nonliving components. A city is made up not only of people but of buildings, power lines, buses, and innumerable other things that are clearly not alive.

These systems, however, carry out the same basic life processes as do lower-level systems with more cohesive components. What is more, the structure of at least some systems at lower levels is less fixed than it appears to be, although components do not freely leave one system to join another, but remain within the system boundaries. Many of the cells in an organism's body are in the process of continual replacement. The white blood cells are much like freeliving amoebas as they move from one part of the body to another to dispose of invading proteins.

Further, systems at levels below the group are not always devoid of nonliving components, although such components are usually less massive as compared with the living components than they are at higher levels. At the organ level, pacemakers keep hearts beating regularly. Prostheses like artificial legs and plastic aortas substitute for missing parts or augment the function of defective components of organisms.

Artifacts in higher-level systems, particularly in systems above the group, are essential parts of systems, but it is the living components that form the living system. An abandoned city is not a living system.

In addition to the greater complexity of certain essential molecules, living systems differ from nonliving in several significant ways.

(a) Living systems are more complex in structure and process. Cells, minute as they are, have an awesome array of structural parts and carry out innumerable chemical reactions. Free-living cells exhibit adaptive behavior of various sorts. Computers are generally agreed to be the most complex machines so far invented. They do not yet approach the complexity of organism nervous systems. The levels above the organism, which are composed of more than one organism, each complete with cells and organs, are necessarily more complex than any system at a lower level.

(b) This greater complexity permits living systems to combat, for varying lengths of time, the inevitable increase in entropy that leads to dissolution of matter-energy of all sorts. Nonliving systems do not do this.

Living systems achieve this temporary victory by taking in matter and energy (matter-energy), using it in their processes, and returning a part of it to the environment. The input substances are lower in entropy than the output. Because they have inputs and outputs, living systems are *open systems*.

(c) Living systems ordinarily process more information than non-living, and, furthermore, animals do more such processing than plants. Information is patterning or order, as distinguished from randomness or disorder. It is the opposite of entropy, that is, negative entropy or negentropy. Information may be conveyed in the shape of a molecule that fits receptors on a cell's surface, making it possible for the molecule to enter the cell. It may be in the patterning of the symbols and words of a letter that allow the receiver to decode its message. The recognizable shape of an object is also information.

Information is not the same as *meaning*, which is the significance of information to a receiving system as shown by immediate or delayed change in the receiver's overt behavior or internal processes.

Steady State

By the input, processing, and output of matter-energy and information, living systems maintain themselves for varying periods of time in *steady states*. The concept of *steady state* is similar to the concepts of *equilibrium* and *homeostasis*. *Homeostasis* is a physiological term that applies to a state of balance of the variables of an organism. An *equilibrium* exists when opposing variables of a system are in balance. If a child on one end of a teeterboard balances the weight of a child on the other, the board can remain level until someone applies force to it. An equilibrium that is preserved in the face of dynamic flux is a *steady state*.

The flows of matter-energy and information into and out of a living system change in nature and in rate as both the environment and the system itself vary. Living systems have *adjustment processes* that allow them to keep many critical variables in steady state ranges in the face of such change.

One example of a steady state that must be maintained by cells and organisms is water balance. These systems must excrete water at about the same rate that they take it in or they suffer damage. Adjustment processes in both cells and organisms increase or decrease water input and output to maintain water balance.

Although no delicate balance is preserved between input and output of information in living systems, both overloads and underloads of information input can stress them.

System change, associated with normal growth and development, pathology, or some environmental event, moves living systems to new, and sometimes very different, overall steady states. A small town that doubles its population as a result of a new factory being located there, a city that is damaged by a tornado, or an insect that undergoes metamorphosis—all must find new steady states.

The Subsystems of Living Things

Living systems at all levels, in order to remain alive and continue beyond a single generation, must be capable of performing certain critical processes or have some other means of achieving the same result. Our general living systems theory identifies 19 of these critical processes, each of which is performed by a set of structural units, or *components*.[4] All the components that together perform a particular process in the system form a *subsystem*, whether or not they are spatially contiguous.

If a system lacks structure for a given subsystem process, it may depend upon a parasitic or symbiotic relationship with another living system or require a favorable environment to provide for it. Examples are plants, which cannot move from place to place and must depend upon bees, wind, or water for fertilization, and human infants who depend upon adults to provide food for them and put it into their mouths.

All subsystems process both matter-energy and information by virtue of being systems in their own right. In the system of which they are components, however, some process primarily matter-energy, others process primarily information, and some process significant amounts of both matter-energy and information. Table 1 lists and defines the 19 subsystems of living systems.

Of the 19 subsystem processes, one, reproduction, is not necessary

Table 1. The 19 Critical Subsystems of a Living System.

Subsystems Which Process Both Matter-Energy and Information

1. *Reproducer*, the subsystem which is capable of giving rise to other systems similar to the one it is in.

2. *Boundary*, the subsystem at the perimeter of a system that holds together the components which make up the system, protects them from environmental stresses, and excludes or permits entry to various sorts of matter-energy and information.

Subsystems Which Process Matter-Energy

3. *Ingestor*, the subsystem which brings matter-energy across the system boundary from the environment.

4. *Distributor*, the subsystem which carries inputs from outside the system or outputs from its subsystems around the system to each component.

5. *Converter*, the subsystem which changes certain inputs to the system into forms more useful for the special processes of that particular system.

6. *Producer*, the subsystem which forms stable associations that endure for significant periods among matter-energy inputs to the system or outputs from its converter, the materials synthesized being for growth, damage repair, or replacement of components of the system, or for providing energy for moving or constituting the system's outputs of products or information markers to its suprasystem.

7. *Matter-energy storage*, the subsystem which retains in the system, for different periods of time, deposits of various sorts of matter-energy.

8. *Extruder*, the subsystem which transmits matter-energy out of the system in the forms of products or wastes.

9. *Motor*, the subsystem which moves the system or parts of it in relation to part or all of its environment or moves components of its environment in relation to each other.

10. *Supporter*, the subsystem which maintains the proper spatial relationships among components of the system, so that they can interact without weighting each other down or crowding each other.

Subsystems Which Process Information

11. *Input transducer*, the sensory subsystem which brings markers bearing information into the system, changing them to other matter-energy forms suitable for transmission within it.

12. *Internal transducer*, the sensory subsystem which receives, from subsystems or components within the system, markers bearing information about significant alterations in those subsystems or components, changing them to other matter-energy forms of a sort which can be transmitted within it.

13. *Channel and net*, the subsystem composed of a single route in physical space, or multiple interconnected routes, by which markers bearing information are transmitted to all parts of the system.

14. *Decoder*, the subsystem which alters the code of information input to it through the input transducer or internal transducer into a "private" code that can be used internally by the system.

15. *Associator*, the subsystem which carries out the first stage of the learning process, forming enduring associations among items of information in the system.

16. *Memory*, the subsystem which carries out the second stage of the learning process, storing various sorts of information in the system for different periods of time.

17. *Decider*, the executive subsystem which receives information inputs from all other subsystems and transmits to them information outputs that control the entire system.

18. *Encoder*, the subsystem which alters the code of information input to it from other information processing subsystems, from a "private" code used internally by the system into a "public" code which can be interpreted by other systems in its environment.

19. *Output transducer*, the subsystem which puts out markers bearing information from the system, changing markers within the system into other matter-energy forms which can be transmitted over channels in the system's environment.

for the survival of individual systems. Reproduction is, however, necessary for the continuance of the species from generation to generation.

The decider in any living system is the essential information-processing subsystem that coordinates and controls systems and determines how their processes operate. This does not imply that living systems always have a single executive component. Coordination and control are decentralized in many systems. Subjective consciousness is not necessarily involved in the determination of system outcomes.

Deciders are usually structured into hierarchically arranged *echelons*, each of which is responsible for certain sorts of decisions. The highest echelon ordinarily has some degree of control over all the others. Lower echelons control more specific and more localized processes. Leaderless groups are living systems with no top echelon in their decider structures. If a group develops two or more echelons, it becomes, by our definition, an organization.

If a living system loses all its decider components, it is no longer a separate system. Parts of the decider process may be taken over by another system, but if a society, for example, is conquered by another society which dissolves its government and dictates its policies and activities, it becomes temporarily or permanently a component of the ruling society.

Each subsystem of a living system maintains the steady states of a number of variables by the use of adjustment processes that alter flows of whatever forms of matter-energy or information are used in that subsystem's processes. Many adjustment processes are negative feedbacks.

At every level of a living system changing values of certain objectively determinable measures or indicators can be used to evaluate the current condition of subsystems, to measure the amount of departure of variables from established norms, or, by extrapolation, to forecast changes in system states in the immediate or more distant future.

Some variables occur in all subsystems at all levels since a number of characteristics of both matter-energy and information flows are similar no matter where they occur. Others are present at some levels or in certain subsystems but not at others. *Rate of processing*, for example, is a variable of all subsystems whether they process matter-energy, information, or both. *Costs* can be assessed for all subsystem processes. *Meaning* variables, *lags*, and *distortions* are characteristic of all information flows. The processes to which a variable relates may be quite different from one level or type of system to another.

System-wide adjustment processes alter matter-energy and information flows among subsystems or change the system's relationship to aspects of its environment. Feedback loops among subsystems, and to and from the environment, are found in all living systems. In general, lower-level systems have a more limited range of adjustments than higher-level systems and, within each level, the more highly evolved systems have a greater range than those below them in the evolutionary scale. Total system variables are measurable in the same way subsystem variables are. Matter-energy and information input-output relationships, for example, are measurable in at least some systems at each level. Within levels, systems can be compared with norms established for their particular types to determine adequacy of adjustment processes. Pathology resulting from lacks or excesses of matter-energy or information inputs, maladaptive information in genes or charter, and abnormalities in internal processing can be discovered in this way at all levels.

Much of the work of biological and social science is concerned with measuring the variables of living systems and establishing normal ranges of variation for them in particular types of systems. It is critical that quantification of as many variables as possible be achieved and it is important that, to the extent possible, measures be in standard units, such as centimeters, grams, and seconds, so that cross-level comparisons are possible and interdisciplinary studies are facilitated.

Development of measures and indicators has proceeded much farther for some levels and types of living systems than for others. At the organism level, for example, values of thousands of matter-energy and information processing variables have been determined, particularly for laboratory animals and human organisms. Measurement of variables of supranational systems has been instituted more recently and is less advanced.

Nonliving Systems

Nonliving systems include the natural physical systems of Earth, considered separately from Earth's living inhabitants, as well as mechanical and electronic artifactual systems without their human producers and operators.

Aside from the attributes that all concrete systems must have, there are few characteristics necessarily common to all nonliving systems. Although no system, except possibly the total universe, is completely closed, nonliving systems can be more closed than living systems since they do not require continual inputs of nutrients in order to "feed on negative entropy" as living systems do. There is more variation in structure and process among nonliving than among living systems. While they may have any of the subsystems necessary to living systems, they need not provide for the limited range of these subsystem processes that plants have or the entire range that animals have.

Nonliving systems, of course, have provisions for control and coordination, but decider and other information processing components are not obligatory aspects of their structure. Computers have components that carry out decision and other information-processing activities, but some other machines do not, and certain man-machine systems have the human components as deciders.

The natural nonliving systems of the Earth, such as those that determine climate, act strictly in response to the mechanical and thermodynamic laws that govern our universe. These laws "decide" when volcanos erupt, the course of winds, and the sudden shifts in forces that cause earthquakes.

The Earth System

Earth is an open system. Its primary input is energy from the sun and from space. Input of matter, in the form of meteors and cosmic dust, is ordinarily not great, although major impacts from planetoids occur every 100 million years or so. Earth outputs heat and light to space, maintaining an approximate overall steady state with respect to energy.

Earth is an intensely energetic system, unlike similar bodies in our solar system.[5] From the moment of its formation, it has been evolving, with the result that its present state is unlike its state in earlier geologic periods. Its future is a matter for speculation. This is in contrast to the moon, Mars, and Mercury, which lack the dynamic processes responsible for the changes that have taken place in the Earth in the estimated 4.6 billion years since its formation.

Scientists have identified several concentric layers of the modern Earth, each with distinct geological and thermal characteristics. The solid crust surrounds a more plastic mantle. Alternative models of the core describe it as entirely or predominantly iron, either in liquid form or with a liquid center surrounded by a solidified layer.[6] Earth scientists agree that the center is hot. Gravitational energy and radioactive decay are considered probable sources of this heat. Earth's strong magnetic field is believed to result from action of the liquid metal in the core as a hydromagnetic dynamo.[7]

Earth has been described as a "heat engine" in which matter is continually cycled by convection from the hot mantle to the crust and atmosphere and back to the mantle. Volcanic eruptions that carry magma from the deep interior to the surface and spew volcanic ash and gases into the atmosphere are part of this cycling process. So too are movements of the great tectonic plates into which the crust is divided. Their movement in relation to each other changes the geography of Earth. Continents change their boundaries and relative positions. Plates collide to build mountains, separate to form new seas, and slide beneath the sea bottom to be melted in the mantle as new crust is formed from upwelling magma. Tectonic strains build up and are reduced in earthquakes. Sea water moves in repetitive cycles between the ocean bottom and hot basaltic rocks below the sea floor, transferring dissolved minerals from lower layers to the sea. Matter circulates at rates and in temporal patterns characteristic of each of these cycles.

Geologic evidence indicates that the heat that drives these cycles and causes development of the crust and atmosphere has declined during the lifetime of the earth.[8] Consequently, cycling of material through the system has slowed. Since, like all physical systems, this one is subject to entropy, Earth will continue to cool.

Powered by radiant energy from the sun, water moves in cycles from sea and land surfaces to the atmosphere, forms clouds, and falls back to the surface as rain or snow. The atmosphere itself is in continual motion as temperature and pressure gradients and the earth's rotation produce winds and air currents.

Subsystems of the Earth system consist of sets of interacting components, each such set concerned with particular processes. Because of interactions, including feedbacks among subsystems, changes in one part of the system may have effects throughout the whole system.

Measures and indicators are available for many variables of the Earth system. New instruments and techniques are being developed to penetrate deep into the crust, explore the sea bottom, and study the processes of sea water and the atmosphere. Except for the first 800 million years of Earth's history, for which the record has been obliterated, the record of the Earth's evolution is stored in its present geological structure, to be read as appropriate methods are developed. Scientists are collecting the data that will increase their understanding of the past and present states of Earth as a system.

Ecological Systems

In ecological systems, living systems at levels from cells to supranational systems interact with each other and with the nonliving environments upon which they depend. Typically, bacteria, other free-living cells, and both plant and animal organisms occupy a region with physical characteristics to which they have adapted, although some parts of Earth are so inhospitable to life that only bacteria survive in them. Local ecosystems are parts of larger systems up to the total ecological system of Earth with all its living and nonliving components. Whether or not this is a hierarchy is unclear.

Life emerged more than 3.8 billion years ago, after a period of chemical evolution, during which the primitive Earth atmosphere that was chemically reducing rather than oxidizing, while availability of appropriate chemical molecules and abundance of energy potent enough to break chemical bonds favored synthesis of the complex molecules necessary for life. Life was "an almost utterly improbable event with almost infinite opportunities of happening."[9] The oldest known bacterial microfossils are found in 3.5 billion-year-old rocks. Nucleated cells were present less than a billion years later.

The first living cells left no fossil record. Although little is known of them, they must have been simpler in structure and process than even the least complex present-day cells.[10] They had, nevertheless, sufficient complexity to provide for the subsystem processes essential for life. Like all cells, they must have had a limiting membrane that enclosed a colloidal ground substance in which molecular reactions occurred and means whereby matter energy exchanges could occur across this boundary. If commonly accepted theories of the nature of the primitive atmosphere are correct, the first cells were anaerobic. They necessarily had a means of converting the radiant energy of the sun into chemical energy. That is, they were photosynthetic. In all their modern descendants, energy conversion involves the formation and hydrolysis of phosphate bonds, commonly adenosine triphosphate.[11] Some provision for coding genetic information into molecular form, duplicating it, and translating it into proteins is essential for all self-replicating cells, including the earliest ones. The DNA-RNA-protein process that characterizes all living cells probably was used by these ancestors as well, although the genome was probably smaller and the translation less precise than in modern cells.[12] This imprecision would lead to a high mutation rate, such as appears to have been the case. During the eons when bacteria were the only form of life on Earth, they evolved into a wide variety of types and radiated over almost the entire Earth, adapting to a great range of different environments.

From the moment of its formation, life interacted with the nonliving physical and chemical systems of Earth, shaping and being shaped by them. Morowitz describes the global ecological system, or biosphere, as:

> *That part of the terrestrial surface which is ordered by the flow of energy mediated by photosynthetic processes. . . .Energy enters the system as photons and is transformed into energetic covalent bonds. All subsequent biochemical changes involve a series of rearrangements which are accompanied by the production of heat. . . .The energy outflow is usually accompanied by the loss of CO_2, water and nitrogenous compounds. This material then moves through the well-known cycles and eventually back into the biosphere.* [13]

Earth is apparently the only body in our solar system with conditions appropriate for the emergence and continuance of life.[14] Its size and mass prevent its volatile materials from escaping into space and its distance from the sun allows water to exist upon it in solid, liquid, and gaseous forms. Its surface temperature has never been too hot or too cold for life, once it had started, to continue.

As Earth evolved, life also evolved, always adapted physically and behaviorally to the climate, atmospheric composition, and chemical make-up of its environment. The view of life as adapting to changes in an environment over which it has little influence has been challenged in recent years, particularly with regard to the highly probable shift from a reducing to an oxidizing atmosphere. Several lines of evidence support such a shift, including the fact that organic syntheses of the sort necessary for life could not have occurred in an oxidizing atmosphere. The change had been considered the result of the breakdown of water vapor in the atmosphere, with the lighter hydrogen atoms escaping to space and the heavier oxygen atoms remaining in the atmosphere. This process would not, however, have produced the quantity of oxygen that, in fact, is present. The alternative, and now commonly accepted view, is that the photosynthetic process, in which carbon is fixed in the substance of living systems and oxygen is released to the environment, was the major influence in the change.

Lovelock regards this atmospheric change, and other aspects of the living system-nonliving environment match, as evidence for a complex interrelationship between living systems and the nonliving physical and chemical systems of Earth.[15] He suggests that the entire range of living matter can be regarded as constituting a single living entity capable of manipulating the atmosphere to suit its needs and "endowed with faculties and powers far beyond those of its constituent parts.[16] This entity, the Earth's biosphere, together with the atmosphere, oceans, and soil, forms a complex cybernetic system which seeks an optimal physical and chemical environment for life. The relatively constant conditions that make life possible are maintained by active control of this system, which he calls *Gaia*, named for the Greek Earth goddess.

Gaia controls the composition of the atmosphere, which can be considered an extension of the biosphere. The amounts of oxygen and nitrogen in the atmosphere do not conform to the expectations of a steady-state chemical equilibrium "by at least 100 orders of magnitude."[17] The amount of ammonia in the atmosphere is just sufficient to maintain the pH of normal rainfall optimal for life. Variables of soil and sea water composition are similarly controlled. Gaia also has an important role in maintaining suitable surface temperatures over most of Earth. Feedbacks in this system correct deviations from acceptable steady-state ranges.

Ecology is fundamentally concerned with the manner in which light is related to ecological systems and with the manner in which energy is transformed in those systems. The steady states of biological systems are highly improbable states. They have a high degree of order. Cells and organisms can sustain such a state only by doing continual work, and for this they require both an energy source and a sink. The stream of radiant energy from the sun and the flow of heat into the environment and, ultimately, into space in the form of infrared radiation provide these. Energy input into these systems is used for system maintenance, synthesis of macromolecules, and the mechanical energy that is expended in motion. Morowitz describes these relationships as follows:

(a) The surface of the earth belongs to that class of physical systems which receives energy from a source and gives up energy to a sink. There is a constant and (on the appropriate time scale) almost steady flow of energy through the system.

(b) This flow of energy is a necessary and, we believe, sufficient condition to lead to molecular organization of the system experiencing the energy flow.

(c) This flow of energy led to the formation of living systems, and ecological process is the continued maintenance of order by the energy flow. Thus, the problem of the origin of life and the development of the global ecosystem merge into one and the same problem.

(d) The flow of energy causes cyclic flow of matter. This cyclic flow is part of the organized behavior of systems undergoing energy flux. The converse is also true; the cyclic flow of matter such as is encountered in biology requires an energy flow in order to take place. The existence of cycles implies that feedback must be operative in the system. Therefore, the general notions of control theory and the general properties of servo networks must be characteristic of biological systems at the most fundamental level of operation.[18]

Ecological Communities

The ultimate ecological system of the whole Earth is composed of smaller ecological systems in which representatives of a number of species interact with each other and with their physical surroundings. In the terminology of ecology, the *community* is the unit of system organization.[19] *Community* is also a standard term in social science, referring to local settlements in which people live and interact, including such human systems as preliterate tribes and primitive villages as well as modern towns, cities, and metropolitan areas. Instead of including such systems at the organization level as has been the practice of many general living systems theorists, some hold that human communities constitute a separate level between the organization and the society.[20]

The concept of *community* as it is used in ecology is more inclusive than it is in social science, referring to all the living systems that interact within a given area of the Earth. Free-living cells, plant and animal organisms, human and animal groups, human organizations, communities, societies, and supranational systems are all components of ecological communities, although the latter may be geographically discontinuous and be located in more than one.

A *major community*, which includes a number of smaller communities, has been defined as:

> *A natural assemblage of organisms [We would say "living systems at any level."] which, together with its habitat, has reached a survival level such that it is relatively independent of adjacent assemblages of equal rank; to this extent, given radiant energy, it is selfsustaining. . . .The formation of the community may be considered as a resultant of ecological selection, in which the building blocks, or organisms [living systems at any level] unable to exist alone, fall into place to produce a self-sustaining whole of remarkable complexity. Organization of such an accumulation is obligatory and the universality of the community is the proof of this general proposition.[21]*

Communities include *populations* of several species which occupy continuous or discontinuous portions of the physiochemical environment known as *habitat niches*. The natural groupings satisfy the requirements for food, shelter, and reproduction of each of the various sorts of living systems in them.

How do communities of this sort relate to the hierarchy of living systems from cells to supranational systems outlined above? A community is a living system with components at more than one level and of several species or types, whereas the seven levels of living systems have their typical components at the next lower level and of the same species or type. That is, animal groups are all wolves or all deer or all some other species, and human groups include only people.

Ecological communities are organized and coordinated largely by matter-energy, rather than information, flows. The bacteria, green plants and algae, protozoa, animal organisms, and higher-level systems that form a community are linked in a complex metabolism of matter-energy. They all participate in *food chains*, which are connected into a *food web* that is analogous in some ways to the distributor for matter-energy in the subsystems. Bacteria in the soil and in aquatic communities are fundamental to the metabolic process since each species is specialized for some critical role in the flow of energy and recycling of matter that makes possible the relative independence of communities. Soil bacteria live by oxidizing inorganic materials like ammonia, carbon monoxide, hydrogen, iron, and sulfur, making them all available for use in organic syntheses by photosynthesizers. Also, they decompose the protoplasm of the dead bodies of plants and animals into simpler organic and inorganic molecules suitable for resynthesis. In the nitrogen cycle, for example, protein from plant and animal tissues is broken down into its constituent amino acids, which are used in chemical reactions that produce ammonia. This is combined into ammonium salts and nitrites and oxidized to nitrates. These successive steps result in fixing nitrogen in the soil and making it usable in synthesis of plant proteins. Other soil bacteria reduce nitrites and nitrates to gaseous oxygen, and still others combine oxygen with other molecules to form amino acids. Some of these nitrogen-fixing bacteria are free-living. Others live symbiotically with the roots of legumes. Their bodies store the amino acids which, at their death, are digested by the bacteria that produce ammonia. In addition to these critical functions, bacteria are food for soil protozoans and zooplankton.

Each successive living system in the food chain breaks energic bonds of molecules in its matter-energy input and synthesizes other forms of matter-energy that are useful for its own metabolism. There is a cost for the process at each step since some energy is degraded into heat.

To avoid a continual loss of energy to the total system, energy must be input directly or indirectly from the sun. Green plants, photosynthetic bacteria, algae, and photoplankton can convert radiant energy to chemical energy and store it within their boundaries. Systems that cannot photosynthesize must consume plants or other animal organisms that consume them, since they are unable to carry out the fundamental chemical reactions that make both matter and energy available to the food chain.

Ecological Community Subsystem Processes

Community metabolism involves many of the subsystem processes found in the seven levels of living systems discussed in this article previously. Ecological systems that include communities and their habitats do not ordinarily have sharply defined boundaries, but grade into each other. The communities they contain, however, have certain *boundary* subsystem processes, like exclusion of species closely equivalent to those already established in niches suitable for both. Bacteria and green plants carry out the *ingesting* process as they bring chemicals from the earth and energy from the sun into the system. The food chain is the *distributor* for matter-energy. *Converting* and *producing* take place at each step in the food chain as cells and organisms break down the matter-energy in their input to repair tissues, grow, and reproduce. Matter-energy is *stored* in various forms in cells and organisms and by multiorganism systems. Finally, matter-energy is returned to the soil and energy is dissipated in the form of heat in the *extruder* process.

The structure of the *supporter* subsystems of communities is determined by the habitats they provide and the species and types of living systems that occupy them. Ordinarily, no niches are unused. Niches in terrestrial communities are found below the surface of the Earth, on the surface where natural shelter is available, in artifacts of various kinds, and on or in living members of the community, like trees or other organisms. Aquatic communities similarly divide their habitats. The Earth, the living systems that are themselves habitats for other systems, and artifacts like nests or hives are supporter components, since they "maintain the spatial relationships among components so that they can interact without weighting each other down or crowding each other" (see Table 1). Communities usually lack *motor* subsystems.

Information flows are less important in these systems than in cells, organisms, and single-species multiorganism systems. Many of the information-processing subsystems are lacking. The *channel and net* for interspecific information transmissions is much less developed, but some communication does take place among organisms of different species. A bird that drags its wing as if it had been broken in order to lead a predator away from her nest is transmitting information and so are animals that warn others away by growls or aggressive displays. Most information, however, is coded for intraspecific transmission. The pheromones, which are chemical messengers, of one species have no effect on the behavior of individuals of even closely related species.

Ecological communities, however, do not lack the essential *decider* subsystem. Decider components are dispersed throughout the system. The decider functions through adjustment processes and feedbacks among components that control system variables and coordinate the system. These are largely matter-energy feedbacks and adjustment processes.

Systemwide Ecological Processes

Both the biotic and the abiotic components of ecological systems are part of the evolutionary process. The structure and processes of living systems have become modified, over time, in ways that suit them to particular environments. Physical differences among closely related species that live in different temperature zones are evidence of such modifications. Migrations of birds, hibernation, and circadian and other biological rhythms adjust the activity of living systems to environmental variables. The biotic components of ecological systems also modify their abiotic environments in various ways and adjust their structures and processes to one another. Species that have evolved together become mutually adapted so that predator and prey, parasite and host, and participants in symbiotic relationships seem made for each other.

Each community has a typical life cycle. It becomes established, develops to maturity, ages, and finally terminates.[22] Some communities end catastrophically, but termination is ordinarily gradual, as natural forces and the activities of living systems alter the environment so that it is no longer suitable for one or more of its species populations. As they die out or move away, competing populations of other species move in. Eventually, historical changes produce a new community. Usually this process is repeated several times, until a relatively stable *climax community* develops.

Each community in this *ecological succession* maintains a large number of variables in steady states by adjustment processes among the living systems that compose it. The relationships among living systems of differing species and types are consequences of the need of each to provide for its essential matter-energy and information processes. Some are mutually beneficial. A herd grazes and its droppings are a source of matter-energy needed by the grass. Bacteria in the intestinal tracts of animal organisms meet all their own needs and are essential to processes of the converter subsystem of the host system. Other relationships involve exploitation of one species by another with no immediate benefit to the exploited system. Such relationships obviously threaten both species. When a parasite destroys its host or a predator kills off a prey species, it may also destroy itself. This sort of thing does happen in nature, but usually when the species involved have had no previous opportunity to become adapted.[23] European mammals introduced into Australia, for example, threaten the existence of native marsupials. More usually, feedback adjustment processes control numbers of each species so that a balance is maintained that avoids Malthusian extremes. Populations rarely approach the limits of their food supplies.[24]

Relationships between predator and prey often take the form of oscillations or cycles.[25] Predators increase until the prey becomes scarce; then the number of predators declines, allowing prey populations to recover. This, in turn, results in increase of the predators, until, again, they have limited their food supply and the cycle is repeated. Some moose that crossed the ice from Canada to Isle Royale early in this century illustrate two different intraspecies relationships, the first with the plants on which they fed, the second with both plants and animals.[26] Since no predators threatened them on the island, their population expanded to the limit of the food supply. Finally, starvation reduced their numbers. When the vegetation had recovered, the moose again prospered and increased. This "boom and bust" cycle was repeated until 1949, when some wolves discovered the same route to the island. Their predation reduced the moose herd to a comfortable 600 to 1000 animals, a number that the vegetation could support. The moose that fell to the wolves were usually young, weak, or sick. The wolf population remained steady at 20 to 25 because moose are hard to catch, and the wolves made a kill only every three days. Vegetation, moose, and wolves remained more or less healthy and the steady state "balance of nature" was preserved.

Variables of Ecological Systems

Many variables of ecological systems can be observed and measured. Variables of nonliving components are such things as physical and chemical compositions of soil, air, or water; the amount of radiant energy that enters the system; air or water and pressure and movement; ambient temperature range; and seasonal changes in weather.

Living system variables include: kinds of living systems in the community, e.g., pine trees, lichens, crustaceans, deer herds, or human settlements; the number, density, or other quantitative measures of species populations or types of systems; the number of individual systems in human or animal groups; the characteristics of species populations, e.g., age or sex distribution; the health of populations; and interspecific community relationships and interactions.

Variables of the mixed living and nonliving ecological system include distribution of living systems within the environment, habitats in use, species that occupy particular habitats, flows of matter-energy and information through the total system or parts of it, effects of living components upon the nonliving environment, and effects of environmental changes on living systems. Table 2 includes representative variables and indicators which measure those variables of ecological systems.

Man and Ecology

Modern *Homo sapiens* is a recent arrival on Earth, having evolved from earlier hominid ancestors in the late Pleistoscene era. Human beings have intelligence, manipulative skills, and the ability to adapt to a wide variety of environments, and so they have been able to exert a profound effect upon the total Earth system in a relatively brief period of several thousand years.

Little is known about the first men, but they must have lived, like other animals, in balance with the ecological communities of which they were a part, subject to similar population-limiting pressures. The discovery of agriculture, which brought the Pleistoscene to an end 10,000 years ago, and the development of industry were step-function changes in human culture that established new and different steady states and made possible an exponential rise in human population as well as the evolution of living systems larger than groups. The effect of this human expansion has been deleterious in many ways to the living and nonliving components of the world system, including human systems. Fyfe says that a man of the modern industrial developed world uses 2×10^7 grams (20 tons) of new mineral material annually. He continues:

> For a billion people, about 15 percent of the global population by 2000, this annual usage (2×10^{16} grams) about equals in mass the most impressive geological processes of our planet, that is, ocean crust formation, erosion, and mountain-building rates. If we add to such a figure the amount of earth moved in agriculture, then there is no doubt that man has become the most important agent modifying the surface of our planet.[27]

Human systems are already exceeding the carrying capacity of some parts of the Earth, including sub-Saharan Africa and parts of Asia, reducing their capacity to support life.[28] They are depleting natural resources faster than they can be replaced. Extruded wastes of human

Table 2. Examples of Variables and Indicators of the Living Systems in the Earth System.

I. Subsystem Variables

Level	Subsystem	Variable	Indicator
Cell	Reproducer	Diatom population number	Number of cells per liter in in lake water
Organ	Channel and net	Information capacity of a neural tract	Maximum number of bits per second transmitted by all-or-none pulses following electrical input of pulses, measured through electrodes at organ output
Organism	Input transducer	Intensity of perceived sensory input	Behavioral responses to varying magnitudes of sensory input
Group	Decider	Group decision time	Time elapsed from addressing a particular type of problem to group agreement on solution
Organization	Producer	Effectiveness	Quantitative relationship of measures of output of producer products to measures of input capital, labor, materials, and energy
Society	Internal transducer	Public attitude toward governmental policy	Public opinion survey using valid statistical sample
Supranational system	Associator	Access to education of citizens of member nations	Average years of schooling in each nation

II. Total System Process Variables

System	Process	Variable	Indicator
Cone cell of retina	Input-output relationship	Color sensitivity	Flow of current in electrode implanted in cell, following inputs of light of different wave lengths
Human organism	Adjustment to increasing flow of information	Accuracy of information output at different rates of input	Percentage of correct responses in total responses to input signals at different rates
Society	Economic input-output process	Flow of goods and services through all sectors of economy	Monetary value of inputs to and outputs from each economic sector
Total human system	Use of natural resources	Rate of depletion of supplies	Proportion of estimated total supply used annually

III. Ecological Systems

System	Variable	Indicator
Community	Species composition	Population counts of component species
Community	Effects of predation on a species population	Percentage of total mortality of prey caused by predators, estimated from total expected mortality of prey and number actually killed
Species population	Species population number	Percentage age distribution of members indicates whether species population number is rising, stable, or falling
Ecosystem, both biotic and abiotic components	Distribution of pollutant through food chain	Concentration of pollutant in soil, water, or atmosphere, and in tissues of biotic components

systems pollute land, air, and water. Pollution and loss of wild habitats are destroying nonhuman living systems at a rate that could extinguish 15-20 percent of all species on Earth by the year 2000.[29] Many of these are tropical forest species that are potential suppliers of foods, pharmaceutical chemicals, specialty woods, fuel, and building materials.

Depletion of Resources

White has described culture as "an elaborate thermodynamic mechanical system" designed to carry on the life processes of man by harnessing and controlling energy.[30] Culture has been said to evolve as the amount of energy harnessed per capita per year increases.[31] Before the domestication of fire, primitive man used only his own physical energy, derived from his food, probably about 2000 calories per person per day. The use of fire may have doubled his energy use. Agricultural societies with domesticated work animals increased their daily per capita energy use to about 12,000 kilocalories. Between 1850 and 1870 developing technology increased per capita daily energy consumption in England, Germany, and the United States to 70,000 kilocalories. Following installation of central electrical power stations in the late 1890s, energy use rose at an increasing rate until, in 1970, the United States, the world's biggest energy user, required about 230,000 kilocalories per capita per day.

The supply of petroleum, upon which the still-increasing world demand for energy at present primarily depends, is exhaustible. By 1968 American oil production was reaching the limits of its capacity. By 1970, it had begun to decline.[32] More recently discovered supplies in the Middle East remain abundant, but the world supply is expected to peak before the end of this century. Already production capacity is increasing more slowly than demand and by 2000 the world's petroleum resources will have declined by at least 50 percent.[33]

Petroleum is necessary not only to fuel the motors of societies, but to make fertilizers and other materials required for producing food, mining, home heating, and other processes. A conservative estimate of world population in the year 2000 is about six billion, a number that would require doubling of the present energy consumption rate to avoid famine and other disastrous consequences. Similar problems exist with nonfuel minerals, metals, and other resources, including fertile land and water.

The depletion of resources and the need for an ever-increasing supply of energy to sustain human life has been interpreted by some as evidence of the entropic degradation of Earth. In this view, history is a reflection of the second law of thermodynamics. Progress in civilization has been made possible not only by the leisure to experiment provided by increasing surpluses in societies but by hardships that have resulted from dissipation of resources. Repeatedly, accumulated increases in entropy change the environment so that a shift to a new source of energy must occur. Each of these shifts is made at the cost of extracting the low-entropy substances with which the Earth is endowed. Georgescu-Roegen's gloomy conclusion is:

> Up to this day, the price of technological progress has meant a shift from the more abundant source of low entropy—the solar radiation—to the less abundant one—the earth's mineral resources. True, without this progress some of these resources would not have come to have any economic value. But this point does not make the balance outlined here less pertinent. Population pressure and technological progress bring ceteris paribus the career of the human species nearer to its end only because both factors cause a speedier decumulation of its dowry.[34]

Pollution

In ecological communities that live in steady states, the number and distribution of organisms is appropriate to the amount of matter-energy available for all essential inputs and to the capacity of the environment to recycle wastes. A balanced-life aquarium, in which fish live without clouding the crystal clarity of the water, is a small-scale model of such a system.

Large human societies, unfortunately, do not maintain a balanced steady state with their living and nonliving environments. In these, organic wastes which, in small primitive systems, can be recycled without damage to the environment, become a problem because the large output cannot be absorbed by soil and water. In addition, chemicals and the products of burning fossil fuels emitted into air, soil, and water further strain global buffer systems. When poisons enter the food chain, they threaten the health and life of living systems at all levels. Nuclear wastes are particularly important because of the difficulty of disposing of them and the extremely long periods of time over which they are dangerous.

Acid rain and snow, effects of atmospheric pollution, are already threatening living systems. They occur when the sulfur dioxide and nitrogen oxides that enter the atmosphere from burning fossil fuels undergo a series of chemical reactions and combine with water to form sulfuric and nitric acid. The average acidity of rain in the United States and Europe has increased 40-fold in the last 50 years.[35]

As a lake's acidity increases, acids leach nutrients and increase the solubility of such toxic metals as mercury. The eggs of salamanders, and then frogs, fail to hatch and those species are lost to the ecosystem. Then bacteria, plankton, and many aquatic plants disappear. Finally the eggs of fish cannot survive. Brook trout and Atlantic salmon are among the vulnerable species. The result is a beautifully clear, blue—and dead—lake. In high concentrations these acids also destroy plant tissue, interfere with photosynthesis, and affect the nitrogen-fixing process in legumes and soybeans.[36]

A second threat to the Earth system is apparent in the increasing amount of carbon dioxide in the atmosphere, also largely a product of the burning of fossil fuels. In the hundred years from 1880 to 1980, atmospheric CO_2 increased from about 300 to 335-340 parts per million. The effect of carbon dioxide is to close the "window" through which thermal radiation from the Earth's surface and lower atmosphere escapes into space so that outgoing radiation must flow from higher, colder atmospheric levels, warming the lower atmosphere and surface by what is known as the "greenhouse effect." Atmospheric CO_2 is expected to reach 600 parts per million in the next century.

If warming from this cause has already begun, it should rise above the noise level of natural climate variability by the end of this century. Atmospheric physicists consider global warming sufficiently likely, however, that a number of global models have been developed to study its probable consequences. These simulate present and past climatic conditions and examine the effects of increased CO_2 on the simulated systems.

A series of models developed by Hansen and his associates predicts global warming of from 1° to 4° C by the end of the next century, depending upon the rate of growth of energy use and the amount of fossil fuel that has been replaced by fuels that do not increase atmospheric CO_2.[37] Among the possible effects of even a relatively moderate warming would be large regional climatic changes that would alter the location of deserts, fertile areas, and marginal lands and cause large-scale dislocation of human settlements and land use.

In addition, since warming at high altitudes would be much greater than the global mean, the world's ice sheets would either shrink or increase in area, depending upon what temperature difference was produced between the ice sheets and the air above them. An increase of five meters would flood many lowlands throughout the world, including heavily settled coastal areas. Hansen and co-authors conclude that (1981, p. 966): "The climate change induced by anthropogenic release of CO_2 is likely to be the most fascinating global geophysical experiment that man will ever conduct."[38]

A "scenario" by Flohn[39] brings together results of a large body of models and researches on possible man-made climatic changes. This also predicts regional changes "more profound than mankind has experienced during the last 10,000 years." Flohn does not consider a rise in sea level as a likely outcome, but considers the risk of a 400 to 800 km. displacement of climatic zones unacceptable because of its effect on mankind as a whole. He warns that the change could occur quite abruptly, in a few decades or less, and would be essentially irreversible since the new steady state would continue for at least 1000 years before the deep ocean could absorb the additional input of CO_2.

Man has certainly not been an unmixed blessing to the Earth system since, in his relatively brief tenure, he has shown an alarming capability to destroy not only himself but also other critical components of the system as a whole. Fyfe says:

> It is only now that we are beginning to study the major geospheres (atmosphere, hydrosphere, biosphere, crust, and mantle). It is these rate processes that ultimately provide the global buffer systems. We now know that man is perturbing some of these rates on a scale that is easily observed.
>
> Almost all the problems associated with understanding the rate processes that control environmental stability concern interfaces. There are the great interfaces between the atmosphere and the oceans, rainwater and the continental crust, ocean water and sediments, the living cell and the hydrosphere, and the crust and the deep interior. We are also concerned with the interface between the atmosphere and the radiation field of space.[40]

Human systems are characterized by an enormous capacity to process and disseminate information. If the ecological system of Earth in all its variety is to be preserved, it is important to collect the information necessary to quantify the variables that control the evolution of our planet and are critical to the environment and to apply it in making rational environmental decisions. Although Earth scientists have greatly expanded knowledge of the system, the amount yet to be learned is awesome. The Earth sciences are now in a period of advance in theory, experiment, observation, and instrumentation that is producing the necessary data.

Human Policy and the Earth System

> The sun will continue to shine on the Earth, perhaps, almost as bright as today even after the extinction of mankind, and will feed with low entropy other species—those with no ambition whatsoever. For we

must not doubt that, man's nature being what it is, the destiny of the human species is to choose a truly great but brief, not a long and dull career.[41]

This is a gloomy view, but it is not unique. In fact, it is hard to find any student of the world system who is really optimistic about the future. One of the most important results of the world models of Forrester, published in the early 1970s, was to make clear how exceedingly difficult it would be to change our complex world system even if a determination to do so was shared by policy makers in all of the separate nations into which the modern world is divided.[42] Because of the complicated feedbacks connecting population, natural resources, capital investment, food supplies, and pollution, change in one may produce unexpected and undesirable consequences in others. In addition, short- and long-term outcomes of attempts to make adjustments were shown to be opposite in effect, with the result that success in the short run in controlling a given variable may, in the long run, lead to its increase beyond its state prior to the intervention.

The simulated world of Forrester, as well as the similar system of Meadows and his colleagues, tends toward equilibrium since growth cannot continue without reaching limits imposed by resource shortage, pollution, crowding, food failure, or some other powerful force.[43]

The conclusion drawn from both simulations is that unless world policy makers choose to suppress growth in the world system, the internal dynamics of the system itself will produce an undesirable equilibrium. Characteristics of a desirable equilibrium, according to Meadows and his colleagues, would be a constant population number, and a constant capital stock. Population, capital, and the ratio between them would be determined in accordance with the society's values. A society could, for example, decide to keep its population lower in order to provide a better standard of living for all. In addition, all input and output rates, such as birth, death, investment, and depreciation would be kept to a minimum.[44] An equilibrium society of this sort would not, they believe, necessarily be stagnant and, in fact, a society based on justice is more likely to develop in such a system.

In its concern for similar problems, the United Nations has sponsored a global input-output analysis and a set of alternative projections of the demographic, economic, and environmental states of the world in 1980, 1990, and 2000, under the direction of Leontief.[45]

This economic model divides the world into 15 regional blocs, each described in terms of 45 sectors of economic activity. Sectors are linked by exports and imports of some 40 classes of goods and services, capital flows and transfers, and foreign interest payments. The model allows detailed analysis of prospective changes in technology, costs of production, and relative prices. It contains 2,625 equations in 15 interconnected sets, one for each of the 15 regional blocs. The solution for the base year, 1970, was made to be consistent with actual data for that year. Estimates for the years 1980, 1990, and 2000 were based on information from national and international statistical and research organizations.

The model was used to project several alternative developmental "scenarios," each derived from a different set of factual assumptions. Some of these scenarios reflect alternative estimates of future values of variables like population growth, gross product per capita, and the total of unexplored reserves of various mineral resources. Others examine the implications of various sets of income targets and the alternative means by which they could be attained. The several solutions describe possible futures of the world and make it possible to determine some of the changes that would be necessary in order to achieve desirable goals for the total world system.

A goal of the United Nations is growth in gross product per capita in the developing countries. If this is to be achieved, increased transfer of technology and/or technical assistance would be necessary. The model showed that implementation of minimum targets of the United Nations until the year 2000 did not diminish the gap in gross product per capita between established and developing countries. It appears that the economies of developing countries will be a problem for the rest of this century.

World population is projected to increase steeply for the remainder of the 20th century, which will put enormous pressure upon societies to produce food. If, however, the land could be fully used and if the technological revolution in agriculture were completely exploited, the task of feeding the multitudes could be accomplished.[46]

A further conclusion of the analysis is that the endowment of mineral resources and fossil fuels is generally adequate to last until the year 2000 and probably into the early part of the next century. Costs of extraction are, however, expected to increase.[47]

The critical questions about pollution abatement are whether increased pollution is avoidable and whether costs are too high, with the result that they would constrain resources for consumption and investment. Leontief finds that, although this is a grave problem available abatement standards do not present unmanageable problems, nor is pollution an insurmountable barrier to economic development of developing regions.[48]

The principal limits to sustained economic growth and accelerated development revealed by this very detailed economic analysis are political, social, and institutional rather than physical.[49] For favorable outcomes in food production, resource availability, and pollution abatement, policies leading to profound political and social changes would necessarily be adopted and implemented.

There is today no worldwide political system with the power to set policy and secure the cooperation of the world's nations in a unified analysis, development of a remedial plan, and implementation of such a plan. Systems at the level of the society are the dominant human political systems. A great deal of supranational decision making goes on in the world in supranational and international organizations, conferences, and meetings among national deciders, but nations comply with decisions of these bodies only when they perceive that the recommended courses of action are in their own best interests. It may well be that securing such cooperation is the most important task now facing human beings.   □

FOOTNOTES

[1] J. G. Miller, *Living Systems*, New York: McGraw-Hill Book Company, 1978, p. 595.

[2] T. Parsons *et al.*, "Some Fundamental Categories of the Theory of Action: A General Statement," in T. Parsons and E. A. Shils, editors, *Toward a General Theory of Action*, Cambridge, MA: Harvard University Press, 1951, p. 26.

[3] R. A. Gardner and B. T. Gardner, "Teaching Sign Language to a Chimpanzee," *Science*, 1969, Vol. 165, pp. 664-672.

[4] J. G. Miller, *op. cit.*, pp. 30-31.

[5] C. L. Drake and J. C. Maxwell, "Geodynamics—Where Are We and What Lies Ahead?," *Science*, 1981, Vol. 213, p. 20.

[6] D. J. Stevenson, "Models of the Earth's Core," *Science*, 1981, Vol. 244, p. 120.

[7] *Ibid.*, p. 617.

[8] *Ibid.*

[9] J. E. Lovelock, *Gaias*, Oxford: Oxford University Press, 1979, p. 14.

[10] C. R. Woese, "Archaebacteria," *Scientific American*, 1981, Vol. 244, p. 120.

[11] H. J. Morowitz, *Energy Flow in Biology*, New York: Academic Press, 1968, p. 55. See also Harold Morowitz, "Two Views of Life—if Life is Inseparable from the Geochemical Processes of the Earth, Then Is the Whole Planet One Great Organism?," *Science 83*, January/February 1983.

[12] Woese, *op. cit.*, p. 129.

[13] Morowitz, *op cit.*, p. 81.

[14] Drake and Maxwell, *op. cit.*

[15] Lovelock, *op. cit.*, p. 11.

[16] *Ibid.*

[17] *Ibid.*, p. 7.

[18] Morowitz, *op. cit.*, p. 120.

[19] W. C. Allee *et al.*, *Principles of Animal Ecology*, Philadelphia: W. B. Saunders, 1949, p. 437.

[20] R. E. Anderson and I. E. Carter, *Human Behavior in the Social Environment*, Chicago: Aldine, 1974, pp. 45-57.

[21] Allee, *op. cit.*, p. 436.

[22] *Ibid.*, p. 563.

[23] *Ibid.*, p. 699.

[24] *Ibid.*, p. 375.

[25] *Ibid.*, p. 374.

[26] E. O. Wilson, *Sociobiology*, Cambridge, MA: Balknap Press, 1975, p. 86.

[27] W. S. Fyfe, "The Environmental Crisis: Quantifying Geosphere Interactions," *Science*, 1969, Vol. 165, p. 105.

[28] U.S. Council on Environmental Quality and the Department of State, *The Global 2000 Report to the President, Volume 1. Entering the Twenty-first Century*, Washington, DC: U.S. Government Printing Office, n.d., p. 37.

[29] *Ibid.*, p. 37.

[30] L. A. White, *The Science of Cultures*, New York: Grove Press, 1949, p. 369.

[31] E. Cook, "The Flow of Energy in an Industrial Society," *Scientific American*, 1971, Vol. 224, p. 135.

[32] R. Stobaugh and D. Yergin, editors, *Energy Futures*, New York: Random House, 1979, p. vii.

[33] U.S. Council on Environmental Quality, *op. cit.*, p. 37.

[34] N. Georgescu-Roegen, *The Entropy Law and the Economic Process*, Cambridge, MA: Harvard University Press, 1971, p. 304.

[35] C. K. Graves, "Rain of Troubles," *Science 80*, 1980, 1, p. 1.

[36] *Ibid.*, pp. 76-77.

[37] J. Hansen, *et al.*, "Climate Impact of Increasing Atmospheric Carbon Dioxide," *Science*, 1981, Vol. 213, p. 964.

[38] *Ibid.*, p. 966.

[39] H. Flohn, *Possible Climatic Consequences of a Man-made Global Warming*, RR-80-30, Laxemburg, Austria: International Institute for Applied Systems Analysis, 1980, p. 71.

[40] Fyfe, *op. cit.*, p. 105.

[41] Georgescu-Roegen, *op. cit.*, p. 304.

[42] J. W. Forrester, *World Dynamics*, Cambridge, MA: Wright-Allen Press, 1971, pp. 94-95.

[43] D. H. Meadows, *et al.*, *Limits to Growth*, New York: Universe Books, 1972, p. 23.

[44] *Ibid.*, pp. 170-175.

[45] W. Leontief, *et al.*, *The Future of the World Economy*, New York: Oxford University Press, 1977.

[46] *Ibid.*, p. 5.

[47] *Ibid.*, p. 6.

[48] *Ibid.*, p. 7.

[49] *Ibid.*, p. 10.

Should the core of a product or the inner space of a building determine its outer form—the "inside-out" approach to design—as the Bauhaus argued? As miniaturization proceeds, is there a limit to the influence of the core on the design of its enclosing shell? Does this then free the designer to express the artist within himself? Are there principles he can invoke to guide this expression? Such are the questions considered in this thought-provoking extract from the author's latest book, Objectology—the Evolving Man-Made Environment.

Chapter 3

THE DETERMINATION OF FORM

Hin Bredendieck

Because form is recognized as an important attribute of any product or entity, a designer is often referred to as a form-giver. But form alone is not all that concerns the designer; it is only one of three basic attributes of any product or entity—the outer boundary taken by a product. A product also possesses an internal arrangement referred to as its structure. And since this internal structure holds a position relative to other structures, there is a third basic attribute of a product that can be termed position. Thus any product or entity has the three attributes

Hin Bredendieck, professor emeritus at the School of Architecture of the Georgia Institute of Technology, spent his formative days in Germany, studying at the art academies of Stuttgart and Hamburg and then earning the Bauhaus diploma. From 1952 until 1971 he headed the industrial design section at the Georgia Institute. Among his designs are the interior lighting of the Corso Theater in Zurich and a range of interiors, furniture, toys and industrial products he did in Chicago while teaching at the New Bauhaus. His address is 2146 McKinley Road, N.W., Atlanta, GA 30318, United States of America.

of form, structure, and position. The task of the designer in the development of a product is to determine the specific characteristics of each of these attributes.

Here I describe these attributes of a product, putting the emphasis on form and referring primarily to enclosure-type products such as appliances and electronic devices, but also to buildings. Although appliances and buildings differ greatly in size, function and complexity they do, nevertheless, have one thing in common: an inner core or operational structure that consists of an interrelated system enclosed by a form and positioned in a given environment. The term "operational structure" refers only to the inner core of the unit and not to its static supporting structure.

The Initial Task in Design

To illustrate how structure, form and position are interrelated, I consider this operational structure as it is found in various enclosure-type products and buildings, for example, the mechanics of a watch, the inner working parts of a telephone, a toaster, or the various space arrangements of rooms, halls, stairways, etc., of a building, each of which is the operational structure that makes the unit workable. The initial task in designing an operational structure is to construct a working unit that is capable of producing a certain specified end result. This applies not only to the engineered components of a product but also to the inner arrangement of a building. The development of such inner structures is well illustrated by the electric bulb and the telephone. Edison's initial goal in developing the incandescent electric bulb was to obtain a unit that would emit light, while Alexander Graham Bell sought to construct a unit that could transmit a voice over distance. Once these initial goals had been achieved to some degree of satisfaction, the task became one of making further improvements in the units. In general such improvements are in the direction of a better relation of the product to the user and of greater compactness of the engineered components. These two aspects strongly influence the configuration of the enclosing form. We see this in the way electric bulbs, motors and other components have been reduced in size over the years.

In developing a product, it is the engineer who takes in hand the inner components while the designer concerns himself with the outer form. In architecture, it is usually one and the same person who determines both the inner spatial arrangement and the outer form. As far as most products are concerned, the components could be used in the form developed by the engineer. Thus, an electric bulb could be used without a fixture and a telephone operated without its enclosing shell. We recognize however that these components are unfinished products requiring further refinements. This is essentially the task of the industrial designer who related the unit more appropriately to the user and his environment.

Unique Role of Designer

The development of a product, from inception through its final introduction into use, requires a succession of steps, each involving the contribution of a particular profession. The final step in this series requires the talents of the industrial designer. To illustrate, development of a product may begin with the location of raw material by the geologist, the biologist, or technologist, then pass through various phases of processing the material, to manufacturing the product and, finally, to incorporating it into the user's environment. Various professions contribute to the steps in this intricate development process. The designer's role is unique in that he, being last in line, becomes the liaison between industry and consumer. He must not only be familiar with the long line of successive steps but, with his intimate awareness of the conditions under which the product is to be used, he must feed back to industry any new requirements that have become apparent as the product is put into use.

Let me illustrate further the difference between the role of the engineer and that of the designer. The engineer aims for "laboratory efficiency" (a measurable quality of performance), while the designer strives to obtain high overall performance of the product in its final place of utilization. The latter is a non-too-measurable quality. The designer may at times have to reduce the "laboratory efficiency" of a component in order to obtain the high overall performance he seeks. For example, the rated "laboratory efficiency" of an electric bulb (the lumen/watt ratio) refers to the naked bulb. To adapt the bulb to man and his environment, i.e., to achieve a desirable degree of overall performance of this bulb as a light source, the designer may have to place the bulb into a suitable fixture. This will, of course, sacrifice some of the bulb's "laboratory efficiency."

How does the designer achieve an improved overall performance? Obviously, he must first familiarize himself with the nature of the component and with details of its operational system, particularly their arrangement. This arrangement is usually one that gives maximal compactness in order to save material, labor and space—a demand of production and distribution rather than of the user. The industrial

designer, however, is consumer-oriented and concerned with performance of the product; he will therefore consider modifying the arrangement of an engineered component the better to fit the user and his
environment. Most engineered components allow considerable freedom
for such rearrangement without interfering with the function of the
operational system. These rearrangements are made with reference to
three types of outer constants: (a) the person who operates or comes
into contact with the product; (b) environmental objects that have
operational, physical or visual relationship to the product; and (c) prevailing conditions that, in one way or another, affect the operational or
physical integrity of the product. Figures 1 and 2 illustrate the influences of these outer constants on the specific arrangement of the details
of the component as well as on its enclosing form.

Figure 1.   Gruen wrist-watch. The specific arrangement of the mechanical component is influenced by the curvature of an arm, an "outer
constant".

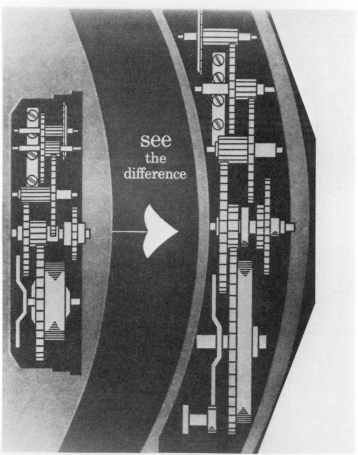

Figure 2. Samson tandem toaster. The inner arrangement of the component resulted from considering the elongated space which may be available on a counter, an "outer constant".

These examples illustrate types of arrangements rather than mere "compactness." They also indicate the advantage in having the designer participate, whenever possible, with the engineer in the final development of the engineered component, particularly in the arrangement of its details.

The Enclosing Form

Having examined this matter of the arrangement of details of a component, we now consider its enclosing form. Whatever form a designer gives his product, it is essentially the result of the design ideologies he entertains. This is so whether he has developed his own concepts or merely adopted them. Although ideologies vary from one designer to another, there are certain generally accepted principles that influence the development of form. We illustrate these by considering buildings as well as products, using the Bauhaus as an historical point of reference.

"Outside-in" Approach

Many buildings of the pre-Bauhaus period were designed with strong emphasis on the façade and the outer form. The underlying principle of

Figure 3. Capitol building, Washington DC. Illustrating the "outside-in" approach to design.

Figure 4. Early radio. Also illustrating the "outside-in" approach.

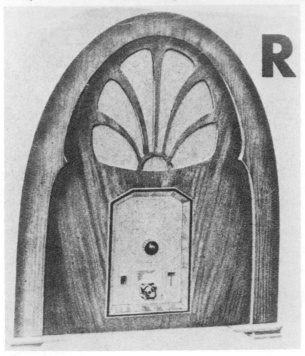

Figure 5. Pendulum clock.

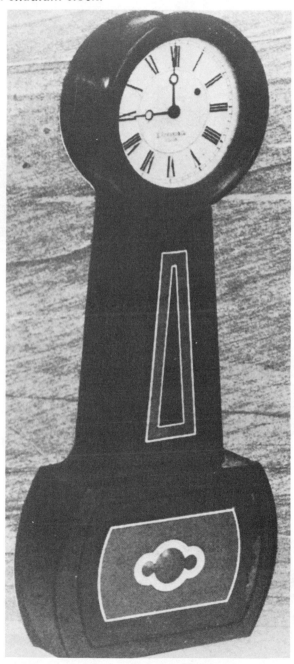

Figure 6.   Werbund Building, Cologne.

Figure 7.   Wolkswagen.

this approach, often carried to extremes, was to superimpose upon an inner core (operational structure) an outer form conceived relatively independently of the characteristics of the inner core. The symmetrical outer form frequently revealed little of the internal arrangements. For example, windows would often be located with total disregard of the internal requirements, these so-called "blind-windows" merely lending a symmetrical design to the façade. This approach can be referred to as an "outside-in" approach because the designer seems to proceed from the outside to the inside of the building. This does not imply that the interior has been ignored but that the outer form, and especially the façade, has dominated the design overriding not only the building's inner core but also its environment.

This "outside-in" approach to design can also be found in some of the products of the early industrial period. When radio appeared, many if not most receivers were designed with this "outside-in" approach. These outer forms, like those of the buildings mentioned above, were generally symmetrical and often dominated the environment in which they were placed.

"Inside-out" Approach

As far as products are concerned, however, this "outside-in" approach was a short-lived and passing phase. Products soon began to reveal more of their inner core. The industrial designer, as we know him today, did not exist at that time; it was the engineer who developed both the inner component and the final enclosing form, his sole aim in choosing an enclosing form being to protect the inner component, and to prevent foreign matter from interfering with the operation of the unit. The inner component dominated the outer form which followed essentially the gross contour of the component. The reader should compare Fig. 5 with Fig. 3 and 4.

The design approach employed with these industrial products was in quite sharp contrast with the approach in architecture. While the latter was dominated by the "outside-in" approach, industrial products were already being developed by the "inside-out" approach. Although these products were multiplying rapidly, they appeared to have little direct influence on the form of buildings. It was only with the advent of the Bauhaus, who followed the "inside-out" approach, that a switch finally occurred in the approach used in architecture. Now the principle became one of having the outer form of a building evolve from its internal structure. The former "outside-in" approach was looked on as superficial and derogatorily referred to as "façade architecture." The newly proclaimed "inside-out" approach was lauded as the logical one. For, argued the Bauhaus, was not the inner core of a product or the interior space of a building the sole reason for developing the unit? Hence, should not this inner core also determine the outer form? The "inside-out" design became known as "honest" because it did not hide the internal parts. Products and buildings began to expose internal aspects as Walter Gropius's 1914 design of the Werkbund Building, Cologne, Federal Republic of Germany (Fig. 6) illustrates so well.

Today the "inside-out" approach is widely practiced both in architecture and in product design. Indeed, at times it is used as the criterion of quality in design. Witness a famous Volkswagen advertisement stating that their car is "designed from the inside-out" (Fig. 7), or the statement by Le Corbusier: ". . .it must grow from the inside out, the concept must be biological, not static. A beautiful seashell is not a façade; it is a shell—this is the essence of architecture."

Interpreting Nature Correctly

Although such reference to natural objects is often made to justify the "inside-out" approach in recognition that nature may indeed provide us with a valid criterion, we must be sure to interpret nature correctly. Statements like the one by Le Corbusier assume that a natural entity evolves only from the inside out. But is this actually the case or does this risk being a superficial observation of nature? Is the seashell's shape determined exclusively by its inner biological structure? We happen to know otherwise. The configuration of the outer form that confines the inner structure—in this case, the animal—actually results from an interaction between the inner nucleus and its external environment. We can state as a fundamental axiom that such an external form can only result from an interaction of inner and outer forces. A form cannot evolve exclusively from unilateral action of something inside or outside! An entity always exists in its environment, living entities in a biological or ecological environment, inanimate entities in a physical ecological environment, and this environment impinges upon and affects the form of the entity. Whether the entity is biological or inanimate, it owes its integrity to the interplay of offensive and defensive forces of action and reaction. Although the entity may be biologically "dead" (for example, a pebble on the beach, a car in the street, or a planet in the universe), it is never physically inert or inactive. Incidentally, we should also note that the "inside-out" principle leads to the notion of an entity with an "absolute integrity"— surely an absurd conclusion.

What, then, accounts for the great popularity of the "inside-out" approach? As with the "outside-in" approach, it is "object-oriented." It focuses on the product itself and treats all other factors as purely incidental. But the inadequacy of this approach is evident when we recall that a product's usefulness always lies in its relation to other objects and to its environment. An object, *per se*, is merely a detail of an operational system which, in turn, is part of a larger system. This being the case, we must move away from this "object-orientation" towards a "system-orientation." Although we cannot deal here with the significance of such a reorientation, it is worthwhile to note that, for the designer, it has a profound impact on the outer form of products and buildings. External factors cannot be treated as incidentals; they must be made an integral part of the design procedure.

Before considering the effects of external factors on the outer form of objects and buildings, we return once more to the inner core of a product. This inner core has certain dimensions and configurations that give it a so-called "volume-form." In the design of the enclosing shell of the product following the *inside-out* approach, this volume-form quite often determines the shape of that shell, particularly if the inner core is relatively large in size.

Influence of Miniaturization of Parts

With the advent of space exploration and the emphasis on miniaturization of parts, internal components for commercial products have also tended to become smaller and smaller. It is interesting to speculate on the influence of this trend on the enclosing shell of these products. Will such components continue to determine the dimensions and configurations of their enclosing forms? That this could hardly be the case may be seen by considering the telephone. Supposing it were possible to reduce the inner core of a telephone to the size of a matchbox, or even smaller, the enclosing form could be correspondingly reduced. But so diminutive an object, when set on a desk, could be easily misplaced and, indeed, difficult to manipulate. Clearly there is a limit to the influence of miniaturization of internal components on the dimensions and configuration of the enclosing shell. At some point, this vital "volume-form" is lost as a design factor and the designer must find new factors obviously external to the unit to guide his decisions on size and form of an enclosing shell.

Bilateral Approach

Each object that is of the enclosure type, whether product or building, has a relationship with what it contains and with that which contains it. In other words, enclosure-type objects are at one and the same time both containers and "contained." It is this twofold relationship that is expressed in the form taken by these products and that is evident in the evolution of biological forms, contrary to Le Corbusier's statement. The design procedure embodying this approach is referred to as "bilateral," because it combines both the "inside-out" and the "outside-in" approach.

Many designers of products and buildings will assert that they always consider the internal and the external factors—that they practice the "bilateral" approach. With the loss of the vital "volume-form" as a factor, however, and because operational and physical requirements are not fully sufficient to determine the outer form of a product, this approach is caught in a controversy over what factors can be considered in determining this outer form. For many designers, the requirements of visual refinement seem appropriate and this has brought a strong emphasis today on visual appearance not only in the design of products but also in architecture. This emphasis has encouraged a widely held notion that this phase of the design procedure should be left to the "artist" in the designer, that this is the place where he should express himself.

Visual Clarity

Other designers have attempted to deal with this non-operational aspect of the design procedure by evolving certain principles relating to the visual aspect of objects. In an article entitled "Aesthetics in Engineering Products" (*IDEA Journal*, 1963), R.H. McKim discussed these principles under the term visual clarity, using this to refer to four different aspects of form: visual clarity of function, of structure, of the producing tool, and of the material.

By visual clarity of function, McKim means that the form of a product or building should express its function—a telephone should reveal what it is, a car show its swift movement, a chair its comfort, and so on. By visual clarity of structure, he suggests that the form of an object should reveal its structural integrity. Visual clarity of the tool holds that the form of an object should show the imprint of the tools and processes used in its production. Finally, by visual clarity of the material, McKim expresses the notion that a material should be used according to its "nature;" that is, that the physical aspect of a material should influence the design of any object fashioned from that material.

My examination of these different notions on visual clarity leads me to find them less than adequate as principles so that the problem of the non-operational aspect of design remains unresolved. Perhaps a more fruitful direction in which to search for principles related to this matter of the non-operational and non-physical aspects of design would be to consider the relationship between the user and objects together with their environment. This relationship can be either direct or sensory (largely visual). Passing over the first, which refers mainly to manipulation of the object, we shall consider the second in some detail.

Ways to Perceive an Object

There are seven possible ways an observer may perceive an object (he may focus on just one of these or on various combinations, depending on his particular interest, inclination and involvement in the situation at hand), which can be listed as follows: (a) the observer may perceive certain physical characteristics of the object (the object as such); (b) the observer may deduce certain environmental characteristics from his visual experience (the object and its environment); (c) the observer may deduce certain traits of the maker of the object (the object and its maker); (d) the observer may deduce certain traits of the user and/or owner of the object (the object and its user); (e) the observer may perceive a message or meaning in his visual experience (the object as a means of communication); (f) the observer's visual experience may evoke a previously encountered personal experience (the object as a personal experience); (g) the observer may experience the object as an integral part of the world around him (the object as an integral part of the total environment).

Among these ways of perceiving an object, the first two refer to an experience of the physical reality of an object or its environment and have to be accepted as facts; these are a part of our daily living. The third and fourth ways listed above refer to the maker and user of an object respectively and suggest that an object, be it a building or a product, may convey to the observer a certain image of the maker or the status of the owner. The possibility of these essentially visual impressions enables a designer to simulate or copy certain aspects of products of established high quality and thereby to evoke a distorted image or arouse false status feelings. This practice must be rejected not so much from a moral point of view but, more important, because this false image or pretended status cannot be maintained over the period of time that the user may possess the product. Such a practice may actually "backfire," resulting in loss of the effect sought by the user.

The fifth listed way of perceiving objects refers to the possibility of finding a message or meaning in the object. Here we are dealing with true symbol, i.e., an object to which a certain message has been deliberately attached for the specific purpose of conveying it to others. The object may, of course, serve a utilitarian purpose at the same time, such as the bishop's mitre, which covers the head but at the same time also symbolizes rank and position. The vast majority of our symbols are without any particular useful purpose, serving only to convey a message. These are our general means of communication. The important characteristic of a symbol is that a message has been deliberately attached to the object whether it has any utility or not. Sometimes buildings and fabricated products are referred to as symbols but this is a somewhat spurious use of the term. Actually, relatively few buildings and products are true symbols, this character being reserved for those that serve certain ceremonial and/or ranking purposes chiefly in religious or military organizations.

Conclusions

What can we conclude from this review and critique of the design process? For one thing, we note the trend towards a holistic approach, so widely found in other fields, now showing up in the practice of those designers who create the forms of our environment. For another, our review of the development of form over a long period of time shows the increasing influence of the consumer. As the cycle of selecting, using, discarding, and then selecting again repeats itself over and over, the consumer exerts his influence on the development of form. What this demonstrates, we believe, is a striving by the consumer to satisfy a still largely unconscious need for harmony with his environment.   □

*The unfathomable complexity of reality drives man to seek prac-
tical accommodation with it. The model serves well in this role. The
mathematical form of a model is unique in permitting mechanization
and automation of man's intellect—indeed in amplifying this capacity.
Many of the greatest discoveries of science turn out to be mathematical
models, generally described as "laws."*

Chapter 4

SOME PRINCIPLES OF MATHEMATICAL MODELING

Blagovest Sendov

The Mechanics of Prediction

The aim of scientific activity of all kinds and human inquiry in
general is to establish methods whereby future events—in the broadest
sense of the term—may be predicted. Man's constant endeavor is to find
ways of understanding the reality which encompasses him without the
need for direct observation.

Every rational action is to some extent based on prediction, the
accuracy of the latter determining the degree of success with which the
objective of the action is obtained. Predictive methods are, moreover,
the only ones that permit the investigation of objects of phenomena

The author is a professor of mathematics who has been teaching computer science
since 1963. His principal publications are in the fields of approximation theory and
mathematical models in biology. Professor Sendov has been a member of his
country's parliament since 1976. Address: Faculty of Mathematics and Mechanics,
Universitet Kliment Ohridski, Boulevard Anton Ivanov 15, Sofia, Bulgaria.

which, by their very nature, defy direct observation. And since the matters investigated by one science or another differ in their complexity, the scope for accurate and reliable prediction varies accordingly.

The fact that it is possible to predict with extreme accuracy many years in advance the moment when the sun will rise is no longer a matter of astonishment. On the other hand, the predictions of geologists with regard to the location and volume of petroleum deposits are by no means a guarantee that oil will actually gush out of every well that is drilled; in this case, the methods of prediction are less reliable and accurate. The same is true as far as meteorological forecasting, medical diagnosis and the like are concerned, while the degree of confidence that can be accorded to predictions related to matters of still greater complexity, such as those involving biological, economic or social phenomena, is even more limited.

Let us consider for a moment the general manner in which a prediction is made with regard to an objective reality.

An Approximation of Reality

The initial stage of our inquiry involves observation and the accumulation of facts; on the basis of the latter, we build up a certain notion of the object we are considering. Although this notion can never amount to more than an approximation of the reality observed, which is of unfathomable complexity, it is nevertheless enough for us to "reason" about the object without pursuing our observation in greater detail. In other words, we have created a model of the object and are reasoning about the model. This process of reasoning can lead us to reach certain conclusions about the model which do not depend on direct observation of the corresponding object. Such conclusions—obtained by a process of reasoning centered on the model, rather than on actual observation of the object—represent our predictions concerning the objective reality.

The process of apperception and the construction of concepts or models related to objective realities takes place in three distinct but consecutive stages: observation and the accumulation of facts; reasoning about the model and the determination of non-observed characteristics; comparison of predictions with reality. This sequence of events corresponds to the classical thesis of materialistic philosophy, according to which one proceeds from active contemplation to abstract thought, and thence to practical application.

From the above, it follows that every prediction is based on a model of some kind. The accuracy of the prediction depends both on the completeness of the model itself, and on our capacity to exploit the model.

A Great Variety of Different Forms

The models used for the predictions of different events or phenomena may assume a great variety of different forms. When the personal record of a worker, for example, is used for the purpose of estimating his future performance and determining the nature of his future assignments, the record constitutes a model, albeit a somewhat simplistic one, for a prediction which—whether or not it proves accurate—in turn leads to a decision. Similarly the charts drawn up by gunners to indicate the possible trajectories of shells fired by a particular piece of artillery constitute models by means of which range can be predicted for certain parameters of fire. Elementary geometry provides a third type of model: for example, knowledge of the height and diameter of a cylindrical vessel makes it possible to predict the amount of liquid which the vessel will hold.

These examples reveal a distinction not only between the degrees of accuracy in the predictions which the models allow, but also between the potential uses which may be made of the models themselves. The worth of a given model depends essentially on the "material" of which it is made, since the latter influences the degree to which the model can be used to determine characteristics which have not been directly observed or which have not been prescribed.

The Mathematical Model

The mathematical model may be described as one whose "material" is of a mathematical nature.

The process of formally determining the properties of any model depends on the rigor with which its different components are identified and put together. This is particularly true as far as mathematical models are concerned. The latter differ essentially from models in general, in that they lend themselves to manipulation with the tools of mathematics. Thus, the predictions obtained from such models amount to logically based, mathematical arguments.

Mathematical models are unique in that they alone permit the mechanization and automation of intellectual activity. Hitherto there have been no effective means available for amplifying man's intellectual capacity; this can be achieved only by using mathematical models and manipulating them with the aid of computers.

The steadily increasing use of mathematical models in the various scientific disciplines constitutes what is frequently called "the mathematization of science."

Although the term "mathematical model" has gained widespread currency in recent years, such models are by no means a modern invention. The greatest discoveries of physics are, essentially, mathematical models, although they are often described as "physical laws."

Physical and Other Sciences

Following the discoveries of Kepler, Newton expressed the law of universal gravitation in the following mathematical equation:

$$F = K \frac{m_1 m_2}{d^2}$$

according to which the force of attraction (F) between any two bodies in the universe is directly proportional to the product of their masses (m_1 and m_2) and inversely proportional to the square of the distance (d) between them.

This law is in fact a typical mathematical model, which can be manipulated in a classically mathematical fashion to produce conclusions which amount to extremely accurate predictions and explanations concerning many aspects of objective reality. Historically, the discovery of the planet Neptune was an outstanding proof of the validity of this model; today, the same model permits the calculation of the complex trajectories of artificial satellites and spacecraft.

The predictions based on Newton's model have proved exceptionally accurate and useful, although modern physicists consider that the law of universal gravitation is not entirely valid, and work with Einstein's law of gravitation.

A Margin of Uncertainty

If we prefer to speak of "mathematical models of physical phenomena," rather than "physical laws," this is not a question of subscribing to fashionable terminology. In describing Newton's discovery as a mathematical model, we naturally allow for a margin of uncertainty concerning the accuracy of the predictions derived therefrom, and acknowledge that there may be room for improvement of the model. On the other hand, if Newton's law is taken as an absolute truth, it follows that any observation which is in contradiction with the law is likely to shake our faith in its veracity. The history of physics is full of traumatic experiences provoked by the dethronement of one theory in favor of another, whereas these "moments of truth" are in reality no more than an inevitable and natural sequence of events related to the progressive refinement of the mathematical models of a given physical phenomenon.

The fact that the accuracy of the mathematical models built by physicists to describe physical phenomena has led to these models being designated as "laws" would be of no account if the question were merely one of terminology, and if the implications of the word used were fully understood. Problems arise, however, when the term "law" is taken in its literal sense, as signifying an unshakeable and absolute truth.

Widely applied in other sciences besides physics, constituting in fact one of the most comprehensive and polyvalent tools of research, mathematical modeling is particularly useful as a less costly and less time-consuming means of verifying hypotheses than the conventional process of experimentation. In this context, investigations of a qualitative or quantitative nature performed on a mathematical model of the phenomenon under consideration, constructed on the basis of a given hypothesis, are a speedy and inexpensive means of determining the validity of such a hypothesis. If the results of these investigations are not in satisfactory agreement with the results of actual observation of the phenomenon, there is a reliable indication that the basic hypothesis is false. On the other hand, good agreement between the results obtained from the model and the results of observation in no way guarantees that the hypothesis is sound; it merely suggests that the hypothesis is plausible and merits further verification through experiment. In other words, mathematical modeling cannot take the place of actual experimentation; it merely rationalizes the latter.

Test Plausibility of Model

Let us suppose that a group of astronomers sets out to investigate the planets of the solar system on the basis of primitive astrological experiments. It is highly unlikely that in the foreseeable future one of them will discover Neptune with his telescope. It is certainly true that visible proof of the planet's existence has indeed been obtained by means of optical observation, but the direction in which the telescope was pointed was no hit-or-miss matter; it was the result of a carefully planned and calculated exercise, using a mathematical model of the solar system based on Newton's hypothesis concerning universal gravitation.

Every actual experiment, even if the scientist involved does not always admit to the fact, is designed to test the plausibility of some kind of model, which is not necessarily a mathematical one. During the course of experimentation, the model itself is inevitably refined. When the experimenter employs a mathematical model in his research, he is able to call upon the latest mathematical and computing techniques in planning his experiments. He no longer has to feel his way blindly in the dark, relying on luck for results.   □

Within any given rigid set of axioms, there are statements which we are incapable of proving or disproving on the basis of the axioms themselves. Thus, we can never be sure that a system—a model—will not contain its own contradictions. This is known as Gödel's Theorem, first published in 1931.

Chapter 5

ON LOGIC, AXIOMS, THEOREMS,
PARADOXES AND PROOFS

Edward Jacobsen

Fifty years ago Kurt Gödel[1] published a paper which ended nearly a century of attempts on the part of mathematicians and logicians to establish a rigorous basis for all mathematics. The theorem which Gödel proved showed, surprisingly, that their quest was impossible. "On Formally Undecidable Propositions in *Principia Mathematica* and Related Systems, I" was published in *Monatshefte für Mathematik und Physik* in 1931. Proposition VI in this paper, usually called Gödel's Theorem, has been stated in ordinary language as "all consistent axiomatic formulations of number theory include undecidable propositions." Expressed even more plainly, Gödel's demonstrable rule contends that within any rigid logical mathematical set of axioms there are statements which can be neither proved nor disproved on the basis of

The author holds advanced degrees in mathematics from the universities of Wisconsin and Kansas. Dr. Jacobsen has taught in Botswana, Kenya, Spain, Turkey and the United States. Now based in Paris, he is responsible for Unesco's programs in mathematical education. He can be reached at the Division of Science, Technical and Vocational Education, 7 place de Fontenoy, 75700 Paris, France.

these axioms. Hence, one can never be certain that a system will not contain contradictions.

This seems interesting to those who concern themselves with the abstractions of the foundations of mathematics. So why mention Gödel, a name unknown to most, in this book devoted to modeling, the link between mathematics and the real world? Gödel's Theorem, is, after all, the mathematical equivalent of the paradox, "I am lying," or "This statement is false," the so-called Epimenides paradox. Let me try to answer the question I have just posed.

Geoffrey Holister's essay, later on, starts with, "In the beginning, there was the word and the word was a model." In the very beginning— mathematically speaking—we have a system of self-governing symbols; meaning arises only when there is an isomorphism between these symbols and things in the real world. Basic isomorphism exists between a system of axioms, usually called the Zermelo-Fraenkel—Skolem (ZFS) axiomatic set, and the natural numbers (or positive integers). It is some of this "set theory" which schoolchildren are asked to learn.

ZFS axiomatic set theory provides the simplest system in which most existing mathematics, but not paradoxes, can be deduced. A familiar example of giving meaning to the set of axioms is geometry. The notions of point, line and space and the resulting theorems are isomorphic to real space. Equally familiar are the different geometries which arise from changing only one axiom, that of parallel lines. Which, then, is the "real" geometry? Various branches of physics use different geometries as their model; hence, we must say that there is not one, real geometry. Similarly, there is not one, real number theory, so we usually use the model which is isomorphic to the ZFS axiom system.

Almost Every Model Has a Mathematical Basis

Interesting examples of the isomorphism between symbols and things in our world are found in Douglas Hofstadter's *Gödel, Escher, Bach: An Eternal Golden Braid*.[2] One of these is how some artists have replaced the traditional expression of ideas and emotions through symbols (sounds, paint) by viewing art or music as not expressing anything, rather as objects in themselves. A painting, that is to say, has no outside meaning; it is simply areas of paint. Music is pure sound, with no symbolic value. Now a much deeper question arises: Do words and thoughts follow rules, or do they not?[3]

The articles in this book show the link between a mathematical model (which is, in turn, a link between a set of objects and a mathematical interpretation) and some object. By carefully selecting meanings for symbols, one can have meaningful interpretations. Concern is shown that the model be *consistent* with the real world, so that the model does not give rise to statements demonstrably false in the real world.

There is another significance of the term *consistency*: internal consistency, so that there are no contradictions within a system. Gödel's consistency theorem means that freedom from contradiction of an axiomatic system can never be verified within the system itself— providing the system itself is powerful enough to develop ordinary arithmetic. Gödel is known for many other theorems in the area of the foundations of mathematics, and he has inspired many other persons to work in this field.

Although the authors in this book do not limit themselves to mathematical modeling, there is obviously a mathematical foundation to virtually all modeling, evoking again the consistency theorem advanced a half-century ago by Kurt Gödel. ☐

FOOTNOTES

[1] Kurt Gödel was born in 1906 in Brno (a city now part of Czechoslovakia). He obtained his doctorate from the University of Vienna, and then spent most of his life at the Institute of Advanced Studies, Princeton. He died in 1980.

[2] The original version of this remarkable book was published in 1979 by Basic Books (New York). The work won for its author a Pulitzer Prize, a major award in journalism and authorship. Hofstadter, a professor of informatics at the university level, presents—informatively, entertainingly and wittily—the relationships between mathematics, language and other symbolic art, and musical constructions. A critical review of Hofstadter's opus appears in *Leonardo, Art and Science*, Vol. 14, No. 2, Spring 1981.

[3] A special treatment of Gödel's theorem as applied to polymorphism in language is found in V. Nalimov, *In the Labyrinths of Language: A Mathematician's Journey*, Philadelphia: ISI Press, 1981, translated from the original Soviet publication, *Veroyatnostnaya Model'yazka*.

Decision-makers and planners seek the aid of models in their need to deal with today's highly complex socio-economic systems. Yet neither objective, mathematical models nor purely scenario-based prospective studies have proved satisfactory. This paper describes a modeling process which combines algorithms and software that the All-Union Scientific Institute for Systems Research finds highly effective for modeling these complicated socio-economic systems; it is a structural description of a computer model.

Chapter 6

AN INTERACTIVE MODELING SYSTEM AS A TOOL FOR ANALYZING COMPLEX SOCIO-ECONOMIC PROBLEMS*

Viktor A. Gelovani

Needed: A Combination of Models and Sciences

Decision-making in contemporary socio-economic systems is a highly complex and responsible affair in view of its far-reaching influence on the phenomenon over which control is being exercised, the strong interdependence of different kinds of problems, and the danger of irreversible changes in a wide range of processes. A thorough analysis of the possible consequences of a decision must rest on a serious study of the phenomenon and the processes involved in it.

Viktor Archilovich Gelovani is head of department of the All-Union Scientific Institute of Systems Research, State Committee for Science and Technology, USSR Academy of Sciences. He holds the degree of doctor of engineering from the Moscow Physics and Technical Institute (1967).

*We gratefully acknowledge assistance in the preparation of this chapter from D. D. Aufenkamp, formerly senior staff associate, dealing with U.S.A.-U.S.S.R. activities, Division of Mathematical and Computer Sciences, National Science Foundation, Washington.——Ed.

Contemporary socio-economic processes and phenomena embrace a wide variety of problems, from the unstructured to the well structured, from political, social and demographic problems to economic, technical and physical ones. Current research on these problems centers either on attempts to build "objective" mathematical models of this broad range of processes or on mainly substantive, purely scenario-based prospective studies of future development. The shortcomings of both these approaches are obvious. The use of purely substantive methods takes no advantage of the large stock of quantitative data, governed by existing and objective scientific laws and relationships, with the result that when the phenomenon under investigation is complex and multiform the findings may be contradictory or conflicting.

The application of purely formal methods to these problems produces the opposite effect, in which the subjective part of the data included in the formal models (and this is inevitable in this approach, since no recognized and tested formalized descriptions exist for many of the problems) exerts greater influence on the result than the objective principles being followed.

What is required is a rational combination of substantive methods with the formal modeling of those aspects of development in which the laws of change are sufficiently well known, i.e., those problems in which the quantitative elements predominate even though the structure is hybrid. (Following Simon's classification,[1] this group of problems, which lends itself to modeling, may be called adequately structured problems.) The range of this group of problems constantly expands as our knowledge of the phenomenon grows.

In this case, research is an iterative process in which the set of substantive scenarios narrows as the formalizable part of the problems is dealt with by means of models and formal scenarios, while at the same time becoming richer through additional quantitative and substantive data, since the model is capable of combining and tracing the interaction of the set of characteristics of the phenomenon under investigation and of providing information that specialists in separate branches of the problem find it difficult to obtain (the integrating effect of the model).

Models Become More Complicated

Methodological and practical problems arise in this mathematical model-building, which includes, in addition to objective principles and tested formalized descriptions, an element of subjective expert information about the phenomenon. The phenomenon itself, a complex dynamic system, possesses different kinds of interacting processes with feedback and time lags, the possibility of modifying the structure in time, etc. The models rapidly tend to become more complicated as effort is made to accommodate in them as many details as possible of these interconnected processes. This attempt to build a "single" all-embracing model capable of simultaneously explaining the whole range of phenomena of a large-scale socio-economic system resembles the trend in technology, physics and so on, where, as knowledge increases, the corresponding models grow more complex. The building of such highly complex models involves considerable expenditure of time and resources. But the use of such models in the decision-making process is justified only when the laws by which the phenomenon under investigation operate are well known, and when widely recognized and pragmatically tested mathematical descriptions are available. In this case, heavy expenditure on the creation of a unique model of this kind may be recouped by prolonged use.

It is doubtful whether this approach to the modeling of the long-term dynamics of large-scale socio-economic systems can be regarded as acceptable at the present time. Attempts to create more or less "universal models" led to such complicated computer programs that researchers could no longer grasp the structure of the model or the initial hypotheses.

Modeling Becomes a Lengthy Search

As in most systems-analysis tasks, each specific goal calls for a model of its own which will be the result of multidisciplinary research by sociologists, scientists and engineers. In this instance, modeling therefore comes down to a lengthy search for a pragmatically realizable series of hypothesis-submodels, making it possible to investigate the major problems for which there are mathematical descriptions both relevant to the research aims and satisfactory to the experts. Thus most of the work in modeling system alternatives essential to decision-making goes into building a special model, which means lengthy and endlessly repeated modifications to its composition and structure. This model-building proceeds through the following stages:

Definition of the limits of the system, choice of the basic variables and structure of the model that will most fully reflect the specifications of the research problem and correspond with existing knowledge and data.

Quantitative description of the chain of cause and effect, writing of the computer programs, collection of statistical data, qualitative investigation of the dynamics of individual submodels.

Combining the finished submodel programs into a single model of the phenomenon being investigated.

Identification of the parameters of the model by statistical and other *a priori* data.

Preparation of a set of alternative scenarios and their formalization.

Analysis of the sensitivity of the modeling results to mistakes in the parameters, review of the adequacy of the model, assessment of modeling accuracy.

Performance of simulation and optimization calculations using different quality criteria.

Collection, processing and storage of the modeling results, their display in suitable form, substantive interpretation of the results.

This enormous volume of work, corresponding to many man-years, often has to be repeated all over again, even for a minor change in the initial statement of the problem. The contradiction between this multiplicity of tasks and the rigid limits on the time available for preparing decisions has evoked the methodological response, first, as mentioned above, of building very complicated models in an attempt to obtain universal models covering a relatively broad range of questions, and then, when this turned out to be a dead-end, of using fairly simple modeling methods (of the "system dynamics" type, the DYNAMO language), enabling specialists who are not well versed in mathematics and computer techniques to build simple models rapidly. This simplicity was gained at the expense of a considerable loss in the potential of the models themselves. Clearly, existing modeling methodology for the range of problems under consideration offers no adequate modeling technique corresponding to practical requirements.

A New Method for Building Models

For this reason a new modeling method is proposed, based on the concept of a *problem-oriented, man-machine modeling system*, i.e. a mathematical, algorithmic, program and information software system enabling experts in conversational mode with a computer to carry out all the processes of building, reviewing and operating the model for a broad range of activities involving the simulation of processes in a given problem area.

The essence of this system is that it does not initially contain a model, but instead a base that lets the expert generate the particular model structure corresponding to his research aims; this structure is then filled in with quantitative relationships describing the links between its elements. These relationships can be contained and stored in the modeling system itself or can be easily written out and fed into the model. The system should also contain and provide ready access to and use of all algorithms and programs needed at the various stages of building, reviewing and operating the model. This should be achieved by automating the routine procedures arising at all modeling stages, taking into account the range of problems specifically being studied.

Attempts to develop or use special software extending the possibilities of modeling and work with models have been the subject of a large number of projects, e.g., the "Systems Dynamics" of Forrester and Meadows;[2] the APT system of Mesarovic;[3] the MODULECO system of the French Institute of Informatics and Automation;[4] the CARPS system produced at the IBM Tokyo Center.[5]

There is also a whole series of modeling languages and simulation systems, designed to perfect the modeling process, which are of interest from the standpoint of systems programming.

These are systems intended for the modeling of discrete and continuous processes and also of mixed systems, such as GPSS, GASP-4, CSSL, WISSIM,[6] PRIZ,[7] etc.

Analysis of existing approaches to the modeling process and of certain modeling languages provides copious material for general conclusions and studies concerning the creation of problem-oriented modeling systems, combining the merits of the various trends and underpinning the full cycle of activities involved in building a machine model.

A Systems Approach

We shall now indicate the basic requirements (the building principles) for a modeling system, which, in our view, reflect a systems approach to the process of building, reviewing and operating the model.[8]

The man-machine approach: all stages in the building, review and operation of the model are carried out in conversational mode between the researcher and the computer.

Universality: i.e., the ability of the system to synthesize models in order to solve a broad range of problems within a particular subject area and to contain the basic data concerning the range of problems under consideration.

Adaptability: the ability to easily reconstruct the initial model as well as research methods to allow for a new statement of the problem.

Combination of quantitative and qualitative research methods: i.e., application of the advantages of both formal modeling and the informal capacities of individuals and incorporation of the greatest possible number of factors bearing on the problem, including phenomena whose dynamics cannot at present be formalized.

Openness: the ability of the system to change, becoming more refined as knowledge increases, through the replacement of existing elements in the system by more advanced ones and through the addition of new blocks.

Cumulativeness: the ability to accumulate knowledge, i.e. model, scenario, algorithmic and statistical information.

Specificity: i.e., the ability to use the general properties of the particular range of problems for which the modeling system was designed, and on the basis of these characteristics to simplify and increase the effectiveness of the algorithms and programs used.

Ease of use: i.e., the accessibility of the system to the researcher at all modeling stages, the possibility of arranging contacts between man and computer in such a way that inquiry and reply take place in language as close as possible to natural language, using terms and categories comprehensible to the researcher. Possibility of working with the model without knowing the details of the actual system and of obtaining intermediate and final data in suitable form for substantive interpretation.

The Modeling System of the All-Union Scientific Institute for Systems Research

The All-Union Scientific Institute for Systems Research has built a modeling system for the study of global development processes. The structure of this system consists of three basic elements: a library, special units and a system control unit (Fig. 1). It is designed to perform all basic operations connected with the modeling of complex socio-economic systems. It makes a clear distinction between the resources required for the two different modeling stages: the model-building stage and the model-review and operation stage. The system is designed for work with dynamic models, described by systems of

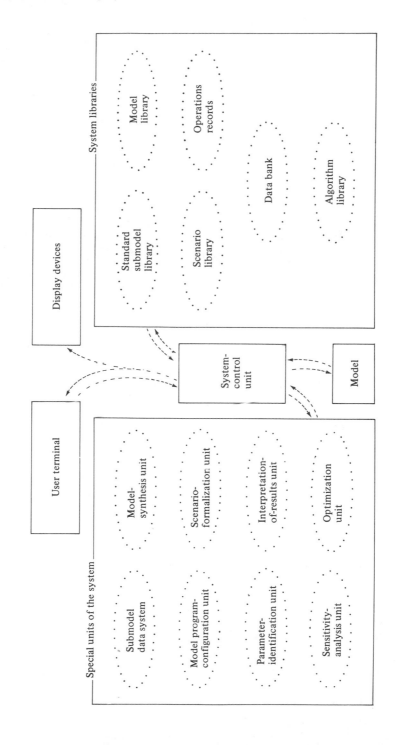

Figure 1. Functional block diagram of an interactive modeling system.

ordinary differential equations, finite difference equations and non-linear functional mapping.

Algorithm library. The modeling process calls for the use of a large number of special algorithms both for building the model and for analyzing and reviewing the finished model. For example, algorithms are needed for assembling the model from the separate submodels, for integration, identification, sensitivity analysis, optimization and so on. These algorithms are constantly being supplemented and renewed.

Statsitical data bank. Data are stored in this bank in a form as close as possible to that in which they were stored in the initial source. Storage in the initial form is important for checking, comparing and updating. The bank also contains data converted to achieve uniformity in units of measurement, contents of variables, etc. The bank has a highly complex structure reflecting the many different origins of the data, corresponding to different organizations and countries.

Scenario library. On the basis of the work of the scenario formalization unit, conceptual scenarios, which are drawn up by specialists, are converted into series of numerical values for the parameters. These series have a complex hierarchical structure. During work with the model the scenarios are collected and stored in the scenario library.

The modeling system's special units consist of a package of relatively self-contained programs that make it possible to unify and simplify such operations as the assembly of a model from separate units, special reviews of the model or its adjustment to study a particular problem. Each of these special programs functions in conversational mode and has its own relatively developed contact language. Unlike ordinary computer-program packages, the special units of the system are designed in advance for work with formalized models. Contact between them and the model and among themselves is effected through the system-control programs.

Submodel library. To ensure the automony of the separate submodels within the modeling system, the concept of a "submodel" is defined as the smallest structural element of the model. The submodel S_i is a map

$$S_i : X_i \rightarrow Y_i$$

of the set of inputs X_i of the submodel to the set of outputs Y_i. The autonomy of the submodels makes it possible to assemble real models at a later stage, using the submodel library. This stores all data concerning the modeled variables and standard submodels, including descriptions of the physical meaning of the variables, a description of the structure of the submodels and the hypotheses on which they are based. The modeled variables are classified in groups (sections) according to the discipline to which they belong and are hierarchically structured. Furthermore, all inputs and outputs of the standard submodels are linked to the modeled variables, with the result that the same variable may be linked to the outputs of many alternative submodels, based on different hypotheses. The submodel library also contains a description of the special links between variables, for example, the differential variables.

By clearly singling out the group of operations concerned with model building from all the operations comprising the modeling process, we can automate to a considerable extent this group, the most labor-consuming part of modeling. Within the man-machine system, a special *model-synthesis subsystem* has been created which considerably increases the general efficiency of the model-building process. It offers the user special language and information software as well as all the necessary means for automating the production of the model's computer programs.

The information software of the model synthesis system makes it possible to accumulate submodel libraries simultaneously with all their possible interconnections. The user can retrieve the description of previous alternative submodels and select those which meet the aims of his research project.

For the modeling of complex socio-economic systems of large dimension, variable structure and random feedback, the algorithmic presentation of the computations, i.e., the construction of the model's computer programs, becomes a difficult problem, the solution of which calls for special language and program software. The use of algorithmic programming languages is ineffective for this purpose. On the other hand, the creation of universal modeling languages capable of describing a broad range of models and the corresponding operations on them leads to excessive complication of the conceptual base.

Some descriptive languages are used to increase the flexibility of the man-machine system. Various modeling languages, best suited to a particular field, may be used for the description of submodels, including universal algorithmic languages. A relatively simple and convenient link language has been worked out to describe the intramodel links between variables and submodels. For the description of operations on models in the corresponding special subsystems of the man-machine system, operation-description languages are used which take into account the mathematical base of each subsystem. Such a division of language software makes the system open with regard to future development and modification.

The model synthesis subsystem enables the researcher to build quickly the model he needs from standard submodels in a process of dialogue with and analysis of the contents of the standard submodel bank. The researcher consults the system about the possibility of modeling the variables in which he is interested and obtains information on all relevant alternative submodels. After choosing the most suitable one, he proceeds to a similar analysis of the submodels linked to it. As a result of this consultation, the model synthesis subsystem generates a description of the model in link language.

The *program-configuration unit* is basically the translator that converts the text of the formal description of the model into a computer program. The work of the configuration unit comes to an end with the automatic production of the computer program for the model. In this way the researcher is entirely freed from the laborious task of reconstructing the computing algorithm and writing the computer program. This program and its reference file, containing all data on the composition and structure of the model, are stored in the model bank and are used in the work of the other special subsystems of the man-machine modeling system.

The scenario-formalization unit converts verbal descriptions by experts into a series of instructions for forming the necessary model structure and assigning the corresponding values to the exogenous variables.

System-control unit. The control unit is the nucleus of the interactive modeling system, linking all its components in a single complex.

This control program provides a two-way exchange of information between the model, the terminal and the other units of the system. It provides the researcher and the special units with standard access to all the model's variables. Concentrating the control of information flow in a single unit makes the system more flexible and facilitates subsequent modification and extension. Receiving instructions from the terminal and the special units, the control program decides the order in which they will be carried out.

This control unit also performs all the auxiliary operations connected with preparing the model for work: namely, computing the essential data, collecting and storing of results. These operations also include: memory loading of the initial values of variables and the model's parameters; selection of the appropriate method for the numerical integration of the model's equations and retrieval of the corresponding subprograms from the algorithm library; definition of the values of the exogenous variables in accordance with the selected scenarios; computation of the variable values with time-lag; solution of the corresponding systems of non-linear equations, for models with feedback; actuation of model operations, and interruption for the collection, processing and storing in the operations records of all essential output data.

Interpretation unit. The substantive interpretation of the modeling results is also a highly complicated task for the expert. The model contains and computes the dynamics of a high number of parameters. The person taking the decisions in conversational mode with the model can become acquainted with only a small proportion of this information. The automatic results-interpretation unit analyzes the dynamics of the whole parameter array, classifies the curves, notes irregularities in particular inequalities and the fulfillment of previously given conditions, and brings into correspondence with the computation dynamics any substantive text concerning events taking place in the phenomenon. This supplementary information greatly facilitates contact between the person taking the decision and the complex mathematical model.

Experience with the prototype modeling system set up at the All-Union Scientific Institute for Systems Research has shown that it is highly effective for modeling complicated socio-economic systems. □

FOOTNOTES

[1] H. Simon and A. Newell, "Heuristic Problem-solving: The Next Advance in Operations Research," *Operations Research*, Vol. 6, January 1958.

[2] P. Koch, *DTSS DYNAMO*, Hanover, N.H.: Dartmouth College, June 1975.

[3] M. Mesarovic, *A Computer-based Policy Analysis Tool (The APT-System) and its Use for US Policy Evaluation in a Global Context*, U.S. Association for the Club of Rome, June 1977.

[4] P. Nepomiastchy, "MODULECO: Software for Macroeconomic Modelling," in S. H. Lavington (ed.), *Information Processing 80*, North Holland/IFIP, 1980.

[5] M. Ohkohchi and M. Udo, *An Interactive Model Operation System for Planning*, Japan: IBM. 1978. (Tokyo Scientific Center Report, GE 18-1880-0.)

[6] J. S. Buehring, *WISSIM: An Interactive Simulation Control Language*, Laxenburg, Austria: International Institute for Applied Systems Analysis, 1976 (RM-76-24).

[7] E. Tyugu, "A Programming System with Automatic Program Synthesis," *Lecture Notes in Computer Science*, Berlin: Springer Verlag, 1977.

[8] V. Gelovani, *Principles for Building a Man-Machine System for Modelling Global Development Processes, Moscow*, VNIISI, 1979. (Collected Studies of the All-Union Scientific Institute for Systems Research, No. 8.)

To delve more deeply

BEER, S., "The Organization of Unthinkable Systems." *Brain of the Firm*, 2nd edition, Chapter 4. New York: John Wiley, 1981.

GELOVANI, V., "On a Control Problem in the Forrester Global Dynamic Model."
  Reports of the USSR Academy of Sciences (Moscow), Vol. 220, No. 3, 1975.
_____. "Modelling the Long-term Development of a Region." *Reports of the USSR
  Academy of Sciences* (Moscow), Vol. 238, No. 3, 1978.
_____. "Methodological Problems in Global Models." *Simulation*, Vol. 33, No. I,
  July 1979.

In the development and application of ecological models in urban and regional planning, the main emphasis has been on sophisticated, integrated modeling techniques. The strength of these techniques lies in their ability to provide a symbolic logic capable of expressing ideas, and particularly relationships, of very great complexity while at the same time retaining a simplicity and parsimony of expression.

Chapter 7

THE DEVELOPMENT OF MODELS IN URBAN
AND REGIONAL PLANNING

J.N.R. Jeffers

The models we seek to construct are basically formal expressions of the essential elements of a problem in either physical or mathematical terms. In the past, much of the emphasis in scientific explanation has been on the use of physical analogs of biological and environmental processes, but today our models are essentially mathematical and abstract. Our use of mathematical notation in the modeling of complex systems is an attempt to provide a representational symbolic logic which simplifies, but does not markedly distort, the underlying relationships. A further condition is that our mathematical representation

John Jeffers was trained as a forester and then as a statistician. He is currently director of the Institute of Terrestrial Ecology, Merlewood Research Station, Grange-over-Sands LA11 6JU (Cumbria), Great Britain, telephone 044-84-2264. This text appeared originally in *Nature and Resources*, Vol. XVII, No. 2, 1981 (a Unesco quarterly).

should enable predictive statements to be derived from the relationships. Without the ability to predict the result of changes in one or
more of the elements in the model, we cannot regard our representation
as belonging to the world of science.

The use of models in modern science is, of course, extensive, and
here I am mainly concerned with their application to urban and
regional planning. My own experience lies mainly in their application to
the problems of ecology in rural land-use and regional planning and it
is inevitable that the views I express are distorted by my orientation.
For example, I have a particular concern about the danger which I see
arising from the fact that our policies for the rural environment and for
regional planning are developed by urban man. Our systems of education and government are almost exclusively developed in an urban
context, and urban man has come to regard the rural environment as a
place largely for his recreation, visual amenity and the conservation of
attractive forms of wildlife. Seldom, if ever, does he see the rural
environment as the primary source of his food, wood-fiber and fuel. I
suspect that urban ideas are given too much emphasis in decisions about
the use of land, particularly close to urban settlements.

The main theme of this chapter, however, is that the development
and application of ecological models must be embedded in the broader
context of the decision making process. The development of models, in
particular, should be determined by the definition and bounding of the
extent of the original problem, so that modeling does not become an
academic and intellectual exercise, which becomes increasingly unrelated to the problem to be solved. Even more importantly, we must
recognize that urban and regional planning is a consultative process, and
that the models we construct should contribute to the discussion and
decision-making phases of that process. In seeking to develop this
thesis, I shall need to describe briefly the role of systems analysis in
environmental research, the identification and choice of families of
mathematical models, and the role of data in their construction, verification and validation.

Systems Analysis

Within Unesco's Man and the Biosphere Program, it has long been
recognized that modeling should be part of the broader systems analysis
of the problem. Various definitions of systems analysis have been
attempted, but in this article I shall assume that systems analysis is the
orderly and logical organization of data and information into models,
followed by the rigorous testing and exploration of these models

necessary for their validation and improvement. Systems analysis provides a framework of thought designed to help decisionmakers to choose a desirable course of action, or to predict the outcome of one or more courses of action that seem desirable to those who have to make the decision. In particularly favorable cases, the course of action that is indicated by the systems analysis will be the "best" choice in some specified or defined way.

Initially, we may identify seven steps in the application of systems analysis to practical problems, and these steps and their interconnections are summarized in the figure below. The process begins with the

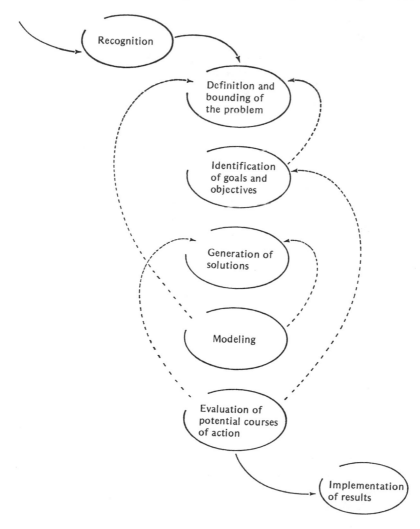

recognition of the existence of a problem or of a constellation of interconnected problems, which may be amenable to analysis. Once the
existence of the problem has been recognized, it is necessary to simplify
it to the point at which it is likely to be capable of analytical solution,
while, on the other hand, preserving all the elements that justify the use
of research resources. The difficult judgment of the relative importance
of the inclusion or exclusion of elements of the problem, and the
balancing of their relevance to the analytical grasp of the situation
against their contribution to complications that may well become
unmanageable, is frequently critical. The delicate balance between
simplification and complexity, while retaining sufficient relationship to
the original problem for the analytical solution to be recognizably
appropriate, will almost certainly determine the success or failure of the
investigation. Once the extent of the problem has been defined and
bounded, it becomes possible to define goals and objectives of the
investigation. Usually, these goals and objectives will form a hierarchy,
with the major objectives progressively subdivided into a series of minor
objectives, and it is important that the priorities assigned to these
various objectives should be defined.

Only then are we in a position to generate a range of possible
solutions to the problem. In general, we will seek an analytical solution
of the greatest possible generality in order to make the best use of
previous work on similar problems, and of the underlying mathematics
of their solution. Ideally, we will develop as wide a range of solutions as
possible at this stage. When the appropriate alternatives have been
examined, and only then, the important phase of modeling the interrelationships between various facets of the problem can begin.

It is particularly important that we should be careful not to allow
ourselves to be carried away by this phase of modeling, in which most
of us are especially interested. Once the modeling has been brought to a
sufficiently advanced stage for the model to be used, even in a preliminary way, we should begin the equally important phase of evaluating
potential courses of action. In making this evaluation, it will usually be
necessary to investigate the sensitivity of the results of the assumptions
made by the model, as it is only when the model begins to be used that
previously unsuspected weaknesses in the assumptions, and in the
model formulation, begin to be revealed. Finally, we may arrive at a
phase in which the implementation of the results that have been derived
from previous phases becomes possible. However, the implementation
may itself demonstrate that various phases of our analyses were
incomplete or need to be revised so that further research and investigation may then be necessary. Indeed, because systems analysis is a

framework of thought rather than a detailed prescription, the whole process should be regarded as iterative, with a necessary return to earlier phases as we realize the inadequacy of our earlier thinking.

In this consideration of systems analysis as a basis for modeling, perhaps the greatest emphasis needs to be placed on the identification of the hierarchy of goals and objectives, and on the definition and bounding of the extent of the problem. There is a long history of research on models or sub-models that have become disconnected from their original problem, so that research continues long after the original problem has either disappeared or changed. Unhappily, the role of academic interest and specialization in our research interests has sometimes had an undesirable effect in placing the greatest emphasis on intellectual achievement rather than on the practical solution of problems. There is perhaps an even longer history of searching for the application of models that have been selected in advance of the identification of a problem!

Families of Models

Despite my emphasis on the identification of goals and the definition and bounding of problems, it is nevertheless possible to identify broad families of mathematical models, which have found application in urban and regional planning. The most popular of these families, because of their academic and intellectual interest, are dynamic models based on the traditions of the Newtonian calculus. These deterministic models draw heavily on the traditional application of mathematics to physics, and are capable of great sophistication. However, they are difficult to communicate to non-mathematicians, and even mathematicians have difficulty in discovering how such models behave as their parameters are changed. Recent discussions, for example, on the behavior of relatively simple predator-prey models, show the extent to which model behavior is counter-intuitive, and sometimes difficult to investigate.

Because of these difficulties, some mathematicians prefer the more formalized matrix models which simplify analysis because eigenvalue solutions sometimes summarize the essential properties of the model. Such models remain deterministic, with severe constraints imposed upon their formulation. However, they are certainly no easier to communicate to the general public and to the non-scientists, with the added disadvantage of the unfamiliarity of matrix notation to non-mathematicians.

Although less popular, stochastic models are probably necessary for the modeling of biological variability in ecological systems. They are also an essential part of the fitting of parameters to other models, and provide for a wide range of possible assumptions. The most popular, and best known, stochastic models are those that are linear and additive, but, more recently, we have seen the development of non-linear models with stochastic properties for ecological processes. An interesting variant, using the convenient properties of matrices, is in the development of Markov models, with their simple assumptions of dependence of dynamic change on transitional probabilities. However, it is doubtful if stochastic models are more readily communicated to the non-scientist, or even to the non-mathematical scientist. Since, regrettably, relatively few of our mathematicians seem to come into contact with statistical theory until late in their careers, there is also some considerable resistance from mathematicians in the use of such models.

Rarer still is the use of multivariate models, with the extension of the stochastic models to situations with large numbers of variables. However, such models are now being widely developed for problems of reification, clustering and discrimination. As such, they are more likely to be used in the preliminary phases of systems analysis than in the final solution. They are certainly no easier to communicate than any of the other model families so far mentioned.

Differential equations
Difference equations
Catastrophe theory
Dynamic
Leslie matrix
Compartment models
Input-output
Topology
Model families
Matrix
Linear programming
Non-linear programming
Dynamic programming
Theory of games
Optimization
Multivariate
Stochastic
Markov models
Reification
Cluster analysis
Discrimination
Linear models
Non-linear models
Distribution models

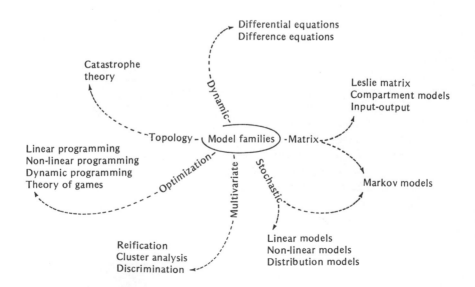

Some of the most widely used models make little attempt to mimic biological or physical processes, but instead concentrate on the search for an optimal solution of a defined system against constraints, as in linear and non-linear programming. Such models begin by the identification of a feasible solution and then seek improved solutions, together with the identification of constraints that must be relaxed to achieve an even better solution. Some large optimization problems can often be reformulated as a series of smaller problems, arranged in sequences of time or space, or both. This search for the best solution at each of a number of stages is known as dynamic programming. Optimization models have a close relationship with the theory of games, from which they are essentially derived, and their wider use may be an essential development in the application of models to urban and regional planning.

Most recently, we have seen the development of topological models for systems with the properties of bimodality, discontinuity, hysteresis and divergence. These catastrophe-theory models have engendered intense interest, possibly because they have a strong visual appeal. However, their dependence on topology limits application to problems with a relatively small number of dimensions. It will be interesting to see whether the intellectual interest in such models is confirmed by their success in the solution of practical problems.

Choice of Models for Development

How do we choose models for the solution of any particular problem? I have already noted an essential condition of systems analysis that we should develop alternative models in the generation of solutions, primarily because it is seldom possible to know in advance which is likely to be the most successful strategy. Only by developing two or more models do we provide ourselves with any flexibility in the evaluation of potential courses of action in the later stages of the analysis. If, therefore, we are using systems analysis as a basis for our search for a solution, we are likely to have two or more models from which to choose at the important stage of the evaluation of results.

Currently, our intellectual and academic preference is for rather complex models, dependent upon advanced mathematics in their assumptions, formulation and solution. Because we are most familiar with particular kinds of mathematics, our preference is for analog solutions based on deterministic functions recognizable as models of physical processes. We are most likely, therefore, to choose solutions that come from the families of dynamic or matrix models. Where we

Models

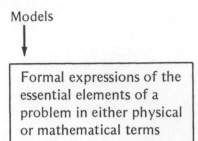

Formal expressions of the
essential elements of a
problem in either physical
or mathematical terms

cannot avoid the untidiness of biological variation, we may turn reluctantly to stochastic and multivariate models, but it is clear that most research workers would prefer to avoid biological variation and its existence than to make use of that variation in a positive way. Since most of us have strongly developed visual imagery, topological models of catastrophe theory also have a marked appeal.

While attractive to the mathematician (and perhaps to scientists seeking advice from mathematicians), such models are "opaque" to the man in the street, difficult to interpret to the general public, to committees of elected representatives and to private landowners, who will make decisions or recommendations. Such people are not content to be told that a particular course of action is best because a mathematical model says so. It is, therefore, especially unfortunate that the mathematical models we would prefer to use present so little opportunity for investigation of their assumptions and constructions or their implications by the users of the results.

An interesting example of these difficulties was experienced in the presentation of the world models by both Forrester and Meadows. Even though Forrester published his model, so that it was conceivably possible for a critic to examine the implications of the model and to

Systems analysis

Orderly and logical organization of data
and information into models, followed by
the rigorous testing and exploration of
these models necessary for their validation
and improvement

criticize them, relatively little of the discussion was focused on the basic assumptions of the model and on changes in those assumptions. There was, however, no possibility of such criticism in the discussion of the *Limits to Growth* by Meadows, because he did not publish an explicit version of the model.

Today, we see increased faith placed in the role of sophisticated interactive modeling, with the use of modern computers providing access to large quantities of data, and enabling complex arithmetic and logical operations to be done at very high speeds. Just as we teach airline pilots to fly on a simulator—essentially a mathematical model of the way in which an airliner flies and is controlled—so we place our faith in our ability to construct simulators for regional planning, urban development, transport management, etc. Such simulators already exist and have been strongly advocated as a basis for solutions to practical problems. The extent to which those being trained can question the adequacy of the simulation is, however, in doubt.

My own experience suggests that we should concentrate on less mathematical and simpler models for regional planning. The main emphasis of the modeling exercise should be on the discussion of the conceptual base of the objectives and on the constraints that must be placed upon the feasible solutions to the problem. Linear programming, with its simple assumptions of linearity of the objective functions and constraints, has proved to be one of the most important families of models upon which to base research on regional planning. Using such models, the discussion of the participants tends to be centered on objectives and on constraints, with many iterations taking place during the time of the investigation, and with little or no barrier to the start of work. Indeed, it is possible to begin the modeling process with only the most elementary of theoretical concepts and to develop both the objective function and the constraints by discussions as the consultative investigation proceeds. In time, and after many iterations, the ideas of the varied group formed to discuss the conceptual solution of the problem converge on an ultimate solution which has come to be defined as "optimum." The feasibility and departure from optimality of alternatives suggested by any member of the group, or indeed by someone joining the group at a later stage, are easily tested. Tests of submodels in time and space, carried out in sequence, help to prevent the foreclosure of future options, while avoiding the mathematical and theoretical complications of dynamic programming.

At an early stage in regional planning, one of the main objectives of modeling may be to reveal to the various agencies concerned with the region that their policies are in direct conflict. From the identification of conflict, it then becomes necessary to develop a strategy for regional planning which combines elements of the various policies of separate agencies in an agreed way. An alternative to linear programming— though closely related methodologically—is that of the theory of games. Through the construction of a game-theory matrix it is frequently possible to define competing strategies in relation to estimates of the outcomes of the intersections of various strategies. When the number of strategies remains small the existence of a saddlepoint in the matrix of outcomes will indicate that there is a unique strategy which should be played by either participant. More usually it will be necessary to identify strategies which should be played according to probabilities which are determined by the relative outcome from competing strategies. This approach to the problem also provides a reasonable measure of uncertainty in the achievement of particular objectives.

The suggestion that we should concentrate on the less mathematical and simpler models for regional planning will perhaps be disappointing to those for whom the main interest, and perhaps future academic status, is linked to increasing complexity and to the development of mathematical expertise. I detect, also, a marked unwillingness amongst applied mathematicians to depart from analogs of physical processes, even where the mathematics of less representational systems of logic are both complex and intellectually challenging. However, the purpose of urban and regional planning is to achieve harmonious development, in full consultation with the elected representatives and with private and public landowners on whom the development impinges. I believe it is necessary to take all these people (or at least their representatives) with us in the development of ecological models for planning. In the Western democracies, at least, it is not sufficient to say: "You must accept what the model says, because it is 'mathematical;' still less because it has been produced with the aid of a computer."

Role of Data

A new and particular problem is emerging from the increasing use of models in urban and regional planning, including such aspects as pollution, resource planning, and public health. This problem results from the dependence of mathematical models on data, first as a data base and, second, for the validation and verification of models. As our interest in mathematical models has increased, together with the realization that we usually have inadequate data upon which to base such models, there is a corresponding increase in popularity of what have come to be called "data banks." Advocates for the creation of data banks assume that, since data will be required for making future decisions, we should now set about collecting the data which will be required for such decisions.

Many individuals and agencies are actively generating and using data. The individuals tend to be oriented towards particular disciplines, like economics or ecology, while the agencies are oriented towards particular missions, like public health or agriculture. In either case, the data they collect are sometimes inadequate for use in broad interdisciplinary environmental studies. Sometimes, the deficiency is imaginary and reflects the fact that individuals are only vaguely aware of available sources of data in other disciplines. Such individuals also often overlook rich sources of information which reside in experienced individuals or organizations.

There are two philosophies behind the collection of data. First, the accounting theory of data collection assumes that a subsequent use of data is independent of the methods used in their collection. An accountant believes that it is possible to collect data in some neutral sense, and that any subsequent manipulation can be justified, if it contributes to the understanding of the problem. Second, the statistical theory of data collection insists on the essential interdependence between the ways in which data are collected and the methods of analyses which are appropriate for these data. The collection methods (including such questions as the population sampled, the sampling units and the scales of measurement) limit the range of analytical methods that may be employed. Alternatively, if we wish to use particular methods of analysis, we must select the appropriate methods of data collection.

Those who advocate the creation of data banks assume the accounting theory of data collection. However, as scientists, we should be concerned that much human effort is currently being wasted in the collection of heterogeneous and ill-assorted data for which little use will be possible in the future.

Our collection of data as a base for mathematical models, and for the validation and verification of such models, should depend upon the statistical theory of data collection. The collection of data, therefore, depends upon well-formulated hypotheses which are to be tested by the collected data, clearly defined populations about which inferences are to be made, and accurately and precisely designated units of sampling. Examples of such data collections include the population censuses of most countries in the world, agricultural censuses and records of various forms of industrial production. Few good examples of adequately defined data collections exist in the environmental sciences, for example in pollution, land use, ecological productivity, etc.

It is perhaps worth mentioning, in passing, that the limitations of available data may well restrict the use of some models which, other-wise, might well appear attractive as a basis for the solution of practical problems. One good example of this constraint is the input-output models for economic and ecological problems. This version of matrix models is exceptionally "data-hungry," demanding large quantities of data and being relatively unreliable where the input-output matrix is incomplete. Another example is in the application of differential or difference equations to the modeling of complete ecosystems. As we discovered during the International Biological Program, attempts to model complete ecosystems are seldom successful, and demand large quantities of data of kinds which are difficult, if not impossible, to collect. However, we should not allow these difficulties to deter us from careful examination and exploration of data that become available through well-defined methods of data collection. It will, of course, be necessary to distinguish between hypothesis testing and hypothesis formulation in such examinations, taking care not to formulate and test hypotheses on the same set of data.

Discussion

I have stressed that the development and application of ecological models for urban and regional planning must be embedded in the broader context of the decision-making process. Ideally, this embedding will be through the use of a clear framework of thought like systems analysis, with special attention being paid to the definition of the problem and to the bounding of its extent. Mathematical modeling must never be allowed to become an academic and intellectual exercise, unrelated to the problems that need to be solved. It is regrettable, but probably true, that we no longer need any more techniques. What we need now is the application of those techniques that already exist to the problems we also already have. This conclusion may be disappoint-ing to those who have to find new topics for scientific research without the necessary access to problems of interest to decision-makers, but it is important to recognize where the real needs exist.

Perhaps our most important need is to recognize that urban and regional planning is essentially a consultative process. If models are to help in this process, they must be seen to contribute to the consulta-tion, and, ideally, to help in directing it. Above all, mathematical models cannot continue to assume an *ex cathedra* role without com-plete loss of practical value—except perhaps as an intellectual exercise.

The role of the electronic computer in the future development of modeling is probably critical. As computers become smaller and cheaper, so that today it is possible to buy yesterday's dream computer for only a few hundred dollars, it is possible to provide an interactive environment for the discussion of urban and regional development policies. The linking of many small computers through telephone networks will provide access to a common model for a large number of agencies and individuals, and, increasingly, to members of an informed general public. Development of computer conferencing will facilitate extensive review and discussion of alternative strategies matched against optimal strategies with varying constraints. The explanation of public policies may also be facilitated, although it is likely that much of the explanation will remain, as today, with the news media.

The future for the development and application of ecological models in urban and regional planning is bright, but only if we are careful to ensure that modeling and systems analysis remain as tools to be used in the larger purposes of man. Our difficulty will be to resist the temptation to erect these intellectual disciplines as monuments to our own (and imagined) cleverness. ☐

As a statement of personal conviction, the author affirms that only the light of reason can pursue the shadows at the furthest reaches of man's existence, and raises warnings about the dangers in social planning. To ward these off, we must break the chain of causality in social facts by taking a view of the future that allows for diversity and facilitates creativity in a society.

History has no meaning.
Karl Popper, *The Open Society and its Enemies*, 1945.

Chapter 8

SOCIAL MODELS: BLUEPRINTS OR PROCESSES?

Graham R. Little

Introduction

The study of societies can be approached in one of two ways: either as autonomous systems inexorably moving from one state to some other, predetermined, state, or as an overlapping of various psychological factors describable by variables that transcend the individual—socialized knowledge, shared attitudes, social norms—and yet fundamentally the collective result of human endeavor and creativity. The first is the position of Karl Marx[1] who accorded meaning to history; the second is the position argued by Karl Popper[2] who accorded history no meaning.

Graham R. Little, Ph.D., B.Sc. (Hons), says that he is a "thinking individual working to shape a career as a writer and philosopher." He is active on the New Zealand energy scene primarily as a commentator with a particular focus on the methodological aspects of energy policy formulation. His address is: 20 Rawene Road, Birkenhead, Auckland 10, New Zealand.

The significance conceded to history is related to the degree of causality perceived in social systems. Thus, if society is considered to be governed by inexorable "social laws," then history obviously provides a guide to the uncovering of those laws. But if history is thought to be merely a backdrop to the stage on which the present is played out, affecting the present and the future only to the extent that it affects our behavior at the moment,[3] then all history can do is merely offer insight into how we have reached our present position without necessarily affecting the choices we make now and hence without necessarily affecting the future. Historicism is the term coined to describe the process of analyzing social forces, identifying the presumed causality of those forces and then projecting the result on to the future as predictions of high certainty. In commenting on historicists, Popper suggested that they appeared to be compensating for their loss of an unchanging world by clinging to the faith that change can be foreseen "because it is ruled by an unchanging law."[4]

The idea that socialism evolves in a predetermined way from capitalism is no longer taken seriously.[5] And while the struggle against this idea (as exemplified by Popper) may be said to have been successful, this idea, like some Janusian beast, persists by presenting a different face under the name of futurology.

The struggle for an open society, for the idea of freedom[6] is a truly enduring problem of philosophy, enduring because forces of suppression, if not of evil, forever lurk in the nearby shadow; philosophical because the struggle is a battle of ideas: a fight for the mind of man. Those who hold ideas to be the true causal factor in the shaping of societies recognize that only the light of reason can pursue the shadows at the furthest reaches of man's existence.[7] In this combat for the mind, the ultimate outcome must be measured in terms of behavior.[8] As words forge the reality of our existence, so it is by their effect on our deeds, by the congruence between word and behavior, that we judge the worth of one philosophy against another. It is this criterion I wish to apply to notions of social planning, social goals, and futurology. In summary, I seek to elucidate the following issue: What alternative conceptions of social planning exist, and what is the integrity of each? (Integrity is defined as the congruence between the stated aims of the philosophy and the behaviors it typically facilitates.) In arguing for a particular program of social reform, Marx contended that it represented the "natural law" of social evolution uncovered as the result of his scientific analysis. Although his argument met with well-known success in the past, today it is unlikely that a similar result can be expected, given the abundance of conflicting data, the many alternative theories and the large number of scholars with opposing prejudices.[9] How ironical, then, that despite these factors and the conceptual decline of historicism, there should arise an even more insidious proposition: that man, being rational, intelligent, clever, knowledgeable and above all a creature of choice, should be able to choose his own destiny!

At an earlier period, Marx sought to uncover the fundamental law of social development and thereby prepared the ground for ambitious politicians who would take actions that could help Nature to get to where she "wanted" to go. But later, when as an aftermath of the work by Popper, Hayek and others, laws gave way to trends and "trend management," the need to provide a goal or target for these trends and their management gave birth to futurism.

Sequence of Steps

The search for utopia is not new to Western philosophy, Plato's *Republic* being one of the earlier attempts. However, the notion of trends backed by the capacities of the electronic computer has in our age given the search for utopia new impetus. This rests conceptually on a very simple sequence of steps, as follows:

Step 1. Identify the social goal or national plan that is to be achieved at some future time. (This is the utopia and may involve a single objective or outline a whole new social order.)

Step 2. Identify the trends that need to be initiated in order to bring society to the desired future.

Step 3. Undertake the actions required to set society's feet on the path marked by these trends so that, at the proper time, a flowering of the "better" society will occur—surely the hope of all the effort.

This simple scheme guides both the idealist and the bureaucratic planner. The idealist fixes his eyes on the vision of this "better" society and passionately proclaims that salvation is at hand if only people will follow him unquestioningly. The bureaucrat, on his part, creates a systematic model incorporating the "significant" trends—too often ignoring, we would note, both the definition and the criteria of "significant"—and trend possibilities (usually subsumed under the dreadful word "scenario") and then turns to the computer for printouts of what needs to be done systematically to set things right. This is the technocratic use of the above scheme. But with what sadness we note that the political consequences of both idealism and central planning are the same, namely, widespread intolerance.

The Fallacy of Composition

The seemingly simple and direct conceptual approach to social development follows from a "common-sense" view of decision making at the personal level. In that view, we simply select our objectives, choose our course of action for achieving them, and then take the steps required; in short, we decide what we want to do and then do it.

There are two fundamental objections, however, to letting this common-sense view guide decision making at the social level. First of all, this simple view itself is flawed; the decision making process at the personal level confuses what we may like to do with what is within our reach, given our resources, commitment and perseverance. There is a big difference between setting out to dig a hole in one's yard to build a swimming pool and attempting single-handedly to shift Mount Everest a meter to the left. Second, and more significant to our argument, there is a flaw in the assumption that the approach to decision making at this personal level will work at the social level. Even though, flaws and all, this approach often works for the individual and gives an appearance of being purposeful as well, to argue that it will work at the social level is to ignore the fallacy of composition, which is that decision making at the social level is not and cannot be regarded as a mere quantitative extension of individual decision making for the same reason that saving in a recession may be good for the individual but is not good for society.

National Goal-Setting

From time to time, a nation does attempt to draw up goals for itself. Taking the United States as an instructive example, we find that former President Eisenhower attempted to "develop a broad outline of co-ordinated national policies and programs" and to "set up a series of goals in various areas of national activity." Later President Johnson established a "Planning-Programming-Budgeting-System" to put the nation's priorities in order. President Nixon after him declared that "it is time we addressed ourselves, consciously and systematically, to the question of what kind of nation we want to be."[10]

In my own country, New Zealand, there have been National Development Conferences, and today, there is a New Zealand Planning Council, a Commission of the Future, and a "Prime Minister's Think Tank." I find that their collective impact has been minimal. Alvin Toffler crystallized the feeling of futility concerning such social goal-setting when he wrote:

> The real, as distinct from the glibly verbalized, goals of any society. . .are already too complex, too transient, and too dependent for their achievement upon the willing participation of the governed to be perceived and defined so easily.[11]

Unfortunately, his critique of a decade ago fell into the age-old conceptual trap of a debate over *who* should rule, a confusion between function and form of government.[12]

To ask the question "who should rule" will inevitably bring psychologically loaded answers. Plato, the philosopher, argued that philosophers should rule; Marx, the communist, argued that communists should rule; Hitler, the Fascist, argued that Fascists should rule; Caesar, the Roman Caesar, said that Roman Caesars should rule. I find it is difficult to accept such relationships as coincidental. The goal-setting approach raises the same question, but merely in different words: who should set the goals?

Unfortunately, concern with this question diverts attention from the truly important issue: Is it possible, in a diverse society, to establish a set of national goals and then implement those goals without reverting to a dictatorship in one form or another?

Methodological Problems

I have treated the issue more fully elsewhere;[13] here I look at the political problems arising from the goal-setting sequence in Steps 1 to 3, above. The principal problem is that the process is implicitly value-laden. Asking a group to decide what it would like the future to be necessarily involves its values. For no matter what its answer is, the group will give priority to objectives it considers most important. This leads to disagreement between groups—environmentalists and developers, for example—and actually aggravates differences by forcing each group to become entrenched in chosen position. The ability to reach any consensus slowly becomes impossible and even a willingness to keep issues open may disappear as one group feels threatened and opts for disruptive tactics. This happens regularly in labor disputes and confrontations with environmental and consumer groups.

A likely result of this inability of groups to agree on goals is for some elite to select the goals: a political party, a group of wealthy individuals, or bureaucrats. Once goals are set this way, dire consequences ensue for the implementation stage: there is limited scope for minority points of view, debate and active dissension are suppressed, and diversity is recognized to be dangerous. After all, what would happen to those who want to implement their plan if diversity should catch on?[14] The "plan" looms so large in the political process that it must be implemented at all costs, whether or not it is still appropriate or useful. The whole goal-setting exercise takes on the set of a uniqueness. Once the goals have been decided, it becomes unnecessary to think and, as for changing one's mind about the desirability of one or other goal. . .?

Given this analysis, debates over who should set the goals seem trivial and pointless, for the very process itself is incongruent with the notions of democracy, individual freedom, and diversity. Can those in positions of political power who claim to be sincere in their advocacy of freedom not see this lack of integrity in goal-setting that renders it a notion to be purged from popular vocabulary and political practice?

The Dilemma Before Us

In response to the question of method, we can now state that in a free society it is not possible to establish a set of national goals and set out to implement these through some plan without destroying the very freedom within which these goals were forged. This is understood intuitively and accounts for the fact that no government dependent on the consent of the governed has ever succeeded even with the first stage of this process. This goal-setting approach leads to the goal becoming a value-laden blueprint for society—a utopia—and that in turn gives rise to an authoritarian political reality. The approach involves insincerity, intellectual expediency and manipulation and is a process without integrity; in other words, the philosophy *qua* behavior is incongruent. The dilemma before us is now clear: How can we conceptualize the future, that is, how can we plan, while maintaining the integrity of our philosophy in the present.

Psychological Theories of Time

A psychological theory of time includes a concept of future time. This is important because ideas shape behavior; how we think today about the future will causally shape that future. The commonly held theory of time considers planning as producing a "blueprint" for the future. This theory has a serious methodological flaw in its tendency to define the future in ever greater detail. This leads to the goal-setting approach to social development.

I wish to consider an alternative to this theory, one that represents time as a "flow of problems." This sees the past as the time when actions were taken to influence future problems, the present as the time when actions are being taken to influence current and future problems, and the future as the time when anticipated potential problems may occur as current problems. This theory not only overcomes the methodological problems inherent in the "future action blueprint" theory, but also offers many advantages. For example, it accurately structures individual behavior in relation to social development, it implicates creativity in social development, and provides a simple conceptual framework within which we can relate human aspirations to environmental constraints and the use of knowledge to overcome these constraints.

This proposed theory also introduces important methodological changes that affect our views of planning and of trends. First of all, planning now becomes a "contingency exercise." In thinking of the future, a planner begins to assess potential problems according to their probability, seriousness, and timing and then gives priority to the most serious and most immediate. This assists the politician and society to take timely action that can counteract tomorrow's unpleasantness. This theory of time sees the future as potential problems derived from today's situations. These potential problems also can provide the criteria for establishing today's priorities. Any change in the problems then alters the future derived from them; no attempt is made to squeeze the present into some predetermined mold. Thus we see how opportunity is intrinsic to the theory.

Second, planning also becomes a cognitive skill.[15] Rather than being a unique exercise, it now becomes a conceptual orientation, a way of thinking, and of organizing behavior.[16]

Third, the problem-flow theory of time affects our view of trends, defining a trend as "the perceived social consequences of a number of people adopting similar behaviors in overcoming a common problem." A trend is thus a description of social development that subsumes social causality. This is similar to the views of Max Weber[17] and contrasts with those of Marx or Durkheim, both of whom placed causality of social facts in earlier social facts.

Changing a Trend

The failure to recognize that trends are abstractions gives rise to an insidious political problem. When a problem is equated with a trend, there is a temptation to find straightforward solutions that purport to get society off the trend line. But, in fact, behavior can be changed in only two ways: by force or by choice. Consider the situation in which planners have come up with the perfect solution to the "trend" problem, but it is not to anyone's liking. By focusing on the trend, we are likely to lose sight of its cause and to forget the fact that to change a trend we must change behavior, that is, we must deal with people, not abstractions.

To employ force in changing a trend is self-defeating and only possible under suppressive regimes. Thus, we are left with choice and the realization that the solution to an intransigent trend is diversity. A multiplicity of solutions to the problem represented by the trend allows individuals freedom of choice and dissipates the distorting impact of the single option, like gasoline-driven motor vehicles as the means of personal transport. However, it is not sufficient for governments simply to seek diversity; they must also facilitate the emergence of creativity from within their people. The quest for our own solutions to our needs is the most powerful social force known, although it does not lead to order.

A free society is a rich tapestry of color, a diversity made one only in its diversity. More than anything else, then, we must learn tolerance. Moreover, if our neighbor is different, we must rejoice in that difference as the expression of our freedom. Freedom is not a license however; it is a responsibility. Rousseau argued that man, to be free, must break society's chain. What he failed to realize is that freedom is not found in severing the chain, but depends rather on who holds the end of it. The truly free man is a slave to the hardest taskmaster of all: himself and his principles. To preserve today's freedoms we must rediscover self-discipline.

Epilogue

The essence of the choice before societies might be said to be between two models: the Marxist vision of the perfect commune or the Popperian one of "piecemeal social engineering;" the one founded on knowledge and reason, the other on uncertainty and the recognition of the limits of knowledge. These alternatives can also be summarized as shown in Table 1.

Goal setting offers a "blueprint" for society, seeking to implement it as an "end;" problem solving, on the other hand, is the implementation of a process: one of seeking out today's problems (wrongs or injustices), attempting to deal with them while knowing full well they will re-emerge tomorrow in some other guise. These opposing points of view are more than mere philosophy; fundamentally, they are applied

Table 1. Two opposing points of view

	Problem-solving (Popper)	Goal-setting (Marx)
Time orientation	Past and present	Present and future
Immediate objective	Define problem	Set objectives
Inherent philosophy	Seeing what is wrong in the present order	How we would like the world to be
Political consequences	Free discussion Access to information Public debate and criticism of government	Implementation of the "plan" Elimination of debate Suppression of diversity
Summary	Elimination of existing evils	Production of a future good

psychology, an analysis of the likely consequences of a socialization under different views of social development.

Blueprints or processes? This is the choice. And in it resides conformity and suppression or diversity and freedom. □

FOOTNOTES

1 See K. Marx and F. Engels, *The Communist Manifesto*, Harmondsworth: Penguin, 1967; translation by Samuel Moore first published in 1888, or K. Marx, *Contribution to the Critique of Political Economy*, Chicago: 1969, for some of Marx's original writings. Alternatively see R.N. Carew Hunt, *The Theory and Practice of Communism*, London: Geoffrey Bles, 1950, for an excellent short account of Marxism. A position similar to Marx's has been argued by many sociologists, for example see Emile Durkheim, *Rules of Sociological Method*, p. 109, New York: Free Press, 1958, where he states that "the determining cause of a social fact must be sought among antecedent social facts and not among states of individual consciousness."

2 K. Popper, *The Open Society and Its Enemies*, London: Routledge & Kegan Paul, 1966 (fifth edition).

3 This is a psychological issue concerning the effect of the "environment" on behavior. For an outline of some of these issues, see A. Bry, *A Primer of Behavioural Psychology*, Mentor Books, 1975; J. McVicker Hunt, "Psychological Development: Early Experience," *Annual Review of Psychology*, Vol. 30, 1979, pp. 103-43; W.F. Hill, *Learning: A Survey of Psychological Interpretations*, San Francisco: Chandler Publishing, 1963.

4 K. Popper, *The Poverty of Historicism*, p. 161, London: Routledge & Kegan Paul, 1957.

5 Many scholars seem to reject historicism without necessarily acknowledging the same; for example, see L. Kolakowski and S. Hampshire (eds.), *The Socialist Idea: A Reappraisal*, Quartet Books, 1977.

6 I reject the intellectual dilettantism that denigrates freedom (for example, Skinner's *Beyond Freedom and Dignity*); it ignores socialized knowledge as a causal factor in forging behavior and social development. At very least "freedom" is an idea, one offering hope; and hope is the stuff of revolutions.

7 See K. Popper, *Objective Knowledge; An Evolutionary Approach*, Oxford: Oxford University Press, 1972; for arguments developing the notion of "knowledge" independent of a particular individual, similar notions are implicit in the writings of Kenneth Boulding, see *Beyond Economics*, Ann Arbor: University of Michigan Press, 1968.

8 Socialized knowledge is a causal factor in shaping behavior while behavior is a causal factor in shaping socialized knowledge. In other words, causality does not involve "antecedent social facts" (Durkheim) or individual states of consciousness. Rather, the causality in social systems involves the exchange between the two. It is this non-lineal nature of causality that has been ill-understood. The second issue implicated is the impact of ideas on behavior. See J. Piaget, *The Origin of Intelligence in the Child*, London: Routledge & Kegan Paul, 1953, for a discussion on the impact of the development of knowledge on the development of behavior. See also E.R. John and E.L. Schwartz, "The neurophysiology of information processing and cognition," *Annual Review of Psychology*, Vol. 29, 1978, pp. 1-29, for a fine review of recent work on the neurophysiological impact of semantic and syntactic variation of verbal stimuli. The overwhelming conclusion is that ideas shape behavior, though we do not know precisely how.

9 See A. Rand, *Atlas Shrugged*, New York: Random House, 1957; Z. Brzezinski, *Between Two Ages*, New York: Viking Press, 1970; F.A. Hayek, *Road to Serfdom*, London: Kegan Paul, 1944.

10 Extracted from Alvin Toffler, *Future Shock*, London: Bodley Head, 1970.

11 *Ibid.*

12 The state, within the theory, is given the status of a Platonic form; it is an idea manifest only in specific examples, in forms of government. Governments consist of men with beliefs, values and prejudices; thus all governments are ideological and all ideologies are a matter of choice. Thus the form of government is a choice but the functions of government are not; rather they are deduced as sociological necessities, derived directly from the question: "Does a society need rules?" The answer can only be "Yes." It follows that societies need some way of managing conflict within its rules; of updating the rules as appropriate; and of ensuring the rules are obeyed. These, then, are the functions of government, referred to in the West as executive, legislature and judiciary. These functions must be performed by all forms of government, whether they be dictatorships, chieftaincies, tribal councils or duly elected representatives of the people.

13 G.R. Little, "'Process' and Problems: A Philosophy of the Future," *World Future Society Bulletin*, Vol. XII, No. 6, November-December 1978, pp. 26-33.

14 It is generally agreed that such consequences arise today in centralized states. See Z. Brzezinski, *Between Two Ages*, New York: Viking Press, 1970; or M. Voslensky, *Nomenklatura—The Ruling Class in the Soviet Union*, Molden Verlag, 1980.

15 A cognitive skill is a systematized sequence used to structure our knowledge and understanding of some situation into a more effective system so as to improve our handling of the situation. See Jill Larkin, "Problem-solving in Physics: Structure, Process and Learning," in J. Scandura and C. Brainerd (eds.), *Structural-Process Models of Complex Human Behaviour*, Sijthoff & Noordhoff, 1978, for a brief discussion on the cognitive skill of "problem-solving in physics."

16 Knowledge, as herein used, is the abstraction from reality used to map behavior back onto the reality; potential problems are knowledge of the future so used. See F. Hayek, *New*

Studies in Philosophy, Politics, Economics and the History of Ideas, London: Routledge & Kegan Paul, 1978.

[17] M. Weber, *The Theory of Social and Economic Organization*, New York: 1974. (Translated by A.M. Henderson and T. Parsons.)

To delve more deeply

HUSAINI, S. "Initiative-innovative Patterns of Socio-cultural Rejuvenation: Islamic Ideological and Technological Modernizations," *Islamic Environmental Systems Engineering*, London: Macmillan, 1980.

PART 2. APPLICATION

It is hard to feel unaffected by pronouncements coming from a global model. Most readers will have experienced this at the time the first global model was described in the Club of Rome report entitled, The Limits to Growth. Advances in global modeling since that time have been many; too many to do more here than provide a brief overview of the major current examples. These fall into three categories: IIASA Conference models, economic models, and politically oriented models. Global modeling in the 1980s can play an important role in shaping our vision of a society that is more humane, sustainable, and equitable.

Chapter 9

GLOBAL MODELING IN THE 1980s

John M. Richardson, Jr.

Introduction

Although global modeling has existed as a distinct activity for about a decade, the field is not well known or understood, even in scientific circles. Nor is it easy to survey briefly. There are now at least twenty

Dr. Richardson is professor of international affairs and applied systems analysis as well as director of the Quantitative Teaching and Research Laboratory, School of International Service, at The American University, Washington, DC. A political scientist who directed the Donald P. Eckman Computing Laboratory at Case-Western Reserve University, the author has published more than twenty papers in the field of system analysis and modeling. He has lectured on modeling throughout the world and is co-author of *Integrated Food Policy Analysis,* a study dealing with the world's food problem. His address is School of International Service, The American University, Washington DC 20016, United States of America.

global modeling projects. Many have been in existence for a number of years. They have produced thousands of pages of "results" and documentation. But only a few global modelers have written books and articles which are widely accessible. Apart from the periodic global modeling conferences at the International Institute for Applied Systems Analysis (IIASA) and their proceedings, there is no single forum or publication in which the state of the art and results of global-modeling projects are widely discussed. As will be seen, global modelers are motivated by different agendas, come from different disciplines, use different methodologies and have widely differing views about the uses to which their work should be put.

The intended audience of the article are readers who are not generally familiar with global modeling or the several reviews of the subjects.[1] For this reason, brief summaries of major projects have been presented. Work not covered in previous reviews has been given somewhat more extensive treatment.

No one who has helped to build a global model, reviewed the field and taken part in many of the forums where global modeling has been discussed, could pretend to present an "unbiased" survey. Here are some of the personal beliefs which affect my view of the field.

I believe that models should be problem oriented, not discipline oriented, and should be motivated by a clearly defined problem. I believe that models should be simple and comprehensible to those who use them. I favor "top-down" rather than "bottom-up" approaches. Although I have used several modeling methodologies, my clear favorite is systems dynamics. I do not regard global modeling as a "normal science" activity.[2] In my view, global models should not only be understood by non-modelers, they should make a difference in their lives.

No doubt, you will see these beliefs and biases reflected in what follows, perhaps in ways that I cannot discern.

A Word About Using Models

Before generalizing about global models and speculating about their future, it is appropriate to discuss how such models should be viewed and used by non-modelers. In a recent survey, Donella Meadows, Gerhart Bruckmann and I tried to provide an answer.[3] We believe our guidelines are relevant to many types of modeling, not only global. Instead of proscribing, we tried to describe what we do when faced with the possibility of using a model as an aid to decision-making.

We keep watching and listening, paying attention to the questions raised by relevant models and the tentative answers put forth.

We ask a lot of questions. We keep insisting that the answers be in plain understandable English. When an answer comes that we do not understand, we say so and ask for a simpler phrasing. If we find a modeler who simply cannot communicate clearly, and if we cannot find anyone who can translate for that modeler understandably, we stop listening.

We try to probe for the biases of each modeler and correct for them. (We would try to do that with any "expert," computer modeler or not.)

We look for and encourage several different models made by different people with different methods and addressing the same problem. If possible, we get them together to work out their differences while we listen and question.

We get information for lots of other sources in addition to the computer model, especially information we know is hard to incorporate in models (information about values and attitudes, about politics and factions, about the feelings and goals of those who will be affected by our decisions.)

We remember that our decisions must come from incomplete, imperfect models in any case and that our mental models have a strong tendency to be biased and illogical.

We try to extract from the computer models general understanding, insights, appreciation for interrelatedness, which we can then apply in our own way to the problems before us. We would never expect the computer to tell us exactly what to do.

Ultimately, we rely on our own judgment, as we always have, hoping that the judgment has become a little more informed and comprehensive by our interaction with the precision and consistency of the computer model.

The "Field" of Global Modeling

Global modeling is distinguishable from other types of modeling primarily by the questions it attempts to answer. Here are some of the questions that have been addressed by global models:

Are current growth patterns of the world's population and capital stock sustainable by the global resource-base and ecosystem?

How could adequate food be provided for another doubling of the world's population?

Is it possible for all basic human needs to be provided for the people of the world by the year 2000? If the answer is "yes," how could this be done?

What will happen to the economies of the currently industrialized
   nations as the currently non-industrialized nations take on a larger
   share of industrial production?
What are the principal strains and stresses, both economic and political,
   with which governments will have to cope during the next twenty-
   five years? Which coping strategies, among the foreseeable options,
   appear most promising?

In all other respects, the methods, strengths and weaknesses of
global models are similar to those of all policy-oriented computer
models. Therefore, if there are any unique properties of global
modeling, they must follow directly from the characteristics of the
problems studied.

Global modeling, as a distinct field of activity, began with publication of *The Limits to Growth* in 1972.[4] In comparison with other types
of modeling, it has been more visible and controversial. This has offered
special opportunities and posed special problems for global modelers.
The field has gained notoriety because many—not all—of the major
global modeling projects have addressed questions which seem fundamental to the well-being and survival of the human species. Posing these
questions has attracted the attention of many individuals, including
high-level officials in business, government and the international community. It is hard to feel unaffected by pronouncements coming from a
global model.

Although the global models are very different in motivation and
methodology, Donella Meadows, Gerhart Bruckmann and I felt, following the Sixth Global Modeling Conference, convened by the International Institute of Applied Systems Analysis (IIASA), that it was
possible to identify some common messages about the state of the
world and possible futures.[5]

There is no known physical or technical reason why basic needs cannot
   be supplied for all the people of the world in the foreseeable future.
   These needs are not being met now because of social and political
   structures, values, norms and world-views, not because of absolute
   physical scarcities.
Population and physical capital cannot grow forever on a finite planet.
There is no reliable and complete information about the degree to
   which the earth's physical environment can absorb and meet the
   needs of further growth in population and capital. There is, however, a great deal of partial information which optimists read
   optimistically and pessimists read pessimistically.

Continuing "business as usual" policies through the next few decades will not lead to a desirable future, or even to meeting basic human needs. Instead, it will result in an increasing gap between rich and poor, problems with resource availability and worsening economic conditions.

Because of these difficulties, continuing of current trends is not a likely future course. Over the next three decades, the world's social and economic systems will be in a period of transition to some state that will be, not only quantitatively, but also qualitatively different than the present.

The exact nature of this future state, and whether it will be better or worse than the present, is not predetermined, but is a function of decisions and changes being made at present.

Owing to the momentum inherent in the world's physical and social processes, policy changes made soon are likely to have more impact with less effort than the same set of changes made later. By the time a problem is obvious to everyone, it is often too late to solve it.

Although technical changes are expected and needed, no set of purely technical changes tested in any of the models was sufficient in itself to bring about a desirable future. Restructuring social, economic and political systems was much more effective.

The interdependencies among peoples and nations over time and space are much greater than commonly imagined. Actions taken at one time and in one part of the world have far-reaching consequences that are impossible to predict intuitively and also impossible to predict with any precision (perhaps none at all) using computer models.

Because of the interdependencies, single, simple measures intended to reach narrowly defined goals are likely to be counter-productive. Decisions should be made within the broadest possible context: across space, time, and areas of knowledge.

Cooperative approaches to achieving individual or national goals usually turn out to be more beneficial in the long run to all parties than competitive approaches.

A Catalog of Global Models

Many readers will inevitably be unfamiliar with some of the global models and with recent surveys. Thus preceding a discussion of "Global Modeling in the 1980s" with a review of major models would seem to be highly desirable. On the other hand, space does not permit even a superficial survey of the purposes, structure, methodology and results of the major models. Here is a compromise approach which may serve our purposes.

Three categories of global models have been defined: (a) the IIASA conference models, (b) global international economic models and (c) politically oriented models. As discussion of models presented at previous IIASA conferences is found in earlier surveys, the presentation here will be extremely brief. A more extensive synopsis will be provided for some models in the second and third categories.

The IIASA Conference Models

As noted above, all but the first (Forrester/Meadows) of the models discussed under this category have been the subject of major presentations at the global modeling conferences sponsored by IIASA. (The Forrester/Meadows models have also been presented at IIASA, but have not been featured at a global modeling conference.) These may not be the best global models, but they have certainly been the most widely discussed. Regular participants in IIASA conferences have become personally acquainted and consider themselves members of an identifiable community.

Forrester/Meadows (World III). The first global model was conceived by Jay Forrester for the Executive Committee of the Club of Rome and developed further by a team at MIT headed by Dennis Meadows. *The Limits to Growth,* certainly the best known book about a global model, is based on this work.[6]

Mesarovic–Pestel (World Integrated Model). This multisectoral, multiregional model was built by cooperating teams at Case-Western Reserve University, Cleveland, Ohio, and the Technical University, Hanover, Federal Republic of Germany, under the direction of Mihalo Mesarovic and Eduard Pestel. A popularly oriented "Report to the Club of Rome," *Mankind at the Turning Point,* is the best known product of this project.[7]

Bariloche (Latin American World Model). This model was built by a group of Latin Americans working at Argentina's Bariloche Foundation under the direction of Amilcar Herrera and Hugo Scolnik. Mathematical programing is used to demonstrate that basic human needs could be met in the Third World shortly after the turn of the century. *Catastrophe or a New Society* is the project's principal publication.[8]

MORIA (Model of International Relations in Agriculture) was developed by cooperating groups at the Free University of Amsterdam and the Agricultural University at Wageningen in the Netherlands. The purposes of the project were to describe the causes of hunger in the world, to recommend remedial policies and to calculate the global-carrying capacity for food production. Both econometric and optimization techniques are used. MOIRA has made a major contribution to IIASA's food and agricultural project, and work also continues in the Netherlands under the auspices of a newly created foundation. The project's principal publication is *MOIRA—Model of International Relations in Agriculture.*[9]

SARUM (Systems Analysis Research Unit Model). As its name implies, this model was developed by the Systems Analysis Research Unit of the United Kingdom Department of the Environment. Peter Roberts was the project director. The primary motivation for building the model was to learn about the problems and difficulties of building global models so that they could be used by the British Government more intelligently. SARUM is multiregional and based on "standard rules of economic behavior" but differs significantly from the economic models discussed below. This model was used by the OECD "Interfutures" project[10] and has been adopted for use by groups in Australia and at the East-West Centre. *SARUM 76—Global Modelling Project,* a government report, is the project's principal publication.[11]

FUGI (Future of Global Interdependence Model) has been developed jointly by university-based teams in Tokyo, Soka and Osaka under the direction of Tokyo University's Yoichi Kaya. It uses input-output and econometric techniques to examine problems associated with future trends of industrialization in developed and developing nations. Present work is focusing on problems of the United Nations ESCAP (Economic and Social Commission of Asia and the Pacific) region. An application to the Indonesian economy is also in progress. There is no single popularly oriented description of the FUGI model in English, but a number of papers have been published.[12]

United Nations World Model was developed under the auspices of the United Nations Centre for Development, Planning, Projections and Policies (CDPPP). Under the direction of Professor Wassily Leontief, work was carried out by teams at Harvard, Brandeis and New York University. The project's purpose was to explore environmental constraints which might affect the United Nations development objectives. The project's principal publication is *The Future of the World Economy.*[13]

Global International Economic Models

The first efforts at global modeling were greeted with strong reservations by professional economists. However, recently, there has been a growing interest in developing or adapting economic models for long-term analyses of global scope. In the summer of 1980, IIASA devoted an entire global modeling conference to the subject of global international economic models. At its conclusion, IIASA's then director, Roger Levien, enthusiastically endorsed the types of global models presented as a promising new trend in the field. Two examples of such models are Project LINK and Dynamics.

Project LINK has been in existence for more than a decade.[14] Under the direction of Nobel Laureate Lawrence Klein of the University of Pennsylvania and Bert Hickman of Stanford University, the project provides an international linkage mechanism for national and regional econometric forecasting models. Models for thirteen "developed market," seven "socialist" and four "developing" nations are at present incorporated within the system. The thirteen developed market models have been built and are maintained by groups within the respective nations. The other models are the responsibility of two United Nations specialized agencies and Wharton Econometric Forecasting Associates. Long-term forecasting has not been the primary purpose of Project LINK, but forecasts from 1978 to 1985 were presented at the IIASA conference and long-term forecasts of fifteen to twenty-five years are being contemplated. The results of scenarios for: (a) investment promotion through coordinated fiscal policies in OECD countries; (b) coordinated expansionary monetary policies in the same countries; and (c) changes in world oil prices were described. Projections indicated that a return to higher economic growth rates in the mid-1980s was not improbable.

Dynamico. This project is a recent activity of the United Nations Department of International Economic and Social Affairs.[15] A ten-region econometric model has been developed with ten economic sectors (activities) identified for each region. The distinguishing characteristic of the model is its use of linear programing to measure the "efficiency" of alternative resource allocation patterns and development programs. Among the "global strategy functions" which have been tested using the model are: (a) maximization of world GNP at a specified time period; (b) minimization of the income gap between rich and poor regions; and (c) minimization of the discounted value for regional consumption. At the time of the Eighth Global Modeling Conference, only results for the period 1970-80 were available; however, ten-year projections, focusing on the efficiency of alternative regional development proposals, are contemplated.

Politically Oriented Global Models

The importance of political phenomena and the difficulty of measuring them have long been recognized by global modelers. Until recently, however, there has been little communication between the engineers and economists whose work is described above and the small number of quantitatively oriented political scientists who are interested in simulation.[16] In the summer of 1980, the Institute for Comparative Social Research of the Science Centre, Berlin, took an important first step by bringing together a small group comprising political scientists, economists, and global modelers to assess recent work in politically oriented global modeling. A brief description of the two models presented follows.

GLOBUS (Generating Long-term Options by Using Simulation). This ambitious project of the Science Centre, Berlin, has been under way for more than six years. It is a descendant of Harold Guetzkow's pioneering work in political simulation and of later work by his student, Stuart Bremer, who now directs the project.[17]

The model is not yet complete; however, its structure is well defined and has been described in a number of papers.[18] The purpose of the model is to describe long-term patterns of global development under the assumption that governments occupy a central position of action and that political factors should be given equal importance with economic ones. The model will comprise twenty-five national government actors functioning in four environments: (a) international political; (b) international economic; (c) domestic political; and (d) domestic economic. Governments are assumed to be motivated by broad goals such as national security, political stability and economic development and to engage in adaptive problem-solving behavior. At present, economic sectors of the model, where considerable previous work existed, are nearing completion. The political sectors are in a somewhat earlier stage, but represent a significant advance in the state of the art over any previous work in political science. In a recent paper, Bremer points out somewhat ruefully that, while in other fields of scholarly endeavor some problems are central and others peripheral, in global modeling, all problems are central.[19] Unlike most of the models described above, GLOBUS is not intended to be a forecasting or planning tool for policy-makers. It is viewed, rather, as making a contribution to social science theory.

SIMPEST (Simulation of Political, Economic and Strategic Inter-actions). This modest but exciting project at the University of Geneva is similar in conception to GLOBUS.[20] SIMPEST is a model of nation-state actors; variables describing politics and government play a major role in determining the model's output. The nations included in the present version of SIMPEST are China, the USSR and the United States. For each nation, an economic, resource, governmental and political sector is defined. At the international level, interaction between nations is both economic (via trade) and governmental. Governments respond to actions of other nations in the international system by developing armaments, restricting trade, giving aid or requesting it. The modeling methodology incorporates elements of both econometrics and engineering-based approaches such as system dynamics. By opting for a somewhat more top-down approach than GLOBUS, the Geneva group has produced a running model, with excellent documentation and a degree of validation for the period 1965-79. Present objectives for the project include adding more regions, improving the estimation of parameters and extending the projections beyond 1985.

Developments in the 1980s

In an earlier review[21] I pointed with some concern to the tendency, in more recent global models, towards shorter time-horizons, less comprehensiveness, more technical complexity and diminished concern with really fundamental issues facing the human race. This trend is exemplified, in my view, by the emergence of global international *economic* modeling as an identifiable activity. This adaptation of economics to long-term global problems is discipline-based, mathematically complex, and, with respect to economic phenomena, highly disaggregated. On the other hand, its time-horizon is short and a number of variables found in earlier models are excluded from consideration. If the papers presented at the Eighth Global Modeling Conference are representative, this approach will neither raise unsettling fundamental questions nor attempt to answer them. Clearly the potential contributions of economic modeling to global modeling should not be ignored, nor have they been; there is much to be learned from decades of modeling experience about technique and methodology. But it would be tragic if global modeling became simply a sub-discipline within economics.

By contrast, the emergence of political global-modeling projects is an exciting and hopeful development. Participants in early global-modeling projects recognized the importance of social and political variables, but were fearful of compromising their credibility by including them. They judged that top-level decision-makers would simply not accept models with a political component. Now, political scientists who have taken the lead in developing global models with a political component are, unlike the economists, proposing structures that are quite comprehensive and eclectic. Their work should lay an important foundation for further developments in the 1980s.

It is interesting to look at which of the early global models are still part of active projects. A conservative, low-key approach which draws heavily on economics plus meticulous documentation have contributed to the use of SARUM. FUGI's regional orientation has made it particularly attractive for application to the ESCAP region. The continued commitment of Professor Kaya and the colleagues who initially developed the model has been an additional source of strength. MOIRA's mathematical sophistication, especially the work of Michiel Keyzer, contributed to its adoption of IIASA. Its concern with hunger and focus on national units has made it attractive in the Netherlands. Project LINK already has a worldwide following among government and business decision-makers who use short-term economic forecasts. It is too soon to tell whether it will become popular for long-range forecasting as well. All of these models as well as, perhaps, the project at the Berlin Science Centre, would seem to have a promising future. The recent publication of the "Interfutures" report,[22] the Brandt Commission Report[23] and the American Government's *Global 2000* study[24] indicate that the interest of decision-makers and the general public for insights into the long-term future at the global level are far from satiated.

Towards A Normative Agenda

An extrapolation of recent trends in the field points to the emergence of additional models which are highly dissaggregated, mathematically complex, relatively short-term and academic. Global modelers appear to be seeking respectability. I am fearful, however, that respectability may be gained at the cost of neglecting or ignoring the long-term problems and issues which really matter. For that reason, I hope that some global modelers will consider a new agenda for the 1980s, an explicitly normative agenda.[25] I believe there should be global modeling projects whose purpose would be to depict a future, concretely and explicitly, which would be in accord with the aspirations of many of the world's peoples.

What I envisage is a global model describing a world in which: (a) war was no longer accepted as an instrument of national policy; (b) no child was born who was not wanted; (c) all people on earth were nourished sufficiently and sustainably; (d) the human race clearly lived in a sustainable relationship with its environment; (e) diverse cultures, values and life-styles flourished in a context of equity and tolerance; and (f) no human being was subject to exploitation by another.

Some global modelers, the Bariloche group especially, have attempted to incorporate in their work some vision of a preferred future and recommendations about how to attain it. Most global modelers are deeply concerned about this. But no global modeling project has yet seriously addressed the question of how to create a new social, economic and political order. The way that global models have been built and their results reported has militated against this. Global modeling projects typically begin by looking at the past and using it as a basis for describing the present. Once a model has been developed, it is used to generate a "baseline" scenario from the present into the future, assuming no fundamental change. The project team then evaluates the scenario, calling attention to trends which appear to have undesirable future consequences. Current policies which are under consideration may also be introduced into the model and their consequences evaluated. Finally recommendations may be offered which, in the view of the modelers, could lead to a more desirable future. What is meant by "desirable" is rarely spelled out clearly. Often it is assumed, by implication, that correction of potential problems identified by the model will lead to a better world. Systems analysts know that this is not necessarily the case. Correction of a specific "wrong" without a clear conception of an alternative "right" can be equivalent to jumping from the proverbial frying pan into the proverbial fire.

Shaping Our Vision of Society

Consider the following alternative approach. The project would begin by identifying all the components which must be included to portray a reasonably complete social, economic and political order on a global level. A set of values, such as those defined above, would be specified as the basis for such an order. A model of how such an order might function would then be built, taking into account relevant physical and biological laws. Experience in the field of design suggests that such a model would be different, in surprising ways, from those developed by extrapolating present trends. In the next stage of the project, a model of the present situation would be developed, incorporating the same dimensions as the ideal model. Next the project would identify possible pathways which could lead from the present to the preferred future. Finally, concrete first steps would be proposed to begin movement in the desired direction.[26]

My proposed agenda for global modeling in the 1980s is based on the belief that we have a much clearer understanding of what is wrong with the present than what could be right about the future. Lacking a clear vision, our approach to dealing with global issues, even at the highest level, is piecemeal, ad hoc and short term. We focus on the short term where the problems are and fail to recognize that it is in the long term where the opportunities are. We will not significantly change the world a day, or even a month, from now; that world has already been shaped by decisions that were made years or decades ago. But the world of the year 2000 or, better yet, 2020 can be, within broad constraints, whatever we decide it will be. In fact, that world will be shaped by our decisions, no matter what. It could be shaped by our vision of a better society and by our commitment to make that society happen.

A clear vision is a powerful thing. Today, our lives are greatly influenced by the vision of Jefferson, Madison and others who wrote the United States' Constitution and Declaration of Independence. The vision of these men changed the world. In the same way, the world has been changed—significantly—by the visions of Marx, Lenin and Mao Tse-tung.

Today, there is a need for new visions. There is a need for clear and powerful visions of a global society which is more humane, sustainable, and equitable.

Global modeling could play an important role in creating these visions. Those who build global models, those who support them and those who use them share responsibility for determining what that role will be.   □

FOOTNOTES

[1] Readily available reviews include, J. Clark and S. Cole, *Global Simulation Models: A Comparative Study*, London: John Wiley, 1975; J.M. Richardson, Jr., "Global Modeling I: The Models," *Futures*, Vol. 10, No. 5, and "Global Modeling II: Where to Now," *Futures*, Vol. 10, No. 6; D.H. Meadows, J.M. Richardson, Jr., and G. Bruckmann, *Groping in the Dark: The First*

Decade of Global Modelling, London: John Wiley, 1981; and Peter C. Roberts, *Modelling Large Systems,* London: Halsted Press, 1978.

[2] "Normal science" is the solving of puzzles deemed to be important within the context of a well-established scientific discipline. See Thomas S. Kuhn, *The Structure of Scientific Revolution,* Chicago: University of Chicago Press, 1962 and 1970.

[3] "A Final Word About Using Models," in Meadows, *et al., Groping in the Dark, op. cit.*

[4] D.H. Meadows, D.L. Meadows, J. Randers and W.W. Behrens, *The Limits to Growth,* Chapter 2, New York: Universe Books, 1972, 1979, 2nd ed.

[5] For a brief history of the IIASA Global Modeling Conferences, see Meadows, Richardson, Jr., and Bruckmann, *op. cit.,* Chapter I. Proceedings for Conferences I-IV are available from Pergamon Press.

[6] Meadows, *et al., The Limits to Growth, op. cit., The Limits to Growth* has been translated into numerous languages. For a complete listing, see Meadows, *et al., Groping in the Dark, op. cit.* Chapter 3. Here also fairly detailed synopses of the IIASA conference models and complete lists of references have been provided. Other relevant references for this project include J. W. Forrester, *World Dynamics,* Cambridge: Wright-Allen Press, 1971; D.L. Meadows, *et al., Dynamics of Growth in a Finite World,* Cambridge: Wright-Allen Press, 1974; and D.L. Meadows and D.H. Meadows (eds.), *Towards Global Equilibrium: Collected Papers,* Cambridge: MIT Press, 1973.

[7] M.D. Mesarovic and E. Pestel, *Mankind at the Turning Point,* New York: Dutton, 1974.

[8] A.D. Herrera and H.D. Scolnik, *et al., Catastrophe or a New Society: A Latin American World Model,* Ottawa: International Development Research Centre, 1976.

[9] H. Linnemann, J. DeHoogh, M. Keyzer and H. Van Heemst, *MOIRA—Model of International Relations in Agriculture,* Amsterdam: North-Holland, 1979.

[10] Interfutures, *Facing the Future: Mastering the Probable and Managing the Unpredictable,* Paris: OECD, 1979.

[11] P. Roberts, *et al., SARUM 76—Global Modelling Project,* London: Department of Environment and Transport, 1977. (Research Report No. 19.)

[12] Probably the best way to obtain information about the FUGI model is by writing to the project director. An early description can be found in Gerhart Bruckmann (ed.), *Input-Output Approaches to Global Modelling* (Proceedings of the Fifth IIASA Global Modeling Conference), London: Pergamon, 1979.

[13] W. Leontief, A. Carter and P. Petri, *The Future of the World Economy: A United Nations Study,* New York: Oxford University Press, 1977.

[14] A useful general reference is Jean L. Waelbroeck, *The Models of Project LINK,* Amsterdam: North-Holland, 1976. For a discussion of long-term forecasting using the LINK system, see Victor Filatov, Bert G. Hickman and Lawrence R. Klein, "Long-Run Simulations with the Project LINK System " (prepared for presentation at the Eighth IIASA Conference on Global Modeling).

[15] See Antonio Maria Costa, "The Interaction of Trade and Development in the Decade of the 1980s: A Model's Normative Interpretation " (prepared for presentation at the Eighth IIASA Conference on Global Modeling).

[16] See K. Deutsch, B. Fritsch, H. Jaguarube and A. Markovits, *Problems of World Modelling,* Cambridge: Ballanger, 1977; also N. Choucri and T. Robinson (eds.), *Forecasting in International Relations: Theory, Methods, Problems, Prospects,* San Francisco: W.H. Freeman & Co., 1978.

[17] See S. Bremer, *Simulated Worlds: A Computer Model of National Decision-Making,* Princeton, NJ: Princeton University Press, 1977. Chapter 1 contains an excellent review of work leading up to this model.

[18] S. Bremer, *The GLOBUS Project: Overview and Update* (publication series of the International Institute for Comparative Social Research, Wissenschaftszentrum, Berlin, 1 March 1981) contains a complete list of references.

[19] *Ibid.*

[20] See U. Luterbacher, P. Allan and A. Imhoff, "SIMPEST: A Simulation Model of Political, Economic and Strategic Interactions Among Major Powers" (prepared for delivery at the Moscow IPSA Congress, 12-18 August 1979).

[21] Richardson, Jr., "Global Modeling II," *op. cit.*

[22] *Ibid.*

[23] *North-South: A Programme for Survival,* Cambridge: MIT Press, 1980.

[24] *The Global 2000 Report to the President: Entering the Twenty-first Century,* Washington, DC: United States Government Printing Office, 1980.

[25] After completing this article, I became aware of a somewhat similar proposal made by Peter Roberts, "Resilience, Transcience and Sustainability," unpublished paper presented at the Seventh IIASA Conference on Global Modeling, October 1979.

[26] This is essentially the approach suggested by Russel L. Ackoff in *Redesigning the Future: A Systems Approach to Societal Problems,* New York: John Wiley, 1974.

Computerized fiscal impact models are the latest in a series of urban planning reforms designed to supplant the politics of land-use decision-making with rational planning technique. These planning models are similar to a variety of other decision support systems developed to improve the quality of information available to decision makers and reduce the role of political or other "nonrational" criteria in decision-making. A case study of one such model indicates that "political rationality" is not only inherent to the use of such models by decision makers, but it is critical to their successful implementation—perhaps more so than technical rationality in highly charged political contexts.

Chapter 10

THE POLITICS OF MODEL IMPLEMENTATION

Kenneth L. Kraemer

Introduction[1]

Modeling is commonly conceived as a two phase process involving development and implementation. Development refers to the steps involved in building a model, whereas implementation refers to the steps involved in introducing, adapting and routinizing a developed

The author is director of the Public Policy Research Organization and professor in the Graduate School of Management at the University of California, Irvine. He is co-author of two recent books, *The Management of Information Systems* and *Computers and Politics,* published by Columbia Press in 1981. He has served as a consultant to the Federal USAC Program and to the OECD.

Note: Reprinted from *Systems, Objectives, Solutions*, November 1981, by permission of North-Holland Publishing Company, The Netherlands.

model in a specific user agency. It is apparent from the literature and research on modeling that the greatest attention and concern has been given to the development rather than to the implementation phase. Some posit that this misplaced attention has resulted in a generally low level of model use and model success.[12]. Moreover there is increasing recognition among various experts, model practitioners, and theorists that knowledge about model development has far outstripped the capabilities for implementing these tools [27]. This recognition is heightened by notable modeling failures and controversies [1,21]. As a consequence, the implementation of models has become a topic of research in recent years.

Although the approaches to implementation research are varied [16], most conceive implementation as a dynamic, multi-stage process of introduction, adaptation, and incorporation. *Introduction* refers to the period during which a model is considered for adoption, some early pilot testing may occur on a small-scale basis, and the results of this pilot test are used to make a decision to adopt the model. *Adaptation* refers to the period during which broader support for the model is developed, plans are made for instructing and training relevant practitioners, the model begins to be used as widely as resources would permit, and the results of use are monitored. *Incorporation* refers to the period in which the model no longer appears as a new innovation *per se*, but becomes part of the common activities of the organization.

These stages are not very well defined, nor do they bear simple relationship to one another. However, they are essentially similar in concept to other lifecycle stages in research on innovation [28], social change [20,22] and MIS implementation [16,23]. The general notion is that the stages in the implementation process have distinctive characteristics, and the stages occur sequentially over time. Moreover, successful implementation requires completion of *all three* stages. As indicated by Yin [28] the successful implementation of any innovation first requires a set of circumstances which is supporting to introduction. During adaptation, if unforseen problems emerge and cannot be dealt with, the innovation may be discontinued—an appropriate outcome because the innovation was found to be inapplicable. For innovations that have been successfully adapted, however, the third stage of incorporation must occur in which the innovation is routinized as part of the on-going activities of the organization in order for the real benefits of the innovation to be realized. Thus, we define routinization as a key measure of implementation success.

There are a variety of dimensions considered important to successful model implementation. These fall under the headings of: (1) the inherent technical characteristics of the model itself, (2) the social setting in which the model is used, and (3) the uses and impacts of the model as experienced by the organization. One of the most interesting hypotheses about the successful implementation of innovations, generally, is that agencies which incorporate innovations into their day-to-day operations do so because these innovations serve political interests. Moreover, such innovations might become incorporated even through no service improvements are clearly evident. But innovations that lead to service improvements might not be incorporated unless they also serve some political interests [10,11,19,28]. In short, politics appears to be an inherent and necessary feature of the successful implementation of innovations. Hence our concern with the politics of model implementation.

This paper explores[2] the politics of modeling by systematic case study of the stages involved in the implementation of a model for assessing the fiscal impacts of alternative urban development plans in the City of Irvine, California (Figure 1). Theoretically, such models are introduced into local governments to improve the ability of policy makers to rationally determine urban development patterns.

Such land-use decisions are among the most politically charged decisions dealt with by American local governments. Consequently, efforts to reform the urban planning process since the 1920s have sought to supplant the "politics" of land-use decision-making with new forms of organization, technically educated professionals, and rational planning techniques. The 1960s in particular witnessed major efforts to introduce rational planning techniques such as economic base analysis, computerized urban databanks, and computerized urban models and simulations [18]. The most recent technique to appear in this history of planning reforms is the computerized fiscal impact model. Fiscal impact models are designed to provide more accurate and objective forecasts about the local government revenue and expenditure implications of alternative land-use decisions [11,13]. Increasingly, these models are computerized to facilitate their use. Thus, these models are similar to a variety of decision-support systems developed to improve the quality of information available to decision-makers, to reduce the role of nonrational criteria such as the relative political influence of various contestants in the decision-making process and, thereby, to improve the rationality of decision-making [14,17].

Although implementation of the Irvine model occurred over a five-year period, we have been fortuitously aided by the presence of extensive documentation, including city clerk records, tape recordings, and video tapes of council meetings, economic consultant reports on the

Figure 1.   Implementation guide to the Irvine economic model.

DIMENSIONS		STAGES		
		INTRODUCTION	ADAPTATION	INCORPORATION
TECHNOLOGY	Model and Computer Support	Generalized cash flow model for estimating capital cost of urban development Consultant control on large time-sharing computer at service bureau	Model adapted to deal with operating, maintenance, and service costs as well as capital costs, of urban development, and with public revenues City staff control on large time-sharing computer at service bureau	Model unchanged, but model use expanded
SOCIAL SETTING	Principal actors	City council, administrative staff, citizens	City council, staff, Citizen Advisory Committee, consultants	City council, computer systems analyst
	Issues/stakes	What framework shall be used in evaluating alternative land use schemes?	How shall land uses be allocated among competing interests and values?	How shall agreed upon land use allocations be timed and phased?
	Objectives and relationships among actors	Conflicting objectives and competition between low-growth and pro-growth factions with the former as the dominant coalition	Negotiation and compromise among actors	Settled agreements among actors for routine model use Negotiation and compromise among actors for "new" uses of the models
USE AND IMPACT	Political Uses	Postpone decision on the general plan Shift responsibility center from council to staff Temporarily suspend competition and conflict Diffuse citizen opposition by coopting representatives to serve on Citizen's Advisory Committee	Confuse citizens and opposition on the council Legitimate decision of the council Speed decision making of the council Build constituency and solidify around general plan preferred by the dominant political coalition	Exact concessions from the developer
	Political Impacts	City gains "information" parity with the developer Council perceived by citizens as independent of the developer	Council gains influence over the developer Council gains prestige Staff gain professional recognition	Access to model controlled by dominant political coalition

model, planning staff studies and analyses using the model, and model operator and model user documentation. In addition, we have relied extensively upon the perceptions of major actors involved during implementation, including city council, city administrator, planning and budget staff, the economic consultants, citizen participants, and the developer.

The paper first describes the governmental and community forces that led to adoption of the Irvine fiscal impact model. It then chronicles the lengthy implementation process leading to the successful incorporation of the model into the government's decision processes, paying close attention to the political use and impacts of the model. Finally, several perspectives are offered about model implementation and about the role of political versus technical rationality in the implementation of computerized models.

Metamorphosis of a Land Barony

Two great tracts of open land lie between the greater Los Angeles and San Diego regions. One is the U.S. Marine Corps' Camp Pendleton; the other is the Irvine Ranch, which straddles the middle of Orange County. The Ranch is owned almost entirely by The Irvine Company (TIC), which David Curry describes as a modern feudal barony:

> The company has conducted its affairs, in many respects, like a modern feudal barony; rich in lands, a patron of the arts, benevolent to its serfs so long as they regularly remit their rents, and often imperious in its dealings with other baronies, such as Orange County and the University of California [9:18].

The Company's chief enterprise, until about twenty years ago, was a mixture of intensive agriculture and cattle-raising. The shift to urban development began in 1959 when the Regents of the University of California approved a site for a new campus on the Irvine Ranch, and TIC and the University then jointly developed master plans for a university-oriented community (with a "built-out" population of 100,000 on 10,000 acres of the 100,000 acre Ranch) [24,25,26]. Construction subsequently proceeded fairly rapidly and by the end of the sixties the resident population was 20,000 and employment was 30,000. The jobs were chiefly in shopping and commercial areas, in the university (with an enrollment of 5,000 students), and in an industrial complex (with 280 firms). The residential development stressed planned villages, usually with single-family dwellings or townhouses on small lots, common open-space areas, and private recreational facilities. In early 1970, however, the scope and scale of development on the Ranch was changed dramatically when TIC announced plans for an expanded City of Irvine—to be the "largest planned city on the North American Continent." The plan called for: extending development to 85 square miles of the Ranch; increasing the planned population to 450,000 by the year 2000; and forming a separately incorporated city.

Incorporation of the City of Irvine was approved in February 1971 and, subsequently, steps were taken to elect a city council and start a city government. The citizens' voting in both the incorporation and council elections had made it clear that the new city officials could not simply be an instrument of the Irvine Company, but had to become a force for planning and development in their own right; thus they began their own general planning program for the city. It soon became clear, however, that neither the council, nor the planning commission, nor the citizens could agree upon a single future for the new city. Consequently, the city adopted a general plan that allowed three different options for future development. All of these options were similar until 1980, but then they varied greatly in terms of the rate of development assumed through the year 2000 (Table 1).

Table 1.   Summary of Irvine General Plan Options.

Option	Population	Description
1	354,000	The so-called moderate growth alternative.
2	450,000	The maximum growth alternative, basically similar to the Irvine Company's plan for the "largest planned city on the North American Continent."
3	171,000	The low growth alternative, which assumed that a major portion of then existing agricultural land would be permanently maintained in that status.
4A	221,000	Preliminary version of "new Option 4."
4B	245,000	The alternative finally selected for the General Plan for the City of Irvine.

By 1975, the practical difficulties, the uncertainty, and the questionable legality of operating under three general plan options became too much for the city planners and top staff. Therefore, the city manager pressed the council to choose a single general plan option—one of the original three options, or a new option involving some combination of the three. The council agreed and further decided that choice among the options should be based on their comparative fiscal impacts.

Model Implementation

"Introduction" of the Irvine Economic Model[3]

As might be expected, the task of determining the respective fiscal impacts of the general plan options was assigned by the council to the planners in the Community Development Department. None of the planners had previous experience with conducting fiscal analyses. But a senior planner had attended an economic seminar in San Francisco where he had heard about fiscal impact models and thought they might constitute the needed tool for the analysis. Since the expertise with such models rested mainly with consultant firms at the time, the planners put together a request for proposals (RFP) for a model that could be used for fiscal analysis of the general plan options.

The RFP called for development of a computerized fiscal impact model that would afford guidance for measuring the "economic" impacts of the various land plan options in the general plan. The consultant was to: include capital costs as well as operating costs in the models; have all of the assumptions in the model approved by the city staff and a Citizen's Advisory Committee (CAC); analyze the three land-use options of the city in terms of their cost and revenue implications for citizens; and provide an economic analysis of the surrounding Orange County.

The principal actors in the decision to adopt the Irvine Economic Model were many, and their objectives divergent. The city council wanted to know the short- and long-run implications of the general plan options. The city staff supported the basic notion of a computerized model in the hope of eventually obtaining a computer that would house the fiscal model and perform many housekeeping functions such as accounting and payroll for the city. Some citizens supported the model because they were concerned with the adequacy of the tax base to support quality schools; some because they were concerned with the already high tax rate and wanted to have development proposals carefully scrutinized; and some because they thought the model might make explicit the capital costs associated with growth such as the implied by TIC's master plan for the city. Finally, TIC supported the model because they felt that it would support their position on development and, therefore, expedite the adoption of their master plan.

Although divergent, the objectives of these actors coalesced remarkably well around the need for a model, owing primarily to the strategies pursued by the two council members who took the lead in advocating model adoption to the rest of the council and to the city staff. Even these two had dissimilar reasons for supporting the model. One wanted to tool for forecasting the future fiscal impacts of development as an aid to decision-making; the other was interested in the computer technology used to implement the models and in "the technological possibilities of computerizing the entire city." But both had an interest in finding a tool that would help to resolve their continuous history of conflicting viewpoints, acrimonious debates, and futuristic speculations about how TIC development plans would affect the tax rate, open space, low-cost housing, housing appreciation, quality of life, and so forth for Irvine citizens. They thought the model might be a means of facilitating compromise by objectively forecasting the fiscal impacts of alternative land-use plans.

Consequently, they joined forces to convince the other council members of the need for a fiscal impact model. Knowing that the issues of concern to themselves were insufficient to motivate the other members to support the model, the two council members appealed to the council's common concern—to better counter the plans, models, and sizeable planning staff of the Irvine Company. As one of them indicated, "this was an extremely sensitive issue to the council because from the very beginning of the city the council and city staff had been out-gunned by the Irvine Company's planners, models, and data, and they were getting fed up; they wanted to be able to equal if not exceed the company's expertise and the economic model looked like a way to do it." They were aided in their efforts by two economists who lived in the city and were members of the CAC formed to advise the council on public opinion about the general plan options. The economists were "turned loose to become very vocal before the council about the need for an economic model." As citizens, these economists were concerned about over-crowding in the schools and about providing sufficient physical infrastructure for the new city (e.g., streets and highways, storm drains, water and sewage facilities, parks, recreation facilities). They felt the model would make explicit the capital costs associated with growth, and that this information would provide a basis for obtaining public funds, or coercing the developer to build the facilities, or discouraging growth.

The two council members also were aided in their efforts by the city manager and administrative services staff. The manager wanted a single general plan and viewed the model as a tool for aiding choice among the options; the manager and administrative services staff also wanted a computer that would serve the financial and administrative operations of the city, and saw the model, which the council wanted, as another possible application requiring an in-house new computer system. Consequently, they lent their support to these council members.

The council decision to adopt a computerized fiscal impact model, and to spend up to $20,000 for a consultant to adapt such a model to the city, was approved unanimously in October 1975 [2]. The three council members who had not actively supported the model acquiesced with little understanding of either computer models or computer technology. They responded to the overwhelming support for the model.

A total of 12 proposals were received from various planning and economic consulting firms. The very fact that a dozen firms bid for the Irvine model reinforced the council's and staff's perception that adequate modeling technology existed. However, in the end, only three proposals were considered technically competitive. Of the three, the proposal from Marshal Kaplan, Gans and Kahn (MKGK) was the uncontested winner. Not only was the MKGK bid considered technically superior to the other proposals, but the firm seemed to best understand what the council wanted and knew how to communicate in language the council could understand. In the words of one councilwoman:

> We felt they would not just talk in complicated economic terms—some economists are just unbelievable when talking to city councils—but would make their points clear to us, and then we could translate it to the community, which is an important thing when you are sitting on the city countil. So we chose them.

The council approved the contract with MKGK in February 1976, and directed that the Citizen's Advisory Committee, which had been established to provide citizen input to the planning process, oversee the model's adaptation to the city.

The very adoption of the model had a powerful political effect. Previously, debate and conflict had characterized city council meetings in the initial deliberations regarding the general plan, as council members argued extensively over the relative costs of open space and housing densities. No one could predict the fiscal impact of decisions that had to be made in the present but that would influence the future of the city and its citizens. Adopting the model permitted a temporary suspension of long-range development decisions until the model would be completed. It also resulted in a suspension of the competition and conflict that such decisions generated, releasing the council to attend to other matters. Moreover, by directing the city staff and citizens to oversee the model adaptation process, the council essentially shifted the responsibility center from itself to the city staff with input from the CAC.

"Adaptation" of the Model for Evaluating General Plan Options

The principal actors in model adaptation were essentially the same as those involved in model adoption, with the addition of the consultants and the CAC. Most of the council's involvement with the actual transfer of the model, however, was through delegated authority—the city staff and the CAC were to be the real participants and were required to report back periodically to the council. Moreover, the council assigned two of its own members to the CAC. The focus of the CAC's and the city staff's activity and attention, then, was on the consultant firm, MKGK.

The Consultant and the Model

MKGK had previous experience with fiscal impact analysis. The firm had used a highly generalized corporate cash-flow model to assess the public and private capital costs of development.[4] But they had never used a model to estimate the public operating and maintenance costs or public revenues associated with private development. Consequently, the Irvine contract represented a major adaptation effort for the company. The key person at MKGK responsible for developing the Irvine model was an economist. His first major task was to totally restructure the model to include government costs and revenues. But the most difficult and time-consuming task was developing the data and assumptions for the model. He worked for three months with the administrative services staff, with various planners in the Community Development Department and with planners in the Irvine Company in order to generate land-use, service-cost, and revenue-base data for the analysis. Cooperation was remarkable. He worked with all major department heads in the city to generate development standards (e.g., the number of park acres to be provided per 1,000 people) and to develop cost and revenue "functions" associated with population, land use, and other development conditions. The total set of assumptions was reviewed five or six times by all of the participants. He also worked with the CAC, which had been created by the council to monitor the model's adaptation, to obtain their "signoff" on all assumptions incorporated in the model.

Use of the Model

These approved assumptions and data[5] were then fed into the computer model to perform the necessary calculations for each year through the year 2000, and to produce 11 different summary tables for each of the three general plan options.[6] Each option was evaluated using four different assumptions of geographic area encompassed by the city because the "final" boundaries of the city were still open for discussion. Thus, a single general plan evaluation consisted of 12 model runs (3 options X 4 boundary alternatives); evaluation of all three alternatives therefore required 36 model runs.

MKGK made two such major runs using the model. The first was midway through the project, in the summer of 1977, for a presentation to the Council; the second was in the fall, to produce data for the final report. At the time of the midway report, the Irvine Company Board of Directors was engaged in a major struggle over ownership and control of the Company. The Irvine Foundation, a nonprofit tax-exempt private foundation and the majority shareholder in the company was forced by Federal tax law to dispose of its interest in TIC. Bidding for the Company was fierce with two major groups vying for ownership and control: Mobil Oil Corporation, and a consortium of developers headed by Alfred Taubman. The ultimate bid of $500 million for the Company was higher than either Company officials or Irvine residents had expected. Among the residents, moreover, the bid generated fears, fed by local newspaper stories, that the new owners would have to begin rapacious development of the Ranch in order to handle interest payments on the money borrowed to purchase the Company and in order to make an adequate return on their investment.

Both the struggle for ownership and the bidding war heightened concerns of Irvine residents and the council regarding general plan Option No. 2 (which followed the Company's master plan and called for an ultimate population of 450,000; see Table 1). In addition, MKGK's midway run showed that Option No. 2 was the least financially favorable both to the city and to the Irvine School District. These data plus the emotion in the city provided the basis for the council to determine that Option 2 should be eliminated from further consideration. The council then instructed the planners to come up with a new Option 4, which would fall between the two remaining options as depicted in Table 2. This was an extremely significant decision. It not only reduced by 100,000 people the upper range population that would be considered for the City of Irvine, but it effectively set the eventual population somewhere between Options 1 and 3 (171,000 and 354,000 respectively; see Table 1) with the most likely option being some sort of middle-ground compromise. As it turned out, Option 4 represented a built-out population of 221,000.

Table 2.   Population Density by Options.

	"New"		"Discontinued"
Option 3	Option 4	Option 1	Option 2
171,000	221,000	354,000	450,000

This midway report convinced the council of the model's utility. Although none of them understood how the model worked, the model results confirmed the fiscal wisdom of the general plan option toward which the city officials and community were moving as a compromise choice—namely the middleground Option 4 and, consequently, they were satisfied with the model. Although the March council meeting where the model and findings had been presented was anticlimactic from a substantive standpoint, it had been dramatic from a symbolic standpoint. An important event during this meeting had been a demonstration by MKGK of how the model could be used by the council to answer their own questions. The firm had brought a computer located in Kansas City into the council chambers and had demonstrated the model's ability to produce results by changing a few of the model's inputs. Initially a wobbly table prevented good electrical connections which in turn produced chaotic numbers. This initially reinforced the sterotype of the fallibility of computers. But after the physical problems were corrected, the demonstration proceeded and, according to one of the council members:

> . . .John and I (asked). . .him if we could then plug in a certain number of acres of apartment units and he said yes. We said 26 units to the acre and we plugged that in—which is pretty dense. As I recall those were the only two variables we gave him. . . . We might have given him a price per unit. . . . Back came the tax rate that those dwellings would necessitate. It was all pretty convincing.

This demonstration crystalized the acceptance of the existence of the Irvine model and was a key event in its implementation. "Seeing is believing," and the council members now had seen a sample of how their commissioned product could be used both now and in the future. The flexibility witnessed at this time further enforced the idea of getting "local control" over the model so that the council and staff could "play with the model" themselves.

Consequently, the council directed the city staff to take the steps required to "assume control of the model" and to operate the model without the consultant's assistance [3,4]. The Council unanimously approved two service contracts to facilitate that effort—one for computer time-sharing services so the city staff could operate the model in-house and another for use of the parent model in which Irvine's economic model was embedded [5]. Since the city lacked any data processing or computer personnel, MKGK encouraged the city to hire someone with such skills to be custodian of the model. This selection of the first city computer personnel was a milestone because it planted the seeds not only for further fiscal impact model development, but also for further computing development within the city.

MKGK's second major evaluation of the three general plan options was bound in a report entitled *Fiscal and Economic Analysis of General Plan Options* [15] and, subsequently (March 31, 1977), a presentation on the report was given by MKGK to city officials at a joint meeting of the Irvine City Council, Community Services Commission, Planning Commission, and Transportation Commission. The report and presentation indicated three important findings:

1. Option 4 was the most favorable option, especially when city and school taxes were viewed in combination.

2. All options presented a tradeoff between population size and open space area. The larger the population, the greater the total taxes, because the taxes required to support school expenditures were six times as much as those required to support city expenditures. The larger the open space area the greater the city expenditures for maintenance. Consequently, by keeping its population relatively low, the city could pay for some of its desired open space by savings on school expenditures.

3. A maximum spread of 11 percent in combined city and school taxes existed at the end of development between the least and most expensive options and boundary conditions studied. In dollar terms, this amounted to about $93 per year on a house with a value of $60,000 in 1976.

The latter finding was the most significant of all. As stated by MKGK in their report, the importance of this finding was that "the [fiscal] differences among any of the alternatives were clearly not so large as to justify constituting the sole or even the major reason for choosing one plan option and boundary condition over another. Quality of life, environmental, social, and other factors need to be considered" [15:5—41].

Training of City Staff to Use the Model

The presentation of MKGK's final report ended the consultant's involvement with the economic model except for training city staff to use the model. It took only a few weeks to train city people to be able to operate the model on the outside time-sharing service. A variety of people were trained in operation of the model, including council members, planning commissioners, CAC members, and city staff. But the task of using the model fell largely to the city's planners, financial analysts, and computer expert. Once the model was accessible to the city staff, it was used periodically to provide information in response to specific questions asked by the council, commissioners, and staff. Usually, these questions had to do with minor adjustments in land-use patterns, population, or development phasing with respect to Option 4.

Adoption of the General Plan

The net effect of the foregoing adjustments to Option 4 was to increase the amount of residential land while decreasing the open space (including agriculture) land, to increase the commercial acreage to support the new residential uses and, by extension, to increase the built-out population of Option 4 to 245,000. Although the council negotiated fiercely over these adjustments, the die was cast and on September 15, 1977, the council selected Option 4 as the General Plan for the City of Irvine.

The model played an important role in the general plan decision. As expressed by the former planning director:

> I think that some councilmembers placed greater importance on the model than others. For example, the final general plan option was approved on a three to two vote. For the three individuals who voted for Option 4, fiscal impact was an important consideration. The other two councilmembers felt there were other things besides economics that you make land use decisions on. Their concern was more with agriculture and open space preservation.

Moreover, the model was used in policy argument between the supporters of Option 4. On the evening of the final vote on the general plan, two councilmen were having a disagreement about the wording of a proposed council resolution regarding land use in one of the villages. The issue was whether the council wanted to make their approval of the land-use plan for the village dependent upon the future development of an industrial complex and the future annexation of the northern area, or not. One councilman wanted to substitute the phrase "may be dependent" for the phrase "shall be dependent" in a resolution drafted by the other. The former argued that there were many contingencies that might result in the need to change the land-use plan for the village in the future and so there was no need to specifically tie that development to what happened in the industrial complex and to annexation of the northern area. The other councilman responded as follows:

> I totally disagree. I think it shall be dependent in both cases because it is dependent. The economic study shows that it is very dependent on what happens in Irvine Industrial Complex-East and what happens with the northern sphere. I'm not saying that, in fact, no development can occur in Village 14 if, for example, all of the property comprising IIC-East is traded to the Marine Corps. This does not mean that Village 14 cannot proceed and be developed and must be left in permanent open space or agriculture. What is means is that that whole land use plan [for Village 14] has to be re-evaluated.
>
> I want it to be perfectly clear that development of Village 14 is dependent on these two items [annexation of the northern sphere and development of IIC-East]. I think that came out loud and clear in the economic study and I don't want that to be lost [6].

Despite these debates, the model was not the critical factor in the selection of Option 4. The key factor was the overwhelming community opinion that the city should not be allowed to grow to half a million people as originally projected in the Irvine Company (TIC) master plan. And, neither TIC, the council, nor any other decision maker could ignore public opinion. As the former President of TIC said:

> The number of half a million just kept eroding by the pragmatics of politics more than anything else. It was just so overwhelming at that time. The city was just starting out, and 500,000 population was just too huge. The number just became politically intolerable.

Still, the model supported community opinion and provided an objective basis for negotiating over the final land-use and population configuration. When actually used to clarify decision consequences on the refinement of general plan Option 4, the model tended to be used by the parties as a means of influencing choices at the margins (such as raising or lowering residential densities and commercial acreage).

But the model also had important political impacts. Earlier, it had supported the position of the low-growth council majority by showing that TIC master plan Option 2 was the most expensive option. Thus, it gave a temporary political edge to that majority. It also set the outside feasible limits within which negotiations about population would take place among the council, and between the council and TIC. Again, this was a strategic advantage to the low-growth majority on the council. Moreover, while the model never reduced decisions to purely technical criteria, it played a role in facilitating compromises among members of the council and between the council and TIC. For example, one councilwoman indicated that:

> The model made it much more difficult to take an extreme position. You couldn't say you wanted all open space because somebody would say let's see how much that'll cost. Nobody ever thought about that before. I mean open spaces are supposed to be free. So it made it very hard to go to that extreme.
>
> It also made it difficult for the Irvine Company to come in and say they needed to develop the city immediately because it's cheaper than dragging it out. You could say let's see about that and we would tell the planning department to scope that one out. What would happen was that your range of alternatives would get narrower and narrower and you would have to pick the one that was the most economically and fiscally appealing to your constituents at that time.

"Incorporation" and Subsequent Use of the Model

The general satisfaction of the council and staff with the role of the model in the adoption of a single option for the general plan assured its incorporation into the local government. Even when the council membership changed (in late 1976 and again in 1978), continuity of support for the model was maintained. The key role in maintaining council support for the model was played by the city staff. The staff was key because the recommendations of the holdover council members would not necessarily be trusted by the new council members. As indicated by one councilwoman, the city staff played a key role in maintaining support after the council changeover of 1976:

They were new and they had just come on and they didn't trust John or me necessarily. What you do in that case is get the staff to recommend to them the appropriate positions. They were doing what the staff recommended at that point, and the staff was behind what had gone before.

The new council members were willing to accept the recommendations of the city staff because they expected the staff to be neutral regarding use of the model and expected the staff to serve their interests at least equally with those of the holdover council members. Moreover, the new council *needed* the city staff to explain the model to them, to train them in its use, and to review how it had been used in the past.

Conversion of the Model to the City's Computer

Nowhere is the continued support for the model better symbolized than in a vote of the council in June 1978, post-Proposition 13. After the general plan debates were over, the model had fallen into disuse since the decision it was meant to resolve was settled [8]. In addition, the data and assumptions were now two years old and it would require considerable staff effort to update them to reflect the current conditions. The model also was considered difficult to access and use by the city staff since it had not been designed for frequent use, but for episodic use such as assessing the general plan. It still was available only via time-sharing. And planned future uses of the model required its adaptation to operate at the village level rather than only on a city-wide basis—a difficult conceptual problem and an even more difficult problem of data collection and data handling. Consequently, the city faced the prospect of considerable expenditure in order to bring the model to a useable stage at a time when post-Proposition 13 pressures seemed to call for "canning the model and putting all of the available planners to work at the computer processing builder's applications so that development would be speeded up and city revenues increased." A motion to do precisely this was proposed before the council but failed for want of support. Rather, the council reaffirmed their support for the model and approved an extensive work program for converting the model to the city's own in-house mini-computer, to update the land-use and cost data for the model, and to adjust the model assumptions to include "new parameters such as Proposition 13, its associated legislation, and the systems development charge" [7].

The MKGK model was converted to the city's computer and most of the data and assumptions were updated during a 14-week study period beginning in July 1978. The conversion was not aimed at changing the model itself (i.e., the relationships in the model). Rather, it was aimed primarily at changing the data structure and data handling to facilitate model use. For example, the model's file structure was changed from a single large data base to seven files; the binary coded input/output was changed to conversational language (i.e.,English-like statements); inputing of data and assumptions was made an online procedure; and the operation and use of the model was made interactive.

Routinization of the Model

In December 1978, the council officially made updating of data and assumptions for the model an annual process. Administrative responsibility for the model was shared between the Administrative Services and Community Development Departments, with the former responsible for support services and the latter responsible for the computer specialist for the model software; a budget analyst for the cost data; and a planner for the land use, community standards, and other planning data and assumptions.

In those areas where the outcomes of model use were routine, the council assigned control to city staff. Two such areas were growth management and budget making. During use of the model for evaluating general plan options, the council and city staff learned that the model provided a useful tool for negotiating with TIC over the amount and timing of specific developments in the city. For example, approval of residential densities in a particular development could be held hostage to provision of commercial activities (within the specific development under consideration) that would provide sales taxes adequate to balance government revenues and costs; or, approval of residential densities could be held hostage to maintaining hilltops and canyons as permanent open space. In this context, the model indicates what population and land-use mix balances government costs and revenues given expected tax rates.

Similarly, the council and city manager discovered that the model could be used in budget making. Essentially, they ran the model for the forthcoming year to determine the overall level of government spending "required" by existing and planned development, and "possible" with expected revenues. This level of expenditure was then proportioned out to the individual departments as a proposed ceiling on their budgets.

Typically, specific model uses for these purposes do not involve conflicts. Situations requiring council intervention can be handled by a council agreement to assign one or two of their members to staff study teams. Consequently, these model uses and decisions are, to a high degree, routinized. However, the council retains control over all other uses either directly by requiring approval for model runs, or indirectly by setting the priorities for computer use which effectively shuts out other uses. Moreover, the council retains control over the model's assumptions and decision rules by requiring a formal procedure and, ultimately, their approval for changes.

The political uses of the model during incorporation appear similar to those during adaptation. The council, in particular, uses the model to: negotiate with TIC by indicating precisely when population or development changes necessitate public facilities, thus requiring the developer to provide them in exchange for plan approval; legitimate decisions made on other grounds by pointing to how the model supports their position; gain support for their position by giving the illusion of reliance on computer output and technical criteria; and confuse public discussion and debate by seemingly complex and technical discussion of the model assumptions or results.

In this use, the model provides a political tool for extracting concessions from TIC and for demonstrating the reasonableness of what is extracted. And, as one observer says, "when problems arise with a particular development, the developer usually ends up paying for resolving the problems." The cost/benefit calculus for the developer is that of delayed decision versus a more costly development project. Since development costs can be passed on to future buyers of commercial and industrial space or of housing, the choice is usually clear—the developer agrees to pay for resolving the problems just to get the development approval. But the developer also gets something in exchange, usually higher density or more commercial area set aside, or more time to bring commercial activities online.

Thus, TIC seems to have accepted the Irvine "Economic" Model as a suitable basis for these negotiations. At least, Company officials have not openly criticized it. Nor have they advocated some other alternative. Moreover, TIC has consistently taken a real interest in the model. It has not only provided land-use data based on its five-year development plans, but has participated in the whole program, reviewing the reports based upon the model and, most recently, providing a very informed critique of the model assumptions.

The former Planning Director thinks that some of the model's findings influenced the timing and sequence of TIC's development, although not necessarily to the city's advantage:

> I can't recall it being used, at least while I was there, as a tool to beat The Irvine Company over the head, for example. However, The Irvine Company took a real interest in participation in the whole program and I think they got some answers for their own corporate planning purposes out of it. And it helped them develop their own strategies of how to deal with the city. That was very apparent to me.
>
> Their corporate plan was a five-year program that said when they were going to build and when and how much. In the case of Village 10, I think the model had something to do with their decision to delay it somewhat. We had done a separate model run on Village 10 after the general plan evaluation was done. It showed a positive result because there was a lot of commercial development in that area. I think that may have influenced their decision to finish up what they were doing in the other villages [on the grounds that Village 10 would eventually produce net revenues for the city].

Regarding a special model run for the Irvine Regional center, he said:

> We also made a special run on the impact of the regional center. That run was an important consideration in the city pushing the heck out of The Irvine Company to get going [on development of the regional center]. It didn't do any good, but. . . .

Thus, TIC probably supports the model's use in part because they can use the results to their own strategic advantage, or ignore the results when they feel it necessary. Perhaps the most important reason for supporting the model's use is that it is better than the most likely alternatives—namely, requiring the Company to pay for all public facilities, or slowing down the rate of development until public monies can be found to pay for needed facilities. And the model might provide a quantitative and seemingly objective basis for negotiations that TIC planners and managers can, in turn, use to justify their decisions to the company's Board of Directors.

The model also appears to have had an impact on bureaucratic politics. The dominant coalition on the council has succeeded in limiting use of the model to those areas where the outcomes are predictable and has obtained the support of the city manager, computer staff, and planners in delaying or denying other uses on the grounds of priority needed for administrative uses of the computer. For example, one Planning Commissioner commented about the problems of gaining access to the model:

> *What I find fascinating is the internal politics about why you can't use the model when you want to use it. They've set up an economy, a token economy, for the computer, which is that there is only so much computer time available for nonoperational functions. So the different department staffs come in and bid for that time, and the Planning Department's use of the computer time for modeling is a low priority. And, computer time for the planning staff to be running the model for the Planning Commission is an even lower priority. So when you ask questions that could be answered by the model, they say we won't be able to run it because we've run out of our tokens to buy time.*
>
> *The reason this came about is that I was saying that we should have fiscal impacts on everything we do. I asked for a fiscal impact analysis on Irvine Town Center; I asked for it on all projects. The Planning Department staff got very concerned because I spent all of this time talking about fiscal impacts at the Planning Commission meetings. Also, the Planning Commissioners who were representatives of the pro-growth faction knew it was going to be embarrassing in many cases if the cost-benefit ratios were made public. So they simply got to their persons on the City Council and said, don't let the model be run without your permission. So, finally, the City Council came down and said that in order to get a model run, you have to get City Council approval of any run. But, the public justification, which is that the city would go broke if we ran the model as much as we want, is a lot of bunk.*

Finally, the model has performed the symbolic political function of showing the citizens of Irvine that the council does not simply bow to the wishes of TIC. Few citizens are able to monitor the council's actions closely enough to know whether the sum of its actions represent capitulation or not. However, the existence and continued use of the model and the exactions that come out of it convey the impression to citizens that the council *does not* capitulate. So long as there is no easy way to determine the actual state of affairs and the council majority can point to the use of the model in their deliberations, they effectively ignore minority claims of a sell-out to TIC.

Perspectives on Model Implemention

The Irvine Case illustrates several important features about the model implementation process and about the politics of implementation. First, model implementation can be usefully conceived as a multi-phased process involving introduction, adaptation, and incorporation as discrete phases. In Irvine, the introduction phase focused on the decision to adopt a fiscal impact model and selection of a specific vendor to build the model. Adaptation focused on the actual construction of the model and its use for informing selection from among the general plan options, including the use of the model both by the consultant and, subsequently, by the in-house staff via time-sharing. Incorporation focused on the city's commitment to continued use of the model, bringing the model in-house on the city's own computer, making the model's update an annual process, and using the model for additional uses besides the general plan evaluation for which it was first intended. Although the model was used successfully during the adaptation stage, implementation was not complete until the model's use was routinized and made an ongoing part of the city's operational and decision-making processes.

Second, if routinization is used as a criterion of success, the Irvine model must be judged as successfully implemented. Not only was the model used for general plan evaluation, but model use was established as an operating procedure for evaluation of all future development projects. Moreover, model use was extended to growth management and to budget preparation activities as well. The temporary period when the model fell into disuse is not significant in judging its success. The model fell into temporary disuse because the question it was originally designed to answer (Which general plan option should the city adopt?) had been settled and because changing environmental conditions required updating of the model's assumptions, inputs, and parameters. When new questions arose, for which the model was deemed helpful, it was immediately put back into operation. Similarly, the council's decision to limit access to the model to only those uses approved by the council probably cannot be considered as more than a flaw in model implementation. While technical rationality suggests the model should be available for any appropriate use, political rationality suggests that it is unlikely that the council could be expected to permit uses that the council did not approve of or could not control. The policy implications of the model were potentially too politically sensitive and the council coalitions on development issues too unstable to permit access to individuals or groups who might increase the already high level of conflict and competition in the council and the community.

Third, the transition from one implementation phase to another is clearly marked by policy decisions and by concomitant allocation of resources (or changes in the level of resources). For example, "introduction" was marked by the council's decision to issue an RFP for development of the model, and subsequently by the award of a consultant contract to MKGK. "Adaptation" was marked by the council's decision to bring the model in-house, and by the allocation of resources for hiring a computer expert, training staff and acquiring time-sharing services. "Incorporation" was marked by the Council's decision to make updating of the model an annual process and to provide resources for data collection, modification of the model's assumptions, and conversion of the model to the city's own computer.

Fourth, agencies which incorporate innovations into their day-to-day operations do so as much, or more, because the innovations serve political rationality as technical rationality. Ostensibly, the council adopted the model to improve the rationality of their own and others' land-use decisions. But, at each phase of implementation the council's decisions were influenced by their perceived future utility of the model as much as, if not more than, by their actual experience with the usefulness of the model. During introduction the council's decision was influenced more by their general belief in computers and in rational management techniques than by knowledge of the benefit of computerized fiscal impact models from their use in other cities. They lacked such knowledge. Similarly, when the council decided to have city staff trained to use the model and to obtain direct access to the model via time-sharing services, the council was influenced more by their expectations about what the computerized model could be used for than by its actual performance at the time of the midway report on the model by MKGK. The consultant had difficulty operating the model, in full view of the council, and the model never was able to be used for questions at the village level in which the council had the greatest interest. Finally, when the council made a commitment to continued use of the model, they were influenced more by their expectations about new and untried uses than they were about their total experience with its use in evaluation of general plan options.

This is a curious phenomenon, especially since the council repeatedly expressed doubt about whether the escalating expenditures for the model were really worthwhile. There are several possible explanations for the apparent logical inconsistency between the council's experience and its beliefs. One is that the council shared an overriding belief in the value of computers and modeling that allowed them to perceive limitations of the model as problems that would eventually be solved (with additional time and resources). Another explanation is that the model had value to the council beyond its use as a rational decision tool. The model was important in affirming the image of competent, professional government in a community dominated by a highly educated, middle-class population of managers, professionals, and technicians working in high technology businesses and industry. Thus, when the MKGK consultant presented his reports on the models it was done in council chambers complete with computer terminals and all; when the city's planners were awarded a commendation by the California Chapter of the American Institute of Planners, the council devoted time at one of their meetings to have the commendation presented; when the city hired their new computer expert, he was introduced at a council meeting. These meetings, like most other council meetings where the model was discussed, could be viewed by citizens through an Irvine Company cable television channel hooked up to every household in the city. The model also had political value in symbolizing the council's freedom from domination by TIC. City officials had been intimidated from the beginning of the community by TIC's ability to out-gun them with the quantity and quality of their planning and analytical staffs. The Company also had a corporate cash flow model which it used in making its five-year and longer-range development plans. With the economic model, the council now appeared to have firepower equal to the Company and in an area where TIC had no parity.

Fifth, the Irvine case illustrates the fact that model implementation can be lengthy and more costly than most participants anticipate. The implementation process in Irvine extended over three years—from the council's decision to allocate funds for model procurement in October 1975 (adoption), through December 1978, when the coucil decided to have the assumptions and data for the model updated annually (incorporation). During that time, the city spent approximately $50,000 in direct costs on the model. The indirect costs associated with the time of city officials, administrators, and staff other than those directly involved with model operation are conservatively estimated at triple the direct costs. None of the participants in the Irvine effort anticipated these costs; few were aware of their cummulative amount, although the council occasionally expressed dissatisfaction with the continual need to appropriate additional monies for the model effort. Despite this experience, the council's perceived need for a "village-level" model has initiated another implementation cycle and additional unspecified costs since such a model cannot simply be a modification of the current model, but must be developed anew.

Sixth, the model package can change and evolve. The Irvine "economic" model changed substantially as it became routinized in the city. However, the change did not occur in the "economics," or mathematics, of the model. It occurred in the physical location, the operators, the computer support, the data handling operations, and the data base.

Most of the changes were aimed at making it easier to use and access the model. They were not aimed at improving the underlying theory or its implementation in the model equations and assumptions. Indeed, the "economics" of the model may be in serious question not only because of continuous changes in the revenue picture for local governments, but also because the changeover of the program to Irvine's computer may have ignored certain subtleties in the original programing, model equations, assumptions, or data. For example, the MKGK economist said:

> I have reservations about the new in-house model. The computer analyst did not understand the economics, and I am not sure what he has done. Most people have no idea how difficult it is to build a model, and how guessy it is when it is done. They don't understand how difficult it is to reduce the acutal situation to a model. They don't know how to maintain the assumptions and the data so that the model can be safely used.

Seventh and finally, the principal actors, the stakes, and the relationships among actors over the stakes can change throughout the Implementation process. The most significant such change in Irvine was in the dominant coalition of the city council—from low-growth to pro-growth partisans. That change was significant not only because of its direct effect on council decision-making regarding the model and urban development, but also because of its secondary effect on the membership and behavior of city boards and commissions appointed by the council. As indicated by one commissioner, the council's influence over the boards it appoints is substantial:

> Publicly we maintain a facade of being friendly to each other and criticizing the city council all we can in public because everybody wants to look like they're independent. The fact of the matter is that each of us gets our marching orders from the council and we do as we're told.

Interestingly, the change in dominant coalition did not change council support for the fiscal impact model; if anything, it stimulated greater support for routine model uses. One reason for the continued support was the role played by city staff during various changes in council membership. The city staff "educated" the new council members about the model, and because staffers were perceived as neutral, they gave the model legitimacy that the continuing council members, who supported it, could not have provided. Another reason for the continued support was the fact that the model facilitated making marginal adjustments in the city's development pattern that were generally perceived as fiscally advantageous to the city.

The extent to which generalizations for successful model implementation can be drawn from a single case is unclear, but several are suggested by the Irvine Case that might be helpful to others considering model implementation in political environments:

1. Policy makers' decisions to adopt a computer model are influenced as much by their general beliefs about the value of computers and modeling as by the demonstrated value of any particular model. Therefore, efforts to implement a model in an enviroment where policy makers have little faith in the technology are likely to be unsuccessful if their approval or participation is required. Adoption is likely to be enhanced if policy makers are favorable to technology and if the model's value can be demonstrated in terms of their specific decision problem, either by reference to other successful implementation efforts in similar contexts, or by "live demonstration" of the model's operation and outputs. Adoption, however, is only the first step in model acceptance and use. In order to maintain the policy makers' support, each subsequent step requires demonstration of the practical value of the model for a real decision problem, even if the full capabilities of the model remain a potentiality.

2. Personal and political agendas of policy makers and other participants in model implementation, while difficult to assess, require explicit consideration and conscious cultivation to insure a stable coalition in support of model implementation, especially when implementation extends over a long time period and involves changes in principal actors. A critical factor in successful implementation is the presence of an individual or group who advocates the model to others and who provides continuity for the effort throughout the implementation process. While the council played an important role in the Irvine Case, it was the administrative and planning staff who initially advocated the model, who secured the support of the first council and subsequent councils (with the support of the holdover council members), and who advocated continuous updating and use of the model in planning decisions.

3. Ease of understanding of a model's outputs and ease of model operation (as facilitated by technical arrangements) may be

more important than the technical quality of the model for implementation success. Few, if any, participants in model implementation will have the technical capability to truly understand the model and will therefore base their trust in the model on the "form" of the model (ease of use, relevance to the decision problem, format of outputs, and methods of communicating the model's results) and the "reasonableness" of its results. Therefore, attention should be placed on improving the comprehensibility of the model and its results to policy makers rather than on technical perfection of the model.

4. In a highly political environment, a model's symbolic value—in lending technical legitimacy to their decision processes, creating an image of professionalism, and raising the perceived level of technical expertise required by their adversaries—can be as important as its substantive value to policy makers. In advocating a model to policy makers throughout implementation, the symbolic value of the model should be communicated, if not apparent. Making explicit the substantive value of the model is also important, but potentially fraught with difficulties when the value is expressed in terms of likely model outcomes rather than in terms of general applicability of the model to the policy makers' concerns. That is, policy makers will support model implementation to the extent that they believe the model might support their predictions (or policies they have already decided), but are likely to discredit the model or oppose it to the extent they believe it might not support their positions. Consequently, for implementation success it is more important to concentrate policy makers' attention on agreement to use of a model as an appropriate aid to their decision-making than to focus on obtaining their agreement to abide by its substantive results.   □

FOOTNOTES

[1] The author acknowledges the helpful comments of William Dutton, Martha Holis, Susan Fallows and Henry Lucas on earlier drafts of this manuscript. This research has been supported by a grant from the Applied Science Research Division of the National Science Foundation (DAR-7817606).

[2] This paper is an exploration only. It is not an attempt to "test" the hypothesis that political interests must be served as a precondition to successful model implementation. Rather, it seeks insight into how political interests might affect implementation at each stage of the process.

³ The "Irvine Economic Model," which is the term used by city officials and staff to refer to the model, is not really a model of the economy of the City of Irvine as the term might suggest. Rather, it is a model that calculates government revenues and expenditures for a given development plan, compares total revenues to total expenditures, and indicates the net fiscal loss or gain to the city. Thus, it is a fiscal impact model.

⁴ The model had originally been developed by the national accounting firm Kenneth Leventhal Company of Kansas City for assisting private developers in determining the economic feasibility of new town development. MKGK had used the model to assess the capital costs associated with building Kairparowitts New Town, a new community associated with the development of a coal mine and power plant in southeastern Utah, and to analyze capital costs of development for Ciudad Guayana, a new industrial city in Venezuela.

⁵ The assumptions and data involved: the amount of land, by type of use, that would be brought into developed status each year through the year 2000; the capital, operating and maintenance costs associated with public physical facilities; the standards for provision of public facilities (e.g., the amount of land devoted to parks and open space per 1,000 people in the community) which would "trigger" capital expenditures at different population levels; the operating costs associated with the provision of public services such as police, fire, education libraries, planning, etc.; and the revenue factors associated with land uses, population, public service fees, and state or Federal subventions.

⁶ Not all of the tables represented model outputs. Rather, some were simply summaries of the data that had been input to the model. The 11 summary tables were as follows: (1) development of city by land use type by period (acreages); (2) cumulative development of city by land use type by period (acreages); (3) cumulative population and housing units in city by land use type; (4) city annual capital expenditures by item type; (5) cumulative city capital expenditures by item type; (6) city periodic maintenance costs; (7) city periodic operating costs; (8) city annual general fund revenues; (9) city cumulative assessed value by land use type; (10) financing of city capital improvement projects by period; and (11) city fiscal impact summary. Table 11 was the "bottom line" because it indicated the "implied property tax rate per $100 assessed value; that is, the tax rate that would be required to meet the excess of expenditures over revenues for any particular development period (Marshall Kaplan, Gans and Kahn, 1976).

References

[1] BREWER, G.D. *Politicians, Bureaucrats, and the Consultant.* New York: Basic Books, 1973.

[2] City of Irvine, Council Meeting Minutes, October 28, 1975.

[3] City of Irivne, Memorandum from the Director of Community Development, "Continued   Use of the Economic Model by City Staff," October 1, 1976.

[4] City of Irvine, Council Meeting Minutes, October 13, 1976.

[5] City of Irvine, Council Meeting Minutes, December 14, 1976.

[6] City of Irvine, Council Meeting Tapes, September 15, 1977.

[7] City of Irvine, Staff report from the Director of Administrative Services and the Director of Community Development, Updated economic model assumptions, (September 22, 1978).

[8] City of Irvine, Staff report from the Director of Administrative Services and the Director of Community Development, Economic model, (May 16, 1979).

[9] CURRY, D. *Irvine: The Case for a New Kind of Planning*, Cry California 6
      (1971), 18-40.
[10] DOWNS, A. "A Realistic Look at the Final Payoffs from Urban Data
      Systems," *Public Administration Review*, 27 (1967) 204-210.
[11] DUTTON, W.H., K.L. KRAEMER and M.S. HOLLIS. "Fiscal Impact Models
      and the Policy Process: Theory and Practice," *The Urban Interest*, 2
      (1980), 66-74.
[12] FROMM, G., W.L. HAMILTON and D.E. HAMILTON. "Federally Supported
      Mathematical Models: Survey and Analysis." Washington, D C : U.S.
      Government Printing Office, 1974.
[13] GALE, D. "The Municipal Impact Evaluation System Computer-Assisted
      Cost/Revenue Analysis of Urban Development," (American Society of
      Planning Officials, Chicago, 1973).
[14] GORRY, G.A. and M.S.S. MORTON. "A framework for management infor-
      mation systems," Sloan School Working Paper, Cambridge, MA: MIT,
      Sloan School of Management (1971, mimeographed), 458-70.
[15] KAPLAN, M., GANS and KAHN. "The Fiscal and Economic Analysis of
      General Plan Options," (San Francisco, CA, November 15, 1976).
[16] KEEN, P. "Implementation Research in OR/MS and MIS: Description versus
      Prescription," Stanford, CA: Graduate School of Business, Stanford
      University, 1977.
[18] KRAEMER, K.L. "The Evolution of Information Systems for Urban Adminis-
      tration," *Public Administration Review*, 29 (1969), 389-402.
[19] KRAEMER, K.L. and W.H. DUTTON. "Computers, Information, and Power:
      The Automation of Bias," *Computers and Politics*, J.N. Danziger, W. H.
      Dutton, R. Kling and K.L. Kraemer. New York: Columbia University
      Press, 1981.
[20] KOLB, D.A. and A.I. FROHMAN. "An Organization Development Approach
      to Consulting," *Sloan Management Review*, 12 (1970), 51-65.
[21] LEE, Jr., D. "Requiem for Large Scale Models," *Journal of the American
      Institute of Planners*, 39 (1973), 136-148.
[22] LEWIN, K. "Group Decision and Social Change," *Readings in Social Psy-
      chology*, Newcomb and Hartley (eds.) New York: Henry Holt and Co.,
      1952.
[23] LUCAS, Jr., H.C. "Behavioral Factors in System Implementation," Stanford,
      CA: Graduate School of Business, Stanford University, 1973.
[24] PEREIA and LUCKMAN. "Campus Site Selection Study," (Los Angeles, CA,
      Pereira and Luckman, 1958).
[25] PEREIRA, W.L. and ASSOCIATES. "A University Campus and Community
      Study: Phase One," (Los Angeles, CA, May, 1959).
[26] PEREIRA, W.L. and ASSOCIATES. "Second Phase Report: A University
      Campus and Community Study," (Los Angeles, CA, May, 1960).
[27] ROTH, R.F., S.I. GASS and A.J. LEMONINE. "Some Considerations for
      Improving Federal Modeling," *Methodology in Systems Modeling and
      Simulation*, B.P. Zeigler, M.S. Elzas, G.J. Klir, and T.I. Oren (eds.).
      Amsterdam: North-Holland Publishing Company, pp. 167-175.

[28] YIN, R.K. "Changing Urban Bureaucracies: How New Practices Become Routinized," Santa Monica, CA: The Rand Corporation, 1978.

Dennis Meadows, co-author with his wife, Donella, and others of the now famous report on the first study commissioned by the Club of Rome, answers questions posed by Geoffrey Holister. Meadows is professor of engineering as well as director of the Resource Policy Center, Dartmouth College, Hanover, New Hampshire.

Chapter 11

ON MODELING, LIMITS AND UNDERSTANDING

Dennis Meadows
interviewed by Geoffrey S. Holister

Questions by Holister

Many of us tend to comment rather harshly on economics as an exact science. My first question therefore is how can you possibly use any economic model in your modeling processes with any confidence at all, considering the rune-casting nature of the discipline?

The author is professor of engineering science at The Open University, Walton Hall, Milton Keynes MK7 6AA (United Kingdom), where he served earlier as the university's first dean of technology. An engineer and physicist, Professor Holister has worked in private industry for fifteen years; he is founding editor of the *Journal of the British Society for Strain Measurement* and currently editor-in-chief of the *International Journal of Fiber Science and Technology,* British editor of the Italian science journal *Newton,* and co-author, with Andrew Porteous, of *The Environment, A Dictionary of the World Around Us,* published in London by Arrow Books in 1976.

Reply by Meadows

Economics involves the study of procedures for allocating resources so as to obtain a set of competing objectives. The field encompasses an enormously diverse body of empirical data, causal hypotheses, normative statements, models, and analytical results. Because most economists have been preoccupied with the dynamics of short-term, monetary flows in Western industrialized societies, much of the field is irrelevant to issues that arise in long-term global models. Nevertheless, many economists have developed shrewd insights and useful generalizations through their studies of resource use. I always found the better economists to offer useful perspectives on issues we addressed through our research into growth limits.

Unfortunately, the limitations inherent in economics as it is most widely practiced today are ones that become very serious in contemplating an end to the expansion phase of the globe's material resources. Assumptions about human goals that served economists well during the period of continuous growth will shed little insight into the behavior of people and institutions during a phase of steady-state behavior in population and capital levels. Techniques like linear regression, which project past behavior into the future, will not provide useful guidance in periods of great discontinuity. Thus one must be careful in mapping the results of economics on to issues quite remote from those from which they were initially derived.

In your seminars, you imply a belief that all social and political issues are at root linked to resource limitations. Now while I am prepared to accept that this would be so if man were a rational animal, I would suggest to you that, in the present world, rational behavior is in rather short supply. If therefore people and nations behave irrationally in prescribed circumstances, does not the whole basis of your modeling process fall apart?

You have just reversed the point I make in my seminars. I explain how physical shortages generally appear in the guise of social problems rather than as physical depletion. There is, for example, great concern currently about the power of OPEC, about inflation, about balance-of-payments difficulties in the Third World, and about economic recession. All these social difficulties are symptoms of the fact that many of the globe's cheap oil deposits have been exploited. Difficulties that arise from physical shortages can always be exacerbated by greed or stupidity—which abounds. But the upper limits of human potential are set in important ways by the globe's physical resource base.

Our model portrays the consequences of factors that set the upper bounds on the potential for expanding human population and material use. We stated explicitly in our reports that our model made optimistic assumptions about human behavior. War, inequity and irrationality are not included in our forecasts. If they persist, they will serve merely to lower real options below those theoretically afforded by the physical resource base. Thus our model is useful, but not as a means of predicting the exact shape of the future. It indicates, as suggested by the title of our book, the upper limits to growth.

Do you believe that modeling as ubiquitous scientific activity should be taught in schools and universities and, if so, in what context and at what levels?

Any mode of human thought that employs labels or causal theories is a form of modeling. Perhaps we could refine your question to focus specifically on mathematical modeling that addresses longer-term social issues. I believe emphatically that this form of modeling should be included in modern curricula. At Dartmouth College we have developed a four-year curriculum that provides students with a comprehensive appreciation of the techniques, the advantages, the limitations, and the results of mathematical modeling studies. Most of our students will never use a computer after they graduate. Instead they take away the results of their study in a form that disciplines their intuition, that affords them a systematic way of appreciating and interpreting the trends and the forces they see in their environment.

In my experience, the students who have responded violently to problems of current societies are those who do not understand the causes of the problems and feel they have no influence over their solution. They are left only with the possibility of destroying the system that is associated with the problem. Students who have shrewd insights into the nature of current social problems are ones more likely to work for peaceful and constructive change within the system. I know that the studying of modeling can give that kind of insight. Thus I believe it is a crucial element in modern education.

Professor Nancy Roberts at MIT has experimented with courses that convey the essential aspects of mathematical modeling to children in the very lowest grades of the American school system. Her results suggest that modeling can profitably be introduced at the start of formal education.

Could you describe the areas of application where, in your experience, your modeling process has been most and least successful?

Over forty books have been published to report on results of system dynamics studies. There are graduate degrees available to those studying application of the technique in universities in several countries. The diversity of work, consequently, is impossible to characterize in a few words here. Perhaps the best way to illustrate some areas for fruitful analysis would be for me to offer your readers a free copy of the list that indicates the publications available from the Resource Policy Center. Our bibliography includes about 160 reports that describe the application of these modeling procedures to a very diverse set of questions:

What factors lock alcoholics into the persistent consumption of alcohol?

What policies could lead harvesting of forests in the United States to stay within sustainable bounds?

What factors cause oscillation in the price, production, and use of agricultural and mineral commodities?

How will current programs impact on the use of fossil fuels by the American transport fleet over the next two decades?

What programs could arrest the disappearance of small farms in the United States?

What policies could ease society's transition from dependence on oil to dominant reliance on alternative energy sources?

I might say, in short, that the understanding of any complex system can be enhanced through use of computer-modeling procedures. On the other hand, no issue can be fully resolved by the use of these techniques. They must be married with intuition, paper-and-pencil calculations, expert judgment and results available from many other disciplines. Nor can any mathematical modeling technique guarantee the production of wisdom by the hand of a fool.

Could you look into the future for us to predict in which areas you believe modeling will have the greatest impact?

The future impact of modeling depends more on trends in economic and political institutions than it does on the characteristics of the modeling methods available. Modeling is like any new technology; its use will tend to grow fastest where it produces an obvious short-term reward to those who must invest in its use. These conditions have typically been best satisfied within the corporate sector and in the military. I suppose these two will continue to be the major users of models. I would much prefer that modeling come to have greater impact at the individual level. The explosion in use of personal micro-computers certainly affords that opportunity, but educational programs will have to be changed for this potential to be realized.   □

In modeling economic behavior all kinds of information should be used, not merely numerical data. Rich stores of information about economic structure and governing policies are available from mental data bases built up from experience and observation. The daily and weekly business press contains information from which a model can bridge from microstructure to macrobehavior. The System Dynamics National Model draws on all classes of information for its structure and policies. The National Model, without exogenous time series inputs, generates 3- to 7-year business cycles, 15- to 25-year capital cycles, 45- to 60-year long waves, and the processes of inflation, unemployment, and stagflation. Such a simulation model, based on a diversity of information sources, can shed new light on economic dynamics.

Chapter 12

INFORMATION SOURCES FOR MODELING

THE NATIONAL ECONOMY

Jay W. Forrester

Introduction

In this paper I have been asked to discuss how various kinds of information can be used in modeling a national economy. Different types of economic models imply different sources and uses of

Jay W. Forrester is Germeshausen Professor of Management at the Massachusetts Institute of Technology, Cambridge, MA 02139. Work on which this paper is based has been supported by the Sponsors of the System Dynamics National Model. The author especially appreciates comments by Martin B. Wilk on drafts of this paper.

Note: Reprinted by permission from an article in the *Journal of the American Statistical Association*, September 1980.

information. Effectiveness of an economic model is largely determined by how it uses the wide range of information arising from the real system. I believe the inadequacies of economic analysis can be substantially attributed to inappropriate and biased use of available information. By inappropriate use of information, I refer to overemphasis on finding statistical relationships between economic variables and underemphasis on the internal causal mechanisms that produce economic behavior. By biased use of information, I refer to overdependence on numerical data and underutilization of information available from written and mental sources. In this paper, I will examine information from the viewpoint that has guided design of the System Dynamics National Model.

In creating a system dynamics model, information is used in a substantially different way from the way it is used in regression analysis and econometrics. The different uses of information arise from a difference in structure between a system dynamics model and an econometric model, from a broader range of information sources used for creating a system dynamics model, from a different way of arriving at parameter values, from a different use of historical time series data, and from a different purpose for which a system dynamics model is intended.

Sources of Information

Information is available from many different sources. Figure 1 suggests three kinds of data bases: mental, written, and numerical. I use the term *data bases* in an extended sense. Those working with statistics may think of data as always coming in measured, numerical form. But my unabridged dictionary (Webster's *Third*) gives no hint that data are restricted to numerical information. Webster's defines *data* as "something that is given from being experientially encountered" and "material serving as a basis for discussion, inference, or determination of policy" and "detailed information of any kind." Within this broad definition, I will include data stored mentally in people's heads, data stored descriptively in writing, and data available numerically.

As suggested by the figure, the amount of available information declines, perhaps by a factor of a million, in going from mental to written information and again by another factor of a million in going from written to numerical information. Furthermore, the character of information content changes as one moves from mental to written to numerical information. Each kind of information can fill a different role in modeling a national economy.

Figure 1. Mental data base and decreasing content of written and numerical data bases.

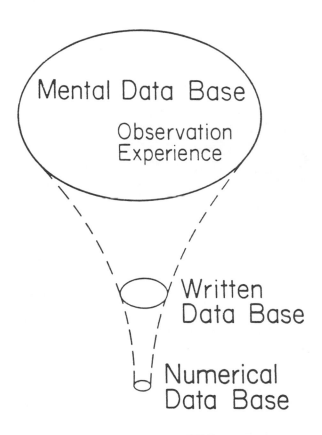

Mental Data

Human affairs are conducted primarily from the mental data base. The mental data base is far more extensive than the other stores of information. Anyone who doubts the dominant scope of remembered information should imagine what would happen to an industrial society if it were deprived of all knowledge in people's heads and if action could be guided only by written policies and numerical information. There is no written description adequate for building an automobile, or managing a family, or governing a country. I am putting special stress in this paper on the mental data base because the significance of that information is not adequately appreciated in the social sciences.

If the mental data base is so important to the conduct of human systems, then I believe a model of such systems must reflect knowledge of policies and structure that resides only in the mental data. Effective model building must draw on the mental data base.

For modeling purposes, mental information can be classified three ways, as shown in Figure 2. The categories differ in reliability and in their role in modeling.

Figure 2. Content of the mental data base as related to components and to behavior of a social system.

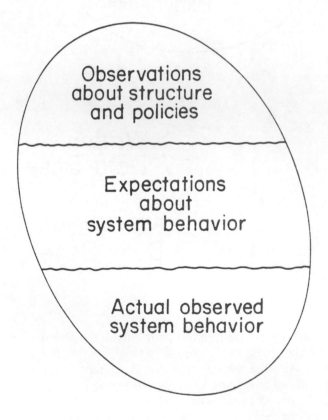

The first category deals with why people act as they do and how the parts of a social system are interconnected. The mental data base contains extensive information about policies and structures, the very things one wants to know to build a system dynamics model. The mental data base is rich in structural detail; in it is knowledge of what information is available at various decision-making points, where people and goods move, and what decisions are made. The mental data base is especially concerned with policy, that is, why people respond as they do, what each decision-making center is trying to accomplish, what are the perceived penalties and rewards of the specific social system, and where self-interest clashes with institutional objectives.

The first category of mental information—information about policy and structure—is directly tapped for transfer into a system dynamics model. In general, the mental data base relating to policy and structure is reliable. Of course, it must be cross-checked. Exaggerations and over-simplifications can exist and must be corrected. Interviewees must be pressed beyond quick first responses. Interrogation must be guided by a knowledge of what different structures imply for dynamic behavior. But from the mental data base, a consensus emerges that is useful and sufficiently correct.

But the second category of mental information is not reliable. The expectations about system behavior are the mental simulations that presumably represent the dynamic consequences of the detailed information in the first category. The second category—the expectations about behavior—represents intuitive solutions to the nonlinear, high-order systems of integral equations that reflect the structure and policies of real systems. Such intuitive solutions to complicated dynamic systems are usually wrong. For example, Congress may pass a law intended to relieve the social and economic distress of cities. The law belongs to the first category in the figure; the law is a statement of policy; that policy is explicit and known. But the expectation that the law will relieve urban distress belongs to the second category; the expectation arises from a judgmental simulation of a complex socio-economic system. Public frustration with government arises largely because such intuitive simulations too often incorrectly interpret the effect of a policy change.

The third category of mental information is useful. It is about past experience with the actual system. From past behavior come the symptoms of difficulty that provide the motivation for a dynamic study and for a model. After a model is operating, behavior of the model can be partially evaluated against knowledge of the past episodes and behavioral characteristics of the real system.

Written Data

The written data base contributes to a dynamic model at several stages. Part of the written store of information is simply a recording of information from the mental store. Another part of the written record contains concepts and abstractions that interpret other information sources.

Published material makes information more widely available than if it remains in the mental stores from which the written record can be drawn. In its totality, the written record is an excellent source of information about system structure and the reasons for decisions. I refer here primarily to the daily and weekly, public and business press, in which current pressures surrounding decisions are revealed.

The temporal nature of a decision sharply restricts the kind of literature in which actual operating policy will be revealed. Decisions control action. Decisions are fleeting. There is only a single instant in time when one can act. That time is now. Action must take place in the present moment that separates history from the future. One cannot act in the past or in the future but only in the present.

The ever-advancing present moment in economic decision making is the businessman's and politician's world of action. It is the world of placing orders, hiring people, buying capital equipment, borrowing money, changing wages in response to union bargaining, shipping goods, setting interest rates, and extending credit. These actions are continuously modulated by changes that occur in system states such as backlogs, inventories, plant capacity, debt, liquidity, and number of employees.

As a consequence of the short life of a decision, it is primarily the literature of the present in which decisions are discussed in terms of goals, threats, limited information, and restraints on action. In economic activity that literature of the present means such publications as the *Wall Street Journal, The Christian Science Monitor, Business Week,* and *Fortune.* The multifaceted conflicting pressures of real decision making are almost absent from economics textbooks and journals. The professional literature emphasizes how decisions should be made rather than how they are made, how equilibrium is determined rather than how dynamic behavior arises, and how macroeconomic theory might apply rather than how the microstructure creates the macrobehavior.

But the current business literature is not easy to use for model building. No single issue of a publication is meaningful by itself. The economic world keeps changing. At any one time, only a subset of possible inputs is important to a particular decision point. At one time, it may be high and rising inventories, at another time falling liquidity, and at still another time the need for more production capacity. Comprehensive policies, suitable for a model that will operate properly over a wide range of conditions, must embody all the considerations that can occur. To be useful, the literature must be pieced together, decisions must be interpreted into policies, and policies and structure must be perceived as causing modes of behavior that may extend over years or decades. One must read between the lines and round out each picture with information from other times and places. It may be that such interpretation of the current business literature cannot be effectively done without first-hand knowledge of the mental data base used by operators in business and politics. Such first-hand knowledge can be obtained only by living and working where the decisions are made and by watching and talking with those who run the economic system.

The written record has two major shortcomings compared with the mental data from which the written data were taken. As a first weakness, the written record usually cannot be queried. Unlike the mental data base, the written record is not responsive to probing by the analyst as he or she searches for a fit between structure, policy, and behavior. As a second deficiency, in being transformed from the mental store to writing, information has already been filtered through the perspective and purposes of the writer. The writer's purpose may have been very different from that of a person seeking the internal causes of a particular dynamic behavior.

Part of the written data base deals with abstractions about structure. An example is the Cobb-Douglas production function. Closely related is the concept of marginal productivity of the factors of production. Such concepts are seldom explicity recognized by practicing management and would not emerge from discussions with those who make economic decisions. The fact that such important concepts are hidden from the practitioner leads to a fundamental issue in designing a system dynamics model.

There are processes that one believes important in real life but that do not enter explicitly into practical decision making. Such processes play a role that is not directly visible. How are such hidden concepts to be handled in a dynamic model? The answer is that they should be included in the structure because they are believed to be real but should be veiled from the decision points of the model as they are obscured in real life. For example, it is generally accepted that marginal productivities do exist for each factor of production. But managers have no way of determining quickly and reliably the values of the marginal productivities. Management does not know with assurance whether money would most effectively be spent for a production worker, a lathe, more raw inventory, a vice president, advertising, or another pilot for the executive jet. Yet if the marginal productivities are seriously out of balance, the underlying truth will gradually be perceived. It emerges from conflicting pleas, from crises, and from repetition of minor bits of evidence. The hidden true marginal productivities are the source of the perceived productivities that eventually diffuse into management awareness.

In the same way, the National Model has a production function that determines present production rate as a direct consequence of the several inventories of the factors of production. In the National Model, a partial derivative of the production function is taken with respect to each factor so the true marginal productivities exist in the model as an underlying basis for generating the delayed and distorted values that will be used in ordering factors of production. But the true values must not be admitted into the ordering of factors of production any more than the true values are available in real life. We believe that an adequate simple approximation to the real process is to assume that true productivities are perceived by management after a substantial time delay. In the National Model, exponential delays, which may be several years long, intervene between the true values and the perceived values. Such delays cannot be directly observed in real life because the inputs to the delays are not known, but their values can be inferred from their effect in generating periodicities and damping cyclic behavior in the National Model that are similar to those observed for the real system.

This handling of marginal productivity illustrates how the modeler must play a dual role in dealing with underlying fundamental concepts in the context of practical decision making. On the one hand the model builder must act as an omniscient observer who puts into the model what must exist in real life. But on the other hand, he or she must degrade information about "true" conditions within the model before it is used in decision making by the model, so as to approximate the distortion that occurs in the actual system.

Numerical Data

The numerical data base is of narrower scope than the written and mental data bases. Missing from numerical data is direct evidence of the structure and policies that created the data. The numerical data do not reveal the cause-to-effect direction between variables. From numerical data one can make statistical analyses to determine which time series data streams correlate with one another, but that still leaves unanswered the question of internal causality.

The numerical data base contains at least three bodies of information that are useful in modeling a national economy.

First, specific numerical information is available on some parameter values. For example, average delivery delay for filling orders exists in corporate records and summaries of business information. Typical ratios of factory inventories to production output can be found. Many normal values, around which variation occurs, are available, such as money balances, inventory coverage, and time to fill job vacancies.

Second, numerical information has been collected by many authors in the economics literature to summarize typical characteristics of economic behavior, such as periodicities, and average phase relationships and their dispersions between variables in an economy. Empirical studies of the Phillips curve are an example. The Phillips curve is a relationship between wage change and unemployment. The puzzling shifts of the Phillips curve, as it moves up and down, right and left, and changes slope, raise questions about economic behavior that a dynamic simulation model should be able to answer.

Third, numerical information contains time series data. In system dynamics modeling, time series data are used much less as the basis for parameter values than in econometric models. But in system dynamics, the simulation model itself generates synthetic output time series data that can be compared in a variety of ways with the real time series data. I believe this independent use of time series data for validating model behavior is less vulnerable to errors in the data than is the econometric use of data for trying to derive meaningful parameters.[1]

System Dynamics

In this paper, information is interpreted from the system dynamics viewpoint. System dynamics is less related to the methodologies of the social sciences than to the methodologies of practicing management and engineering. In the system dynamics approach, the methods of management have been extended and improved by methodologies developed in engineering. System dynamics can be described as a substantial extension of the case-study approach, as that term is used in management education.

Background

As shown in Figure 3, system dynamics grows out of three prior activities—traditional management, feedback systems or cybernetics, and computer simulation.

By traditional management, I mean the way people have managed families, businesses, and nations since the beginning of human society.

Figure 3. Three prior background developments from which system
dynamics emerges.

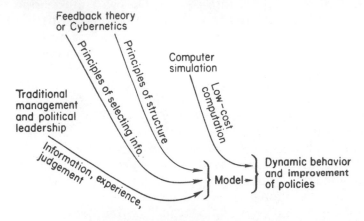

The great strength of traditional management lies in the tremendous
data base to which it has access. Most of the data base exists in people's
heads. The data base records experience, observation, and participation
in life. The mental data base is rich in knowledge about structure, that
is, how the system is organized and how it is connected. The mental
data base contains the most directly accessible information about
policies that govern decisions. But traditional management suffers from
three weaknesses.

First, traditional management is overwhelmed by too much information. As one of its contributions, feedback theory provides principles
for choosing relevant information and rejecting the preponderance of
information that would be useless for constructing a dynamic model.

As the second weakness, traditional management lacks organizing
principles to guide how information should be assembled into an effective framework. That is, traditional management has no theory for
assembling an appropriate model. As a second contribution, feedback
theory supplies principles about structure to guide the organization of
information into a model.

As the third weakness, traditional management has had no way to
manipulate its mental models except by intuition. There has been no
reliable way to determine the behavior implied by the available knowledge about structure and policies. Probably no mathematician would
presume to solve by inspection even a simple fourth-order linear differential equation. By contrast, the working environment of a manager or
politician is far more complex; he or she is undertaking to solve, by

discussion and compromise, systems that are highly nonlinear and of at least hundredth order. The task is nearly impossible. But now, computer simulation can do perfectly the formerly impossible task of revealing the dynamic behavior implicit in a complex model.

Use of Information

The preceding discussion of information and methodology leads to the modeling process shown in Figure 4. From the mental data base first comes the purpose of a model. The motivation usually arises from troublesome behavior of the real system. In a corporation, perhaps market share has been falling, or employment has been fluctuating more widely than for other companies in the industry. For a national economy, the motivation could come from controversies over inflation or a steadily increasing amplitude of the business cycle as has occurred during the last 15 years. Such a model of the national economy would be expected to explain troublesome behavior, not merely in the sense of correlations between historical variables, but instead by actually generating the troublesome symptoms from the same underlying structural and policy mechanisms that generate the real-life symptoms.

Figure 4. Creating a system dynamics model.

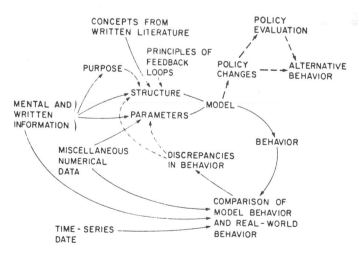

During model construction, the central focus is on information available from mental and written sources and numerical information other than time series data. Such other numerical data include, for example, average delays in filling orders, typical ratios of inventory to sales rate, relative costs of production inputs, and lead times for ordering factors of production.

The full range of information and the purpose, along with appropriate modeling concepts, are interpreted through principles from feedback-loop theory to yield a model structure.

Parameters are also usually derived directly and individually from the mental, written, and numerical data bases. I believe that in the social sciences too sharp a distinction is drawn between structure and parameters. The distinction is fluid. For a simple model to be used over a short time span, certain quantities can be considered constants that for a model dealing with a longer time horizon should be converted into variables. Those new variables would in turn depend on more enduring parameters. For example, a policy for reordering goods for inventory might in the short run suffice if it sought to maintain a specified number of units in inventory. But for a model that was intended to be valid over a longer run, sales might change substantially, and a constant inventory would no longer be appropriate. The policy for managing inventory might instead be cast in terms of a variable target inventory that would try to maintain inventory equal to a specified number of weeks of average sales. Weeks of sales covered by inventory is a more enduring parameter than an absolute level of desired inventory. In creating a structure of variables and the associated parameters, one must continuously decide what will be considered a variable and what a parameter.

In a system dynamics model, every parameter should have meaning in the real-life setting. Its numerical value should be discussable with operating people in that part of the real system where the parameter is relevant. A plausible range for each parameter can be initially estimated from field information. Then, simulation tests can help to refine a parameter value within its plausible range. A particular parameter is likely to influence primarily a single dynamic mode of the system and some specific behavior within that mode. Because two parameters seldom have the same effect on system behavior, a change in one parameter will not often substitute for a change in another parameter. Sensitivity testing, with results interpreted against a wide array of real-life data, tend to converge toward a rather well-defined set of parameters. Further sensitivity testing will usually show that a choice between policy alternatives is not likely to be affected by reasonable changes in parameters.

A preliminary determination of structure and parameters yields a model. But, as suggested in the figure, an initial model formulation is only the beginning of the system dynamics process. Model behavior is generated in the form of time series data for as many of the model variables as one chooses to plot. The diversity of variables makes possible a multitude of comparisons between the model as the real system.[2]

Model behavior can be compared with the many kinds of behavioral information from real life. Available information will include knowledge of logical possibilities. For example, real inventories do not go negative even though model inventories often do in dynamic models with inadequate shipping functions. When such a finding is traced back to its cause in the model, a weakness is revealed, or an intended shortcut in model construction is shown to be unacceptable.

Time series data are used primarily in comparing the time series output of a model with the time series output of real life. Because of the way randomness in decision making influences both the real world and a model of that real world, one does not expect model output and historical data to match on a point-by-point basis. Instead, one looks at the behavioral characteristics of the time series data stream from the model and compares them with the corresponding characteristics of the real data. For example, what are the typical time lags in the business-cycle mode between variables and what is the statistical dispersion in those lags, or what are the relative amplitudes of fluctuation of different variables?

The comparison of real-world behavior with model behavior will reveal discrepancies. Each discrepancy must be evaluated to judge whether it justifies the time and effort to make a correction. Discrepancies become the sign posts that lead back through the prior stages of model formulation. The discrepancies create a new perspective from which to reevaluate the mental, written, and numerical data bases; to test parameters for their effect on behavior; and to modify structure so its behavior aligns better with the real system.

After a model has been judged satisfactory for its particular purpose, the model can then be used for policy analysis. A policy change, which is usually a parameter change in a policy statement, is made, and a new simulation run obtained. Behavior from the new policy is compared with behavior from the old policy to evaluate relative desirabilities of the policies.

It is not only those in system dynamics who argue that models should be based on far more observation of how economic affairs are actually conducted. Phelps Brown in his presidential address to the Royal Economic Society in 1971 said:

For our knowledge of the behaviour of economic agents we must rely mainly on the patient accumulation of direct observations. . . . Where an economic problem arises, let us observe whatever seems significant, and follow clues to causes wherever they may lead. . . . The findings of those who have been at pains to ask businessmen what they actually do, have been smiled at as impressionistic, as somehow unprofessional. In the present stage of our science, at least, I believe that this relative valuation should be inverted: we ought to value powers of observation more highly than powers of abstraction, and the insight of the historian more than the rigour of the mathematicians.[3]

The mental and written data bases of businessmen can yield the structure and policies and parameters of a model that will behave like the real system. We have made the transformation from descriptive information to effective models many times in applying system dynamics to understanding the consequences of corporate policies. One can go into a corporation that has serious and widely known difficulties. The symptom might be a substantial fluctuation of employment with peaks several years apart. Or the symptom might be falling market share. The symptoms are often unique to the one company in the industry, indicating that the trouble must arise from internal policies rather than from the external environment. In the process of finding valuable insights in the mental data store, one talks to a variety of people in the company, maybe for many days, possibly spread over many months. The discussion is filtered through one's catalog of feedback structures into which the behavioral symptoms and the discussion of structure and policy might fit. The process converges toward an explicit simulation model. The policies in the model are those that people assert they are following; in fact, the emphasis is often on the policies they are following in an effort to alleviate the great difficulty.

When the model is put on a computer, the simulation results show that the model itself generates the same difficulty that prompted the modeling. In other words, the very policies people are intentionally following in hope of solving the problem are sufficient, when interconnected, to cause the problem. The situation is deceptive. People believe they know the solution and act accordingly. They do not perceive that their actions are causing the problem. As the situation becomes worse, they apply more of the assumed solution, which makes matters still worse. A downward spiral can develop. Application of the policies worsens the situation, which in turn is taken as need for more vigorous application of the policies. As an example, if profits decline, financial pressures develop and lead to emphasis on tighter control of inventories; lower inventories leave a narrower range of products available in a more limited number of sales outlets so market share falls; and profits decline still further. The policies aimed at relieving the financial stress can create the unfavorable financial symptoms. At each point in such a corporate system, people are doing what they say they are doing and doing it because they believe the action will help solve the problem. But no one perceives that the unfavorable consequences are being created by the ensemble of known and intended policies.

We embarked on the National Model expecting that well-known policies and structures in industry and government would be found to create the observed economic difficulties.[4] Such seems to be true. Quite ordinary managerial policies in industry can create business cycles and longer disturbances. National policies for perpetuating prosperity can accentuate major depressions. Energy policies, such as holding down the price of energy, are encouraging energy use and discouraging energy supply, with even greater pressures leading to still more counterproductive policies. Inflation is being increased by policies intended to reduce inflation.

The System Dynamics National Model

The System Dynamics National Model is a simulation model for replicating in the laboratory the behavior of a national economy.[5] Its purpose is, first, to serve as a tool for achieving a better understanding of economic behavior. Second, the National Model is intended for evaluating alternative corporate and national policies.

For the last seven years at the Sloan School of Management at MIT, we have been developing the National Model. The work is supported by 30 sponsors, about equally divided among corporations, foundations, and private individuals. I believe most sponsors are attracted to the program because they are deeply concerned about puzzling and unfavorable economic trends, they find that traditional economic analysis is not providing the guidance that is needed, and they see the National Model as a promising way to understand economic behavior.

The National Model brings the structure and policies of the national economy into the laboratory where controlled experiments can be performed. As a replica of the economy, the National Model generates the broad range of behavior seen in the real economy. The model exhibits such realistic behavior without depending on exogenous inputs. By generating macroeconomic behavior from internal microstructure, the National Model shows how the many policies in industry, banking, and government interact to create troublesome behavior of the total socioeconomic system.

The National Model is not yet fully assembled. It now exists in various partial assemblies that can already address several major economic issues.

Description of the National Model

The full National Model will contain a set of production sectors.[6] A labor mobility network moves people between production sectors. The financial sector makes long- and short-term loans, sets interest rates, and manages a government securities market, and the monetary authority controls credit in response to economic conditions. The government sector issues debt, levies taxes, and pays for government services, military expenditures, and transfer payments. The household-consumption sectors receive personal income, buy goods and services, pay taxes, save, and determine labor force participation. A demographic sector will generate births and deaths and produce a varying age distribution to use in evaluating the viability of Social Security and private retirement plans when population growth slows and the average age rises. The foreign-trade sector will permit transfer of goods and payments and will generate the balance of international payments and shifting exchange rates.

When fully assembled, the National Model will include 15 production sectors, such as consumer durables, manufacture of capital equipment, agriculture, housing construction, services, and energy. Each production sector will order and use some 12 factors of production. Real flows are handled separately from their financial representations. Each sector generates a full balance sheet and profit-and-loss statement. Prices and wages are generated at each sector.

> Note: The original paper continued with a section on economic behavior of the national model. Following is Professor Forrester's summary for the complete paper:

In summary, I believe that

1. Modeling a national economy is not being hampered by a shortage of data.
2. Rich data sources exist in mental data stores and in the current business literature.

3. Known structure and policies do cause the economic behavior that has been so puzzling.

4. Statistical correlations have often incorrectly been interpreted as identifying causal relationships and have misled public policy.

5. A comprehensive system dynamics type of simulation model allows controlled laboratory experiments to show how misleading data are produced by known generating mechanisms.

6. Real time series data are most useful for judging model-generated output.

7. Ensembles of economic conditions generated by a model can be used to identify previously unrecognized economic syndromes, that is, combinations of interrelated symptoms arising from a previously unidentified mode of behavior.

8. Empirical regularities are easily misinterpreted as being guides to economic policy. One must understand how the regularity is generated before a direction of causality can be assumed.

9. Within time series data are hidden contributions from many different modes of economic behavior. A variable that is induced to change by one mode may belong to an entirely different mode when used as a policy control lever.

From all this, I hope to have left an impression that rich information sources exist for modeling a national economy, that a dynamic simulation model can communicate with all kinds of information, and that the results promise to unify and clarify the economic debate.   □

FOOTNOTES

[1] Senge illustrates the use of time series data for hypothesis testing in system dynamics models. (Peter M. Senge, *The System Dynamics National Model Investment Function: A Comparison to the Neoclassical Investment Function*, Ph.D. thesis, Massachusetts Institute of Technology, Sloan School of Management, 1978.) Senge shows possible errors in econometric estimates arising from errors in time series data. (Peter M. Senge, Statistical Estimation of Feedback Models. *Simulation*, 1977, 28, pp. 177-184.)

[2] Jay W. Forrester and Peter M. Senge, "Testing for Building Confidence in System Dynamics Models," in Augusto A. Legasto, Jr., Jay W. Forrester and James Lyneis, *System Dynamics*, New York: Elsevier, 1981.

[3] E.H. Phelps Brown, "The Underdevelopment of Economics," *Economic Journal*, 1972, 82, pp. 1-10.

[4] Jay W. Forrester, "An Alternative Approach to Economic Policy—Macrobehavior from Microstructure," in Nake Kamrany and Richard Day, *Economic Issues of the Eighties*, Baltimore: Johns Hopkins University Press, 1979, pp. 80-108.

⁵ Jay W. Forrester, Nathaniel J. Mass and Charles J. Ryan, "The System Dynamics National Model: Understanding Socioeconomic Behavior and Policy Alternatives," *Technological Forecasting and Social Change*, 1976,9, pp. 51-68.

Some major issues of concern in the production, dissemination and use of knowledge are reviewed, and a conceptual framework is proposed for further investigation of society's exploitation of research in science and technology. The author is concerned with national/political systems and their decision-making potential for both formulating and attaining goals associated with the promotion of welfare and progress, worldwide.

Chapter 13

SOCIETAL USE OF SCIENTIFIC AND TECHNICAL RESEARCH: EXISTING AND ALTERNATIVE MODELS

Veronica Stolte-Heiskanen

Society's Use of Research and Development: Concepts

Any discussion of the use of scientific and technological knowledge must recognize that the concepts refer to a complex set of multidimensional phenomena. Utilization may vary, in terms of scope, from

The author, who was born in Hungary, studied at Columbia University and the University of Chicago before obtaining the doctorate in social sciences at the University of Helsinki. She is professor of sociology at the University of Tampere. Dr. Stolte-Heiskanen is concerned primarily with the organization of research and the study of science policy. She is a member of the International Sociological Association's Research Committees as well as consultant to Unesco and member of the Finnish National Commission for Unesco. Address: Pitkänsillanranta 17C25, Helsinki 53, Finland; telephone (90) 710081.

Note: This chapter has been adapted from *Societal Utilization of Scientific and Technological Research* (Science Policy Studies and Documents, No. 47), Paris, Unesco, 1981, based on an original manuscript prepared by K.D. Knorr (Austria), V. Stolte-Heiskanen (Finland) and Y. de Hemptinne (Unesco).

the use of problem-solving techniques in a wide variety of so-called applied areas, to the formulation of alternative policy options in R&D involving long-range and sometimes large-scale consequences. Correspondingly, the objectives governing the utilization of scientific and technological research may range from the development of some product or process to the solution of long-range problems confronting mankind. In addition, "societal utilization" may be differentiated also by the *way* scientific knowledge is used.[1] According to some statements appearing in the modern literature, scientific/technological research may be utilized for "legitimizing"—sometimes ex-post facto—decisions taken independently and outside the sphere of science; or it may be "instrumental" in solving a problem; or it may be used for conceptual clarification in an "enlightening" way (particularly in the social sciences).

Awareness of the complexity of the issue of utilization of R&D makes the traditional distinction between pure and applied research less and less useful because it largely rests on the personal motivations of the researchers themselves on the one hand, and on the goals of the organizational environment wherein research takes place, on the other.[2]

A further distinction which encompasses both science and technology categorizes research into *discipline-oriented* R&D and *mission-oriented* R&D. From the point of view of the present study the focus is on "useful science" or, if one prefers, on mission-oriented R&D, whatever motivating force drives the research worker. In other words, *societal utilization of R&D is considered to take place when the research serves in its problem-solving* (or anticipating) *capacity and the results are—or may be—put to use to improve mankind's predicament.*[3] Although the purely symbolic manifestations of utilization are thus by definition excluded from the concerns of the present study, any investigation of the problem of utilization from a societal perspective must necessarily also pay attention to the problems of non-utilization of potential results. Furthermore, the focus on "useful science" is not meant to imply that fundamental, basic, or theoretical research is not considered useful. Indeed, the question of what is the appropriate balance between research oriented towards long- vs. short-term consequences of results, or alternatively between discipline- vs. mission-oriented research, is one of the major science policy issues where options taken will have significant consequences on the societal utilization of R&D.

The focus on the utilization of science and technology in a societally beneficial way has raised a host of new questions about the relationship between science, research results, and their applications in practice. If "societal utilization" is concerned with scientific and technological research carried out in the context of organized societies with the purpose of acquiring and applying knowledge (and know-how) that is necessary in order to satisfy the needs and aspirations of the peoples, at least *three aspects* must be taken into account:

— forecasting and identification of emerging issues and problems in society (societal awareness), as well as in science itself (scientific awareness)—realistic appraisal of social goals and societal needs to which science and technology can be expected to contribute

— the creation or development of relevant knowledge (R&D)—the potential of the science and technology system for generating relevant knowledge

— the practical application of R&D results—application and its consequences

The first concerns the normative-political context and the decision-making structure of society that defines the desirable ends, the range and priority of needs and the spectrum of beneficiaries of expected progress. The production of research results of societal relevance depends on the stage of internal development of a given scientific field, on the extent societal needs are communicated to scientists, and on the scientific ideology that defines what are legitimate goals for R&D. The practical application of relevant research results calls attention to the actual process of utilization, how research results are transformed into practice and the evaluation of the consequences.

In order to conceive this over-all process one must develop an understanding of how the national R&D (sub)system on the one hand, and the corresponding (national) societal system on the other hand, operate. And perhaps more important, to develop an understanding of how the interaction, interdependency and transformations of goals (aspirations and concrete objectives) are mediated and negotiated between the two.

In the following sections some of the existing models of societal utilization of R&D are reviewed. An alternative approach is then suggested, which takes into account the three aspects of societal utilization outlined above.

Existing Models of Social Use of Scientific and Technical Research, and Some Implications

The concept of societal utilization of R&D as outlined above was linked to the three-pronged question of societal application of the scientific approach to emerging national (or global) issues. Depending on what assumptions are made about the relationship between the stages of such a scientific approach and the systems involved (R&D and national) and depending on the degree to which investigation of these stages and systems is included or excluded from the analysis, different conceputal models of the process of societal utilization of R&D have been developed and realized in the past. Particularly a review of the *implementation* and *transformation* models is of relevance to the present study.

The implementation model is based on the assumption that scientific-technological R&D results are produced in the scientific community *independently* of their utilization or of their potential applicability. Results are subsequently "applied" to societal goals and practical problems. The criteria which govern the generation and control of findings are thought to be *internal* to science, i.e., they are thought to be exclusively determined by the knowledge and methodology in a specialty field or discipline. In accordance with an exclusively internal view of R&D, only research scientists are granted the right to evaluate the quality of scientific results. "Autonomy of science" based on the classical laissez-faire model of the Polanyi school is advocated.[4]

Not surprisingly, this conception often goes hand in hand with a rigid adherence to the distinction between basic (scientific) research and applied (technological) research which is equated with the dichotomy between production and implementation of knowledge. Thus, there is a tendency to regard technological research as ruled by mechanisms of result-production which differ in principle from those of scientific research, and to consider the latter as a necessary precondition of the former.[5] With regard to the societal utilization of research results the "implementation" model conceives the problem as one of *adaptation* and adaptability of scientific findings to a practical situation, and identifies the relevant mechanisms as those of *communication* and *application* of results.[6] The model matches the situation of *information in search of a use,* equally described as "knowledge-driven" or as one of "knowledge/technology push."

In contrast to the "knowledge push" implementation models, "demand pull" approaches are based on the assumption that utilization is a process that starts before research efforts are initiated.[7] Consequently, *transformation models* conceive the process of utilization of R&D in terms of *input-output* in which some "external" goals are "internalized" and transformed into scientific descriptions of the issues at hand, which are then examined within the R&D system (production of *relevant* knowledge). The results of the examination are eventually translated back into practical action "external" to the R&D system. In the simplest version of this model, only the relationship between external goals and the production of relevant knowledge is analyzed.

The "utilization cycle" is seen in terms of questions of transformation: "How is a practical problem *translated* into search for pertinent knowledge?" and "How is the unavoidable gap between knowledge and action *bridged* by additional considerations so that recommendations can be produced to help with the solution to the problem at hand?"[8]

In *more elaborate versions of the model,* the process is described as follows: "A need or deficiency is recognized; the extent of the problem is assessed and its causes diagnosed; basic or applied research is conducted or retrieved to find ways of ameliorating the problem; technology is invented or improved—either 'hard' technology in the form of devices, or 'soft' technology in the form of programs and human services; institutions are created or modified to provide the technology or services."[9] The number of steps which surround the linkages between the external world and scientific production of knowledge may be increased in more elaborate versions of this model, and sometimes a self-regulating mechanism is built into it.[10]

The transformation model ties in with a *producer-consumer* conception of the relationship between scientists and their political, economic or social counterparts, a view which matches the frequent situation of *contract research* from which it seems to originate. The emphasis is on the interaction between two systems (the "external," societal, political or economic system of the nation concerned and the "internal" R&D system of science and technology) whose modes of operation and production (decisions in the political system and discoveries or inventions in the case of R&D) are not themselves made part of the analysis. Despite the fact that external influence on R&D is recognized (through societal goals or practical problems calling for an answer on the part of scientific and technological research), the question of *how* external variables materialize in R&D—the very question of "transformation"—is not in itself investigated.[11] This "black-boxism"[12] with regard to the production of knowledge can be compared to the separation that exists between economic production of goods on the one hand and their circulation on the other, which is characteristic of many modern societies.[13] It was reflected not only in research into the question of societal utilization of R&D, but in social studies of science in general up to very recently.[14] Needless to say, this black-boxism will have to be overcome if genuine insights into how societal utilization of R&D has worked—and may work in future—are to be gained.

In summary, the idea of putting existing scientific knowledge to some practical use (implementation model), for which it had (or had not) been specifically developed, without a definite connection with those concerned by the findings, has led to many efforts toward societal utilization of R&D.[15] In contrast, the utilization procedures underlying the transformation model described above can be observed in most cases where research is carried out on a customer/contractor basis; depending on the interests and awareness of producers and customers of R&D results, various degrees of elaboration and sophistication of these procedures are observed.[16]

The predominance of one or the other of these models of application of research results is also related to different historical epochs and conceptions of science policy. Thus the "implementation" model and the attempt to draw a rigid distinction between basic and applied research in terms of the motivation of researchers and of their management, design and execution, or of the practical significance of the results obtained, might be related to the dominance of academic science and the "ivory tower" situation which appears to have characterized much of scientific life up to the Second World War. It corresponds to the liberal conception of non-intervention in scientific production by external policy formulation and stresses the exclusively autonomous development. However, it has been increasingly recognized that the laissez-faire conception of the autonomy of science today is no more tenable than the original economic model to which it was analogous. Moreover, the self-generating activities of science do not bear a structural resemblance to economic laissez-faire.

In contrast, the "transformation" model seems to capture the spirit of increasing use of R&D as a tool for economic, political or social goals as *mediated* by the policy system, i.e., by science and technology policy since the Second World War. The simple version corresponds to big-scale organization of research activities and the growing institutionalization of contract research, which was further carried over into a more general veiw labeled "technocratization of science".[17]

The instrumental use of R&D that had earlier mainly occurred at the level of the industrial enterprise[18] has been extended to the overall R&D system through the "sectoralizing principle" recently pursued by science policies of some West European countries. Sectoralization means a compartmentalization of the national R&D system according to ministerial departments and in accordance with their politically determined social objectives, out of which spring the "sectoral" programs for scientific and technological research. The "societal direction of science" is interpreted to mean that representatives of various organized social interests have *direct* leadership over research programs and dictate the research efforts of scientists. Consequently the necessary distinction between the "inner" and "outer" steering problems of research tends to be eliminated. If sectoralization predominantly affects the rules and standards for accepting or rejecting new knowledge within science, the traditional principle of "autonomy of science" must be seen as seriously undermined and even totally jeopardized.[19]

Nevertheless, despite the internal logic of scientific advances and their undeniable character of unpredictability or serendipity which certainly calls for a certain degree of internal autonomy at the various levels of the R&D system, research policies can be formulated so as to influence appreciably the direction in which scientific efforts are oriented in order to contribute to the solution of the most pressing problem of a nation or of mankind as a whole. It implies the formulation of research policies that take into account the developmental actions oriented by governments towards both long-term and short-term objectives, and the integration of science and technology policy into overall national development policy. In this respect the significant question again becomes the achievement of the proper balance between sectoralization and integration of a nation's research efforts, the contradictory and complementary tendencies in the dialectic of contemporary scientific development.

Alternative Approach to "Societal Use of R&D"

The proposed working framework for further study of "societal utilization of R&D" is based on the assumption that *interaction* between (external) societal needs and wants, and the national R&D system (factors internal to the production of knowledge) should be made the focus of research in its own right. According to this approach, external goals are transmitted into R&D through principles and directives which orient national development, i.e., principles which determine the extrinsic objectives of R&D, the criteria for evaluating the successfulness of R&D efforts, and what counts as a "solution." More concretely, there is a transformation of *societal goals* into R&D policy programs and budgets, and finally into projects on the side of the societal system, which is matched by a similar transformation on the side of the R&D system. Here, relevance criteria deriving from societal goals are concretized in terms of directives for research-orientation (R&D objectives) and for the allocation of R&D resources; and finally into guidance for overall scientific/technological development.

The practical application of the results of R&D is a function of the nature of the scientific-technological inputs, and of the structure and application mechanisms of the interested societal sectors. If the relevant results are applied in practice with beneficial consequences one can say that societal utilization of R&D has indeed occurred.

Within this framework, the study of societal utilization focuses on the interaction and interrelationship of the R&D system with concerned societal structures on the three levels of the overall process outlined *in fine* of the introduction: the identification of emerging issues and problems, the creation and development of knowledge, and the practical application of the results. Within each level, the major concern is with the internal and external constraints which affect the process.

The overall conceptual scheme of the utilization process is outlined below. The different components are then discussed in greater detail.

Identification of Emerging Issues or Problems: The Transformation of Societal Goals into Science and Technology Policy Decisions

Worldwide recognition of the societal role of R&D has brought a new emphasis on evaluating the claims of research for resource-allocation by governments and on the question of how to efficiently direct R&D and the application of existing scientific and technological knowledge to desired ends. The notion of "desired ends" already implicitly contains the assumption that societal goals and ways of utilizing scientific and technological research are *as such* important in their social and human consequences, and that these "desired ends" cannot be inferred from science/technology itself. It therefore follows that any *in vivo* evaluation of the societal utilization of R&D is ultimately and essentially normative.

Although the notion of "societal goals" is central to any analysis of societal utilization of R&D, a precise definition of such goals is difficult to agree upon at national, regional and global levels. At the highest echelon of planning the societal goals are derived from *ultimate ends*. For example, at the global level, survival and justice may constitute ultimate ends; these are at the same time basic human values. "Knowledge" is an ultimate end which the scientific community strives to attain and a human value in itself.

In order to promote progress toward the achievement of ultimate ends, these must be given the form of transient ends, i.e., *goals*, through which the universe of tangible and verifiable benefits can be defined. Increasing national productivity, improving the physical welfare of the members of a given society, "The New International Economic Order,"

Figure 1.   Identification of emerging issues or problems.

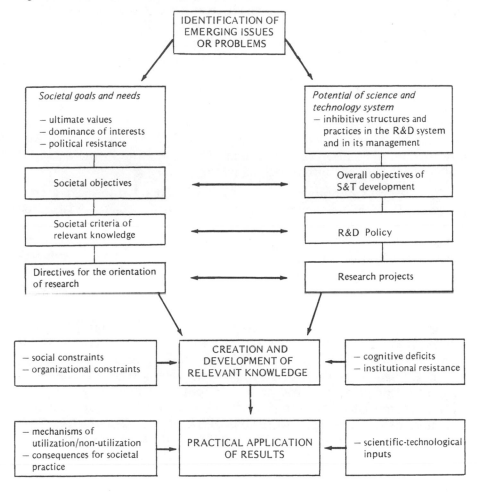

are examples of such goals, which may subsume a varied group of objectives and activities.

Such goals are established usually as a result of a complex set of social and political processes which involve dynamic interaction between interest groups and actors that may—or may not—include also direct scientific interests. For example, Van den Daele, et al. have extensively shown the varying degrees of influence exerted by societal and scientific authorities involved in the "transformation of political into scientific goals." Some of the most striking illustrations of the process of goal determination can be seen e.g., from studies of the Manhattan project, the Apollo Mission, or the US Cancer Program.

The precise content, processes and mechanisms in the identification, definition and redefinition of societal goals is a complex process that is a function of prevailing social relations. First of all, within the context of the ultimate ends of a society many alternative societal goals may be formulated. However, at any given time only a limited portion is recognized as an urgent problem, and only a part of these are defined as societal goals in terms of problem oriented activities. The outcome of this selection process (i.e., what are urgent problems, what problems demand societal action) is determined by the existing economic and political relations, which in turn are a function of the structures of power, dominant interests and extent of participation in the decision-making process by different societal groups.

Science and technology are not necessarily expected to make a contribution to the attainment of all the defined societal goals. For example, the reduction of social inequality may require primarily a political solution. Which societal goals of a given country should call for the contribution of science and technology in order to solve the underlying practical problems, depends on the potential of the national R&D system on the one hand, and on the sources of perception of problems and dominant societal interests, on the other.

New goals may arise for a variety of reasons. The perception and normative definition of a societal problem that requires scientific "solutions" may come from a variety of sources within any given society. An awareness or formulation of a problem may come from the sphere of the institutionalized political or governmental structure (e.g., administration), some part of the organized public realm (e.g., trade unions), the more diffuse and less institutionalized sector of society (e.g., "the public"), or even from the sphere of R&D itself. From a more international perspective, societal goals of science and technology may arise from a shift in the structural interdependency among countries or regions of the world, or from an international awareness of issues of global concern to humanity (e.g., the environmental crisis, earthquake prediction, drought or famine forecasting, etc.).

One fundamental aspect of the understanding of the processes of societal utilization of scientific and technological research thus involves the identification of the relevant societal goals as they find expression in the formal statements concerning science and technology policies. While the underlying ideology may not be explicitly stated as such, it is reflected in the viewpoints and arguments on how science and technology interact with society, how the current state of that interaction is defined, what national importance is given to the development of R&D,

what the relative importance is of various branches of science or technology for the achievement of national/societal goals, and what should be done to foster various kinds of research activity.

Once formulated, societal goals are then mediated through different scientific, socio-economic and political considerations that may be expressed at varying levels of generality. The transformation of societal goals into research goals such as takes place in the planning, programing and budgeting for science and technology may be determined by a variety of societal factors. Dominant and possibly conflicting interests and value orientations may act as structural constraints that selectively determine which societal goals can be transformed into research goals. In the presence of conflicting interests, the transformation of societal problems into research goals may reflect only an artificial solution to reduce or avoid societal or political conflict without real expectations for potential solutions of problems. As such, not only the pronounced "official" goals, but the mechanisms, structural context and dynamics of the transformation of societal goals into actual research plans, budgets, programs and projects need to be extensively analyzed.

In short, at the societal initiation end of the "utilization cycle," the processes of the establishment of goals, their content, and their mediation into research programs need to be understood in *real-life societal contexts* in order to isolate the factors that determine the success or failure of societal needs and objectives to find expression in scientific or technological research.

The Potential of the National R&D System to Generate Societally Relevant Knowledge: The Context of a Field or Discipline

Understanding the process of societal utilization of R&D and the difficulties it is fraught with requires not only an understanding of *how* relevant knowledge is *produced* in the laboratory, it also requires a workable conceptualization on a more general level of *how* the national R&D system *operates.* In order to capture phenomena like the resistance and evasiveness of scientists with respect to treating certain questions, the proliferation of research projects in some rather than other research areas, etc., it is necessary to understand how research operates in the context of a scientific (or technological) field or discipline. In accordance with some recent theories a field or discipline is defined as the locus of an "agonistic[20] struggle for the monopoly of scientific credit;[21] this credit is a symbolic capital which is at the *same time* scientific (technical, cognitive) competence *and* social authority.

It is very important to see that the currently predominant additive (or at best interactive) model which conceives of social factors as acting on top of, or in addition to, cognitive factors is rejected here in favor of a conception which holds the so-called cognitive and social factors to be facets of the *same* phenomenon with the R&D (sub)system, which emerge when looked at from a certain angle or in the light of a specific perspective. Thus the use of a highly expensive laser-electron microscope is a technical solution to the cognitive problem of determining the molecular structure of proteins, but it is *at the same time* the social element of a career-promoting move of the scientist concerned, since the use of (and competence in dealing with) this scarce and expensive equipment eases access to publication of results and to certain career positions. In the above context, it should be stressed that what counts as a successful research finding that can be published is determined by the field and by the individual scientist's position in the field. As a social sphere, the field is constituted by the research scientists, groups and organizations working in an area. As a regulating force which structures and orients the perceptions and decisons of scientific researchers, the field operates through its "scriptures," a body of writings considered to be authoritative. The writings are structured by indicators having different values, such as the names of authors, journals or publishing companies, citation indexes, and the date of appearance or of circulation. In academic research these writings—together with what cognizant research scientists say about their current undertakings—constitute traditionally the agonistic *context* in which research decisions are embedded. In the case of a technological R&D group in industry, this context will have to be respecified so as to include conditions set by the enterprise and by the agonistic market conditions which presumably are only incompletely mapped into the technological literature of the area.

Thus, cognitive approaches and attitudes within scientific research must be seen *at the same time* as social strategies within the competitive struggle of the scientists and institutions active in a certain field or discipline. In addition, evidence emerging from observational studies of certain scientific laboratories suggest that there is no core of internal "scientific" decisions about R&D which could *in principle* be exempted from societal (or external) consideration. It also seems that selections made "a priori" between alternative approaches do not unequivocally determine procedures which follow later on in the research process.

With regard to the above conception this means that one cannot expect to identify a hierarchy of decision criteria which can be partitioned exclusively according to the cognitive-societal and internal-external dichotomies and which would definitely specify the process underlying the societal utilization of research. Rather, one might have to associate different kinds of scientific products (such as a gas law or a method of protein separation) with various modes of carrying out research in different *contexts* (defined as cognitive and social) and, at the same time, also with *societal goals* which cannot be reduced to a simple set of parameters whatever their range and generality.

The Creation or Development of Relevant Knowledge

Cognitive Deficiencies and Institutional Resistances

One of the problems which have long been haunting science and technology policy-makers is the phenomenon of institutional resistance vis-a-vis attempts at orienting R&D towards the forecasting, identification and solution of practical problems or societal goals, and the question of how to select, promote and assess the cognitive potential of national R&D in science and technology that could adequately deal with these questions. It seems reasonable to assume that the phenomenon of evasiveness of scientists who may feel inclined to use contract research money in order to pursue their own rather than the financing agency's interests, can be linked to the scientific or technological field and to its associated career-promoting mechanisms. What is less clear is how phenomena of institutionalization and de-institutionalization, but also of increasing differentiation and segmentation into sub-specialties, affect the mechanisms underlying the development of a given field or a discipline. Furthermore it is open to speculation whether or not these phenomena lead to different degrees of possible societal utilization of R&D at different points in time. Finally, it is not clear whether the "state of knowledge" of a field, i.e., the amount and the quality of facts and techniques, must be associated with a differentiated feasibility and ease of application of science and technology for practical and societal purposes.

In a recent attempt to conceive some of these factors in the light of societal utilization of R&D, a model has been proposed which came to be known as the theory of finalization. For the present purpose, the theory serves as an example for a further kind of analysis which will be called for in connection with the scientific/technological field or discipline and with respect to the question of societal utilization of R&D: an analysis of *how* different stages of cognitive development (as they appear from different forms and degrees of institutionalization) affect the applicability of the scientific approach to societal problem-solving.

The theory of finalization postulates a three-stage model of the development of a scientific discipline: a "pre-paradigmatic" stage of trial and error in which there is no commonly agreed-upon theory or paradigm which could consolidate the various efforts; a stage or "paradigmatization" or theoretical development; and a stage of "finalization" in which theoretical development reaches completion and is no longer pushed further. During the pre-paradigmatic stage societal needs can—but must not—be taken into account or met by a discipline. During the stage of paradigmatization science has and needs autonomy to settle its internal theoretical problems; it should not receive extrinsic orientation and guidance. During the stage of "finalization" the situation of the discipline does not any longer yield criteria of problem selection and specification from the intrinsic scientific point of view, which means that societal and practical issues can (and should) take over the role of pushing the development further. In sum, societal application of the scientific approach is predominantly possible at the third stage (finalization) of a discipline's development; the link between science or technology and society will be particularly strong and justified (because it enhances a further development in an otherwise "complete" area) in the last stage, a stage which many disciplines are thought to have entered into by now.

The theory of "finalization" has been a focus of discussions with inconclusive results during the last couple of years, and was recently criticized for legitimizing the ever increasing instrumentalization of science independently of whether it is beneficial for man or not. The discussion raised once again the question of the social responsibility of research scientists both for the kind of results they generate and with respect to the way these results are societally utilized. In light of the "finalization" theory, this responsibility would be linked to the stage of development of a field. In a more comprehensive study of societal utilization of R&D, the issue will have to be analyzed in the light of the power attributed to individual human values of scientific researchers (which is often overestimated when scientists are urged to show more societal responsibility) in face of the internal dynamics of a field, and with a view to a possible change of such dynamics, which would call upon a higher degree of societal responsibility on the part of the researcher.

Apart from the above considerations and from more theoretical objections to the somewhat simple evolutionary model of the "finalization" theory, it is clear that the claims it makes cannot be empirically (or experimentally) validated as long as no criteria for when a scientific discipline is complete—or when it is preparadigmatic—are offered. The question of whether the state of knowledge in a given area or discipline is relevant for the degree of societal knowledge (or R&D) utilization as put forward by the "finalization" theory, will have to be addressed in any further study of the process of societal application of the scientific (R&D) approach.

Societal utilization of R&D is thus understood as the production of research results in a context which is at least partly determined by the conditions governing prevailing scientific practices. Since science proceeds by international change, it may be useful to conceive of this context as constantly fostering *differences* to occur between what is the case and what appears to be possible. A new scientific fact that has practical relevance can be equated to materializing some such possibilities. The difference produced by the emergence of a new scientific fact in the prevailing contextual situation determines the value of the finding and measures the change of state of the context or field. Differentiation and institutionalization of contexts—in science marked by the emergence of professional associations, of specialized journals, of positions, etc.—must be associated with selective change of state in a scientific/technological field. Some of our present knowledge and institutions with regard to the characteristics of these contexts in academic research have been discussed above, but clearly more insights will have to be gained about them.

Social Constraints and Rewards, and Organizational Factors

The receptivity and resistances on the part of the scientific community toward the creation and development of societally relevant knowledge must also be analyzed from the perspective of social and political constraints prevailing in the particular socio-political system wherein science operates. The significant question is: to what extent do the external interests and perceptions that are steering scientific activity run parallel, reinforce or contradict the internal perceptions and interests of the scientific community.

The structures of power and sources of dominant interests vary from one societal model to another, and the role and position of the scientific community may vary accordingly. Thus in pluralistic societies characterized by openly conflicting opinions and situations, the scientific community may be caught between rival interest of multiple centers of power (e.g., bureaucratic, political, economic), or between the interests of different social groups. Science may be faced with the choice between the interests of the "rulers" and the "ruled," and scientific "neutrality" may act in practice to the advantage of the "rulers," the "ruled" being too weak to utilize the scientific results. On the other hand, to favor the "ruled" may mean engaging in activities considered to be outside the traditionally accepted definition of scientific work. Under these conditions, resistance to mission-oriented research and the re-emphasis of the principle of "autonomy of science" may at first represent a "negative" attitude but, ultimately, it may promote fruitful societal utilization.

On the opposite side of constraints are the rewards. At the level of the individual scientists, the question is: to what extent are scientists motivated through financial support, social prestige or recognition to pursue research of high societal relevance? Perhaps even more important are the reward structures of society that reinforce the internal interests, orientations and capacity of the R&D system so as to promote the performance of research oriented toward extra-scientific goals. At the most general level this raises the question of the social status of science in a particular cultural setting. This implies the need to study questions such as the extent of participation possibilities of the scientific community in the definition and transformation of societal objectives into R&D policy; the degree of autonomy of the R&D system in the management of its internal affairs, and the extent of support given to the long-range prerequisites of national scientific development such as the training of qualified research workers and the building of appropriate scientific institutions.

Science also has a social structure with its particular modes of organization, interactions, and composition. A fundamental aspect of improved understanding of the societal utilization process thus involves the identification of organizational forms and institutional structures conducive to the performance of societally relevant research, but at the same time compatible with other types of research activities. For example, with the institutionalization of project-oriented R&D, the "hybridization" of modern research communities has been noted to occur, as researchers turn half administrators, half researchers, or the reverse. This type of organization often comes into conflict with discipline-oriented research. The appropriate balance between the organizational needs of mission-oriented and discipline-oriented research is thus one of the factors of relevance to the understanding of the utilization process.

Societally Beneficial Utilization of R&D Results

A critical scrutiny of the criteria used in decisions regarding scientific-technological solutions to societal problems, implies going beyond analyses of the "external" orientation of scientific research, integration of societal goals in the research process and attainment of societally relevant scientific results. The analyses must include issues concerning the practical application (utilization) of the research results in a *societally beneficial way*.[22]

Prevalent interpretation of the use or non-use of scientific knowledge fall into three types. According to "knowledge specific theories" the main reasons of non-utilization are inherent in the nature of scientific results or in the inclinations of the scientists themselves. "Two-community" theories are based on an argument similar to C.P. Snow's *Two Cultures* to explain the communication gap between scientists and practitioners. Finally, "policy-maker constraint theories" stress that "non-utilization of results mainly occurs because of the constraints under which policy-makers operate." Within the present framework it is maintained that these different interpretations are not alternative explanations, but point to problems that may be simultaneously present to varying degrees and as such need to be investigated in further research on the utilization process.

It has often been pointed out that the formal links between societal decision-making structures and scientific research present a variety of unresolved problems in organization and communication. So far, satisfactory methods of feeding societal needs and wants into the R&D decision-making processes have been far from sufficiently elaborated and political leaders or decision-makers "continue to feel that their concerns are insufficiently recognized by scientists." (The opposite is also true.) Although it is frequently said that they live in separate worlds, there is some evidence from empirical research that the perceptions and concerns of scientists and practitioners correspond rather closely to each other. Both feel however, that effective communication between them constitutes a major problem, although practitioners tend to see the source of the problem more in the attitudes of scientists, while researchers point to the lack of institutionalized communication patterns.

At the very least, societally beneficial utilization of research results implies that the responsible decision-making structures are *aware* of existing and relevant research results. Thus the relations, mechanisms and existing structures for transmission (and often translation) of research results from the knowledge producers to the users of scientific knowledge, also constitutes an aspect of the problem of societal utilization of R&D that calls for further systematic study. In this respect a reconceptualization by scientists of scientific-technological inputs that go beyond traditional research "products" (e.g., books, articles, prototypes, etc.) also seems to be necessary. The role of less conventional inputs, such as the political role of scientists, their informal interaction with practitioners, their formal participation in decision-making structures and other types of active involvement in the utilization of the research results will need to be analyzed in greater detail. In this context considerably greater attention must be paid to the potentials and implications of various types of "activist" feedback alternatives and to the possibilities of creating or strengthening such channels.

Organizational constraints and communication barriers are some of the manifestations of the problems posed by societal utilization of R&D. However, a critical approach can no longer take the formal pronouncements of policy-making structures at face value, no more than one can take the "value-free" theory of science for granted. One must go beyond the overt objectives of the societal decision-making structures to the *potential or latent intentions of initiating "societally relevant" research programs.* For example, when the political structure defines a certain "legitimate" societal goal, and accordingly supports corresponding research programs, it often appears that research is in fact being supported under such goals in pursuance of other covert purposes. Research programs may be initiated not for the expected utilization of the actual results but for the side effects such programs may have, e.g., for economic development, increase in the qualification of manpower, or to promote certain political goals or economic policies. Alternatively, the underlying purpose may be "legitimation," i.e., when science is called upon to give greater credibility and power of conviction to political decisions. Furthermore, research programs may be supported to demonstrate that "something is being done about the problem." All these examples are illustrations of "utilization" of R&D that cannot be overlooked in further analyses of actual (or potential) "societal utilization" of R&D as are being proposed in this study.

Scientific or technological results—new knowledge—may however turn against "legitimation" or be contrary to the interests of existing power structures. If such new knowledge is made available to the public (or to conflicting interest groups) it may have a "delegitimizing" effect on the existing decision-making structure and thereby call into question existing social relations. In the international context one hardly needs to search for examples of selective use or availability of "knowledge" in order to maintain the status quo (for example, the alleged destruction of the "ozone-layer" by the supersonic plane Concorde or the carcinogenic effect of saccharine). All this implies that the same structural constraints that were discussed in connection with the identification of emerging issues and problems in any society must be also taken into account in the analysis of the practical application phase of the utilization cycle.

This brings us to the final and most problematic question of societal utilization of scientific and technological research: *for whom is societally relevant research useful?* Obviously the term "society" in the foregoing discussion of societal goals and societal utilization implies a broad concept of "mankind," "people" or "populations," both in the national or international contexts. The extent to which clear choices can be made by the policy-making structures, both nationally and internationally, about societal goals in support of which scientific research should be utilized, is linked to the utimate question of what are the social or international relations that provide an adequate basis for the beneficial utilization of the achievements of science and technology. This question obviously lies beyond the scope of the present study. The problem can, however, be restated by attempting to define the domains where the societal consequences of research may be the broadest and most significant for the material and spiritual welfare of peoples, and where decisive contributions can be made to the survival and development of mankind.

Global Problems of Societal Relevance; Corresponding Research Areas

Obviously it is not possible, and—as will be argued below—hardly desirable, to reach an agreement on all specific problem areas where societal utilization of R&D needs attention. As a starting point, one can nevertheless point to some global problems—often formulated in different ways depending on the concrete historical context of a given society—that are undoubtedly of universal concern at the present time. From a societal point of view these global problems can be defined in terms of *homeostasis i.e., the ways in which human beings and societies can regulate and stabilize their living conditions (physical, physiological, psychological, social, etc.) so as to make their existence both possible and acceptable.* Even though the most common and obvious criteria for homeostasis is that of biological necessity, the conditions involved are not only—nor simply—biological. Moreover, although the origin of the homeostasis concept is linked with biological processes, it can usefully be considered as a distinctive function in society. Social homeostasis aptly describes "course of life" needs—i.e., needs for living in a certain manner.

Although there are different views concerning the criteria that should be used in defining the conditions and parameters of societal homeostasis, the underlying principle in general is that they are connected with the more general notion of *welfare*. It is primarily in connection with concern about welfare and "level of living" that various organs of the United Nations (especially UNRISD)[23] have evolved a theory based on the idea that men have rather unchanging and similar homeostasis patterns. The emphasis in this approach is on international comparability while at the same time it recognizes that comparability does not necessarily require complete equality of the homeostatic conditions, but only that those conditions should vary between nations in a known fashion.

In the work of UNRISD the level-of-living concepts were explicitly elaborated with reference to the level of satisfaction of needs and wants and of the corresponding component areas thereof:

a) *Physical areas,* which include food, housing, health.

b) *Cultural areas,* which include education, leisure, recreation and security.

Although the delineation of these areas has undergone a number of modifications, the central basic components that have remained during the various phases of inquiry were nutrition, housing, health, and education. Today it is generally agreed that concerted efforts to create homeostatic conditions in these areas is both a national and international obligation of all societies. Conversely, it can also be said that the satisfaction of (or the elimination of existing threats to) these principal components of societal homeostasis constitutes a major "global problem" for mankind.

From the point of view of societal utilization of science and technology it thus seems that the most urgent issues of effective utilization concern those research areas and disciplines that can most immediately contribute to the solution of global problems directly related to societal homeostasis. These have often been expressed in terms of the following four "challenges":

1. The population challenge—implying the need for medical and pharmaceutical research for raising health standards, the need for agricultural and related research oriented towards problems of nutrition.

2. The energy challenge—implying the need for research into post-fission nuclear resources and non-conventional renewable sources of energy.

3. The environment challenge—implying the need to develop economical methods of environmental protection.

4. The nuclear challenge—implying the need for research on reactor safety, nuclear waste disposal, and on the geography and economy of the exploitation of nuclear resources.

In many of the research domains pertaining to these four challenges, efforts should be made to redirect current trends of research away from areas where utilization might seriously threaten the homeostasis—or even survival—of mankind as a whole.

The devastating possibilities of nuclear weapons are known to everyone. Mathematical engineering has developed vast computers whose information storage and retrieval capacity has a wide range of significant applications, but at the same time contains the potential of endangering the privacy of individuals. While the potential societal contributions of biology, biochemistry, etc. hardly need to be emphasized, the hazards of biological engineering have been drawn to the attention of the public by the self-imposed moratorium of research scientists which discontinued for a while certain types of genetic experiments. The overriding importance of medical research, too, often pushes to the background the important ethical issues involved in many research areas, such as, e.g., those related to transplantations, embryology, and therapeutic techniques.

In view of what has been said above, it thus seems that one approach, both theoretically and practically justifiable, to the further study of societal utilization of science and technology, would be to focus on areas crucial to societal homeostasis. Obviously the magnitude of the societal problems and the urgency of the "challenges" vary from one country to the other, and there are undoubtedly also corresponding differences in the research efforts devoted to the various areas. Nutrition and health are currently more universal problems, and of greater concern particularly to the nations of the Third World, than the nuclear challenge (from a non-military perspective) or the waste disposal and environmental control challenges, the latter being for the moment of more immediate concern to the highly industrialized nations. Nevertheless, all of these problems relate to all segments of the population in all countries. And ultimately the efforts devoted to their solution as well as the outcome of such efforts certainly have implications for the entire international community. □

FOOTNOTES

[1] The term "societal" here refers to the larger context of a society, including its needs and problems as well as its national decision-making structures (political, legislative, administrative and consultative) and the related corrective feedback processes. The term "societal utilization of R&D" consequently refers to the scientific and technological research carried out in the context of organized societies with the purpose of acquiring and applying the knowledge and know-how that is necessary in order to satisfy the needs and aspirations of peoples. The term "social" is used in this document mainly to refer to the social mechanisms on the basis of which national R&D subsystems operate, in contrast to the cognitive mechanisms and models underlying their functioning.

[2] R. Richta, "The Scientific and Technological Revolution and the Prospects of Social Development," in R. Dahrendorf, et al., Scientific-Technological Revolution: Social Aspects, London: Sage Publications, Ltd., 1977.

[3] This has also been called "the product value of science;" cf. P. Weingart, "Science Policy and the Development of Science," in S. Blume (ed.), Perspectives in the Sociology of Science, Chichester: John Wiley & Sons, 1977.

[4] M. Polanyi, The Republic of Science: Its Political and Economic Theory, Chicago: University of Chicago Press, 1962.

[5] See G. Radnitzky, "Prinzipielle Problemstellungen der Forschungspolitik," in Zeitschrift für allgemeine Wissenschaftstheorie, No. 7, 1976, p. 403; he claims that all important technological innovations originated from previous developments in basic science—a thesis which, in the light of recent historical studies, must be regarded as at least controversial. See also R. Strichweh, Ausdifferenzierung der Wissenschaft—Eine Analyse am deutschen Beispiel (Report Wissenschaftsforschung 8), Bielefeld: University of Bielefeld, Forschungsschwerpunkt Wissenschaftsforschung, 1977. Radnitzky also asks that in applied research at least a minimum of "scientific" quality be required, implying that the criteria and procedures of the applied sciences do not regularly meet the standards of a "science."

[6] See, for example, R. Havelock and F. Mann, Research and Development Laboratory Management—Knowledge Utilization Study, Ann Arbor: CRUSK, 1968, and R. Havelock, Planning for Innovation through Dissemination and Utilization of Knowledge, Ann Arbor: CRUSK, 1973.

[7] Evidence comes from the way effective research "utilization" was achieved during the Second World War when there was convergence of political, military, industrial and scientific efforts. Quantitative evidence is available from studies of successful and unsuccessful innovations on the economic market (see, for example, Marquis, D. "The Anatomy of Successful Innovations," Innovation, No. 7, 1969) and from studies tracing the interaction between science and policy; these have shown that influence on the conception of a research effort before the execution of the research work itself is a good predictor of the degree of use of results (cf. K. Knorr, et al., Erkenntnis und Verwertungsbedingungen sozialwissenschaftlicher Forschung in Oesterreich, Vienna: Forschungsbericht des Instituts für Höhere Studien, 1978.

[8] Cf. P. Lazarsfeld, J. Reitz, A. Pasanella, Introduction to Applied Sociology, New York: Elsevier Press, 1975.

[9] Cf. D. Pelz, Utilization of Knowledge on Management of R&D Units, Ann Arbor: CRUSK, 1977.

[10] The scheme is adapted from Lazarsfeld, et al., q.v. For more elaborate schemes of the process, see Havelock, op. cit.

[11] This has to do with the fact that the up-to-recently dominant functionalist approach to science of science studies defined its topic as: the social system of science and its functional mechanisms of internal organization and control. This approach considers cognitive processes in research and external factors as more or less irrelevant. It was only after Thomas Kuhn's theory on the structure of scientific revolutions (1962, 1970) had been absorbed, mostly via European

studies on the "science of science," that a redefinition of the field occurred; this considered cognitive and external variables as being of vital interest.

[12] See R. Whitley, "Black Boxism and the Sociology of Science: A Discussion of Major Developments in the Field," in P. Halmos (ed.), *The Sociology of Science* (Monograph 18), University of Keele, 1972.

[13] N. Luhman, "Theoretische und praktische Probleme der anwendungsbezogene Sozialwissenschaften: Zur Einführung," in Wissenschaftszentrum Berlin (ed.), *Interaktion von Wissenschaft und Politik*, Frankfurt-am-Main and New York: Atheneum Fischer Verlag, 1977.

[14] In programmatic form, the criticism of black-boxism appears first in the literature of the early 1970s, e.g., in R. Whitley, *op. cit.*, and P. Weingart (ed.), *Wissenschaftssoziologie 1, Wissenschaftliche Entwicklung als sozialer Prozess*, Frankfurt-am-Main: Atheneum Fischer Taschenbuch Verlag, 1972.

[15] The study published by Havelock and Mann (*op. cit.*) investigates this mode of utilization.

[16] Such a model (the political utilization of social science) is reflected in N. Caplan, *et al.*, *The Use of Social Science Knowledge in Policy Decisions at the National Level*, Ann Arbor: Institute for Social Research, 1975. For a general discussion of the growing use of contract research in daily practice, see G. Radnitzky and G. Andersson, "Wissenschaftspolitik und Organizationsformen der Forschung," in A. Weinberg (ed.), *Probleme der Grossforschung*, Frankfurt-am-Main: Atheneum Fischer Verlag, 1970.

[17] M. Blissett, *Politics in Science*, Boston: Little, Brown, 1972.

[18] For an overview of this development and a tentative assessment of the future situation, see Salomon, J.-J. "Science Policy Studies and the Development of Science Policy," in I. Spiegel-Rösing and D. Solla Price (eds.), *Science, Technology and Society*, London and Beverly Hills: Sage Publications, 1976.

[19] See A. Elzinga, "Science Studies in Sweden," *Social Studies of Science*, Vol. 10, 1980, and G. Radnitzsky (*op. cit.*).

[20] The term agonistic is used here in the Greek sense to describe a context of *generalized* competitive rather than direct individual conflict. For example, in order to compete successfully in their field, scientists are at the same time antagonists and accomplices, arguing against each other's products though drawing on these products.

[21] The notion of *scientific credit* is not to be confused with the "recognition" or "reputation" in studies of scientific communities. Credit is a commodity which can be exchanged for different kinds of resources (project money, assistant scientists, etc.). Furthermore, credit is linked to the promise of future or ongoing research work, on the basis of which resources and opportunities are allocated rather than exclusively to past achievements.

[22] Purposeful non-utilization should also be considered; in this connection one must recognize the beneficial effects of intentional non-utilization of research results that are potentially harmful for the welfare of mankind.

[23] United Nations Research Institute for Social Development.

A sociologist of science examines the possible advantages and short-comings to a nation's scientific community in terms of its access to study and training abroad. He takes as model the case of Hungary in the postwar years, from the 1950s to the 1980s. His findings help to under-score the supranational character of the scientific enterprise today.

Chapter 14

SIMULATING A SMALL NATION'S INTERNATIONAL SCIENTIFIC CONTACTS: AN EVALUATIVE ANALYSIS

Pál Tamás

By Way of Introduction

The observation that science is national, and even supranational, has in a certain sense been the cornerstone of the pertinent literature over the past 400 years. It has also been obvious that progress in scientific research has been determined by the immediate social medium of scientists. Indeed, the various science and technology policies of governments treat research as a kind of national resource.

The approach used in social studies of science has recognized this contradiction as a consequence of the immanent, dual structure of

---

Dr. Pál Tamás is a social scientist concerned with the human dynamics and cultural trade-offs of scientific research in the international realm. He wrote this chapter expressly for inclusion in *Models of Reality: Shaping Thought and Action*. His address is Institute of Sociology, Magyar Tudomanyos Akademia, Uri Utca 49, 1014 Budapest, Hungary.

science, whereby the production of knowledge is a national social phenomenon but the product itself is international in character. Yet two other, important elements are rarely mentioned in such studies.

The first of these deals with the hypothesis that the relations between "center" and "periphery" appear in the process of producing scientific knowledge. (I have borrowed these terms from political science.) The center can be construed as the core of the world's science in a given age (for instance, Italy in the 17th century), within a given discipline (theoretical physics, for example, at the time of the Weimar Republic), or at the focus of the organization of national scientific endeavor (such as the Academies of Science in Eastern European countries) within the overall scientific network.

The locus of the center is not determined once and for all; it changes, partly under the impact of political and economic processes, and partly under the influence of the turning points in the history of science. Thus the scientific center will not necessarily coincide with the current cores of the world economy. And for the sake of simplicity, we call here "peripheries" all those entities having a complicated hierarchical relationship among themselves but remaining, at a given moment, outside the center.

The relations between center and periphery can be interpreted in two ways. The first, discriminatory, views the periphery *a priori* as inferior, less interesting and secondary to the center. Yet this perspective does not exclude the possibility that, in societies whose science is secondary (from the point of view of international science), the knowledge produced at the periphery becomes a prime factor in the satisfaction of local economic or other social needs.

The second interpretation (my preference) does not refute the first; rather, it complements the first view by averring that being on the periphery may have its advantages. The efforts to overcome a (false?) inferiority complex may lead to genuine quality in research. Those situated on the periphery have not much to lose, so perhaps they can risk more; they have a relatively greater chance of reaching original solutions. The leading centers exert little pressure, and their momentarily valid paradigms have little force on the periphery. These are both factors which can help the periphery to accomplish more. We are dealing here only with possibilities, however, so that only a small part of the periphery can make use of them. Once the periphery becomes successful, it then becomes part of a new core or center.

At any rate, those who stand on the periphery (whether they make headway or not) attach great value to international relations. The importance of outward contacts is clear to both researchers and decision makers involved with science policy. Science studies concerning international relations seem to follow two distinct lines: (a) where international scientific relations are means of foreign affairs and diplomacy, and (b) where such relations are examined in the broad context of communication, neglecting their political and societal dimensions.

Our purpose here is an experiment seen from two points of view. We wish to increase, first, the number of papers describing the periphery because these are fairly rare in the literature. We are convinced that the patterns of the institutionalization of science are different from those at the core. The difference is especially marked in the evaluation of the role of international scientific contacts. We conceive of these relations, secondly, as resources; and "peripheral" science suffers from the (imagined or real) absence of such resources. Social and especially power relations within science play a major role in the distribution of the limited resources available.

Our approach is an empirical demonstration of our propositions, with the aid of the situation in Hungarian science during the 1970s and 1980s.

Specialization, System and Foreign Contacts

Correlations in the hypothesis described above were tested in a survey involving 1300 scientists.[1] Because of its empirical nature, the survey embraced a broad range of questions concerning research policy and the organization of science. Here, I wish to limit myself to a few problems related to international scientific contacts.

Our starting point was this: In the case of a relatively modestly staffed research base, delimited by national borders and operating on the periphery of the world's economy, international professional relations will have high prestige—regardless of whether the research base produces scientific knowledge of value to the center or of relevance only to the periphery. Hidden from view are the complicated networks of real and presumed needs, State strategies of development, political preferences and economic considerations, and personal ambitions. We have no intention here of untangling this web; we limit ourselves, rather, to stating the possible major reasons or listing the principal determinants. These follow.

As a consequence of the international division of labor in research, the major markets of existing knowledge—the places where knowledge is categorized and qualified—are situated outside the country. This is practically true of all research done in Hungary, with the exceptions of some agricultural research and work related directly to the study of the nation's culture or certain social applications.

As a result of specialization, small research groups are responsible for entire spheres of science. On the domestic scientific market, this leads (in the worst case) to the emergence of professional monopolies or (in a better case) to the creation of oligopolistic relations. In such conditions, the utilization of international relations becomes a particular means for maintaining these monopolies. On the other hand, however, the same network of relations offers itself to groups representing alternative values. For the latter, this opportunity is a kind of lifejacket and, at the same time, a means to reorganize the power relationships within domestic science.

Regardless of its system of scientific institutions, and given the country's size and geographic location, travel abroad (especially as a means of gaining experience, rather than as recreation), Hungary's relations with people abroad have become an integral part of the way of life of the intelligentsia of one country—especially of a small country in the peripheral zone. Yet, at the same time and notwithstanding constraints of a financial nature, the relatively poor command of languages by some persons presents certain intellectual barriers.

Public opinion among scientists attributes a high value to professional relationships abroad because of another factor. Regardless of the social need and individual ambitions already cited, such relations have not been possible during certain periods in modern Hungarian history or among certain institutions (although these organizations needed them). This led to a "communication hunger" which produced, in turn, the typical analogy of "overeating" or at least the intention of doing so in certain periods, posts or organizations (each of which could more or less satisfy these demands).

Because of all these reasons, foreign contacts have become "scarce material," hence the rules of economic shortage have prevailed. This manifests itself particularly in the Hungarian setting because, again, two other factors are involved—apart from the logic and needs of research. The first of these factors is the balance of power and its distribution throughout the world of science. Other Hungarian contributions to the social sciences have shown, incidentally, the particularly strong connection between achievement and power in the motivation of success. The second factor is, naturally, the knowledge of languages. According to the findings in all sociological studies of the Hungarian intelligentsia, a knowledge of languages is closely correlated to the social origins of those investigated. This means that language knowledge acquired in traditional middle-class families is an advantage not easily gained by those stemming from other social strata.

Pecking Order and its Governing Constraints

There follow some characteristics of the specially structured   network of international contacts of which I am speaking, where we limit ourselves to demonstration of single-variable interrelations. First, we surveyed the basic distribution of contacts according to some personal parameters: age, sex, rank, scientific degrees. This was to determine who can accede to what type of international contact and, thus, who is left out for one reason or another. Then we interpreted scientific experience in its broadest sense, according to which international experience should consist of the following: participation in foreign university or post-graduate training, study tours or professional trips of some length, work assignments abroad for longer periods, and regular participation in conferences or shorter meetings.

Table 1 shows an important negative fact: 57 percent of all scientists in the sample and, within these, 50 percent of the researchers at the Hungarian Academy of Sciences (considered the most efficient part of the national research potential) have no significant international experience. The breakdown by institutional system reveals that, even so, the Academy enjoys a much better position (in terms of international relations) than industry or the universities. The Academy's staff has twice as many foreign scientific degrees and has attended 1.6 times as many foreign universities as the sample's average. The same applies to the possibilities for long trips and conference participation: the Academy has most of the advantages.

We attempted to treat relations with socialist and non-socialist States separately. We were not moved by purely political considerations. Owing to variations in the aims of science policy, foreign currency and other considerations, the conditions for cooperation and how this is realized are different in the two cases. Furthermore, different groups of researchers have varying possibilities of access to these two types of relationship.

During the past thirty years, study in foreign universities has meant chiefly attendance at institutions of other socialist countries, especially the U.S.S.R. Apart from special cases (such as the children of diplomats accredited abroad), there has been no possibility to study in other politico-geographic zones. There are no Hungarian state scholarships to such universities, and Hungarian citizens cannot accept, in principle, support for university studies from foreign sources—whether institutional or individual.

The number of Hungarian students in universities and colleges of other SEV (or "Comecon") countries, especially the Soviet Union, has

Table 1. Scientific experience abroad, by type of research institution.

Experience	Academy	University	Industry	Totals
Higher education in socialist country	11.5	9.0	4.2	7.23
Higher education in non-socialist country	0.5	2.3	0.8	0.92
Post-graduate studies (first, second degree) in socialist country	4.1	1.1	1.0	2.00
Long scientific trip to non-socialist country	20.9	16.4	6.9	12.69
Long residence for scientific and other purpose in non-socialist country	3.4	1.1	5.5	4.23
Regular participation in international scientific meetings	33.6	22.6	18.6	23.9
No significant international experience	50.1	55.4	61.6	57.08

been more or less the same for fifteen years.[2] Many of our researchers, especially those aged 30-39 years, obtained their diplomas in another socialist country. Their ratio in this age group is significantly above the sample's average. In all the other age groups, however, their ratio is below the sample's average. Among older scholars, the number of non-Hungarian Eastern European university graduates is obviously small,[3] although the first scholarship-holders must have been 22-24 years old when they returned from the U.S.S.R. in 1953—and this generation is now near the retirement age!

Another thing strikes the eye. While the number of students at foreign universities remained fairly constant, their proportion is much smaller among the younger researchers aged 20-30. The survey data offered no explanation of this phenomenon, but we have some ideas based on the results of complementary interviews. A reason for the change may be the professional reorientation of Hungarian graduates by socialist (i.e., practically, Soviet) university influence. Instead of the predominantly theoretical subjects studied in previous years, Hungarian students in the 1970s pursued their work mostly in the technological disciplines. And perhaps the level of ability of the Hungarian students in foreign institutions may have changed, too. Another reason may be that, in the last ten years, it has become easier to be admitted to engineering and other technological faculties in Hungary. Furthermore, the loss of prestige suffered by Soviet technology among some professional groups made technical studies in that country less attractive.

Social Roots of Professional Scientists

As a consequence of all these factors, our young students who are prepared for higher learning and who in the past opted to go abroad tend now to remain in Hungarian universities; they will be replaced in the foreign schools by other groups of scholarship-holders. But then, our own research institutes will be less keen than before to take on these stay-at-homes. It may be difficult to demonstrate all this with figures, but I believe that—despite the general decisions taken in regard to science policy—the factors mentioned hamper the establishment of sounder relations between Hungarian research and its primary "natural environment," the science of the other Eastern European countries.

In terms of scientific relations with Western Europe and North America, the absence of a group of young Hungarian scientists trained in Western universities is even more conspicuous. During the four-to-five years spent at institutions in this region, the young specialists would have acquired local knowledge and built personal relationships. This disproportion has become all the more conspicuous during the past 10 to 15 years, when the weight of Western countries has greatly increased in Hungary's system of foreign relations—not only in the scientific but also in the economic sphere.

The social origins of scientists, as those of other members of the intelligentsia subsequent to the major restructuration that took place in the 1940s and 1950s, determine their behavior patterns within the world of science (and in everday life, too) to a considerable extent. The differences are also significant in the distribution of the international experiences of scientists (Table 2). Analysis of the data shows that the ratio of students from workers' families is somewhat higher than the sample's average among graduates of universities in the Comecon region, mainly the U.S.S.R. The reason for this varies according to the age group. In the 1950s and 1960s, studying in the Soviet Union was

Table 2. Scientific experience abroad, by social background of respondents.

Experience	a	b	c	d	e	f	g	Totals
Higher education in socialist country	5.32	20.21	5.32	17.02	38.30	2.13	11.70	100.00
Higher education in non-socialist country	0.00	16.67	8.33	8.33	41.67	16.67	8.33	100.00
Graduate studies (first, second degree) in socialist country	3.85	30.77	3.85	15.38	38.46	0.00	7.69	100.00
Long scientific trip to non-socialist country	3.03	18.79	3.03	22.42	38.79	3.64	10.30	100.00
Long residence for scientific and other purposes in non-socialist country	1.82	14.55	1.82	27.27	43.64	1.82	9.09	100.00
Regular participation in international scientific meetings	4.50	18.01	6.75	22.19	38.26	2.25	8.04	100.00
No significant international experience	2.70	18.06	7.68	20.49	38.68	3.37	9.03	100.00
Sample structure	4.08	18.49	6.70	20.57	38.29	3.16	8.71	100.00

Notes: a -- No answer
b -- Blue-collar workers
c -- Farmers
d -- White-collar workers without higher education
e -- Professionals
f -- Private entrepreneurs
g -- Non-employed, retired

meant to be a "political act," in the eyes of both public opinion and State policy. Hence part of the scholarships went directly to students coming from workers' families. In the 1970s and 1980s, State scholarships are enabling many students to study abroad who would not be able, financially, to afford university studies in Hungary.[4] Proof of this lies in the somewhat higher ratio of economically inactive or retired parents (category *g* of the table).

The proportion of scientists with a worker's background is remarkably high among those who have acquired a scientific degree abroad, notably among the "candidates" (equivalent to holders of the Anglo-American Ph.D.). Their ratio is one and one-half of the sample's average, and one of the likely reasons is that the possibility of obtaining a scientific degree abroad is even more limited to the U.S.S.R. than in the case of higher studies in general. The majority of those opting for a scientific degree are one-time students, coming mostly from a working man's background. A second reason is that the candidates' three years of study abroad reduce the standard of the applicants and the quality of life to which they are accustomed; this is not so with undergraduates.[5]

Other empirical experiences, not confirmed by our investigation, lead us to hazard the following statement: After graduation, the independent existence of young researchers depends mainly on the acquisition of an apartment of their own. This is a central, often unsolved problem for Hungary's young generation, and its solution will depend mostly on the help the young can obtain from their parents.

This kind of inequality is advantageous for young people whose parents emerged from the upper middle-class or certain peasant elements. Living conditions for young scientists belonging to this group are much better at about age 30 (when they apply for candidate studies) than those of their colleagues from other social strata.[6] The latter are more willing to accept a deterioration in their living conditions, typifying their stay abroad.

The Significance of Knowing a Foreign Tongue

We found that among newcomers to the intelligentsia their international scientific experiences corresponded to the sample's average; those coming from peasant families did not quite reach the sample's average. And contrary to our expectations, representation of the traditional intellectuals' background differed little from the average with regard to all types of international contacts—yet the percentage is very high (40 percent). The ratio of those with some experience in non-socialist countries is also higher than in the sample's ratio. The difference is relatively small, however, and I think that the result is not attributable to social origin. The probable truth is that second-generation intellectuals tend to concentrate in internationally better known institutions or prestigious research centers. It is therefore easier to be sent on long study tours if one comes from such organizations.

As to the knowledge of foreign languages by scientists, in a small nation such as Hungary (with its own isolated language) this is an essential factor in the relations outside one's immediate environment (*cf.* the data in Table 3). In our investigation, we left it to the researchers to assess their own linguistic ability since we had no way of confirming their declarations. Language knowledge has a value of high prestige at all strata of Hungarian society. Given our everyday experience with language, therefore, the index numbers indicated seem very high—even if we accept No. 3, "developed active knowledge," for the real ability.

One survey of the command of languages led us to conclude that the order of popularity of foreign languages is English, German, Russian and French. This order is significantly different from the order of learning languages in school;[7] I do not mean the high ratio of English and German, but rather the relative eclipse of Russian.[8] As to the various institutional elements of our model, the command of languages is better at the Academy of Sciences than elsewhere in the sample. An active knowledge of English is 2.7 times and of Russian 2.4 times higher than in industrial research establishments. It is quite remarkable that the difference in favor of the Academy as to language matters is much greater than for direct relations abroad. Regular conference participation, for example, is a ratio of 1.8, of longer tours abroad 0.62. (See Table 3.)

International experience in terms of the age of researchers is shown in Table 4. The proportion of Comecon-trained candidates of science is remarkably high among 40-50 year-olds. This age group is linked with the dynamic growth of Soviet science during the first half of the 1960s, and it played a major role in the large-scale modernization of the Hungarian research system completed in 1970-72. The distribution of long professional trips abroad is very unequal, according to age. Under 35 years, the index number is very low indeed, but between 35 and 50 years this number is well above the sample's average. (The rates are 1.7 for age group 35-39, 1.6 for age group 40-44 and 1.55 for the 45-49 group.) As we have said before, Hungarian researchers have had no opportunity in recent decades to obtain Western university diplomas, hence long professional trips are important for getting acquainted with the major scientific centers in the West.

Table 3.   Knowledge of foreign languages by level and respondents' type of research institution (percent).

	Academy			
	Russian	English	French	German
a	16.79	6.47	76.02	47.48
b	22.06	3.84	6.47	11.99
c	31.89	35.25	10.79	16.31
d	29.26	54.44	6.71	24.22
Totals	100.00	100.00	100.00	100.00

	Universities			
	Russian	English	French	German
a	21.47	25.42	84.75	30.51
b	28.25	3.95	3.95	13.56
c	39.55	46.33	6.21	23.16
d	10.73	24.29	5.08	32.77
Totals	100.00	100.00	100.00	100.00

	Industry			
	Russian	English	French	German
a	32.29	31.16	83.00	47.45
b	27.90	8.92	5.52	14.02
c	27.88	39.80	6.37	21.67
d	12.32	20.11	5.10	16.86
Totals	100.00	100.00	100.00	100.00

Notes: a -- No significant knowledge
        b -- Elementary knowledge (school level)
        c -- Developed, passive knowledge
        d -- Developed, active knowledge

Number of persons asked = 1300

Table 4.   Scientific experience abroad, by age of respondents (percent).

Age	a	b	c	d	e	f	g	Total
20-24	6.38	8.33	0.00	0.51	3.64	1.29	9.30	7.00
25-29	21.28	25.00	3.85	7.88	10.91	9.65	29.25	23.15
30-34	30.85	8.33	30.77	19.39	18.18	22.19	24.53	23.00
35-39	17.02	16.67	11.54	24.85	18.18	17.68	13.48	14.62
40-44	10.64	8.33	34.62	20.00	16.36	20.90	9.43	13.69
45-49	8.51	25.00	19.23	16.36	18.18	14.79	8.63	10.54
50	1.06	8.33	0.00	7.88	7.27	7.40	2.43	3.58
More than 50	1.06	0.00	0.00	1.82	7.27	5.14	1.75	2.69
Totals:	100.00	100.00	100.00	100.00	100.00	100.00	100.00	100.00

Number of persons asked = 1300.   No answer: 1.46 percent of respondents.

Notes: a -- Higher education in socialist country
         b -- Higher education in non-socialist country
         c -- Graduate studies (first, second degree) in socialist country
         d -- Long scientific trip to non-socialist country
         e -- Long residence for scientific and other purposes in non-socialist
                 country
         f -- Regular participation in international scientific meetings
         g -- No significant international experience

   We did not ask—and thus we do not know—the ages of scientists at
the time of their long stays abroad.[9] The deprivation of the present
young generation in this respect is not predominantly the consequence
of change in Hungarian science policy; it results from less willingness on
the part of Western partners to receive them. During the postwar
decades, most such tours were financed by Western sources. The growing need for lecturers in the expanding universities of the West during
the 1960s, and then political détente between East and West, created
good conditions for the development of this kind of research relations.
But the economic and political changes since 1977-8 have generally

hindered this form of international scientific exchange (except in a few special fields, such as mathematics and theoretical physics).

So conditions hamper today's young generation of scientists in traveling abroad for professional improvement. The disadvantages are augmented by reductions in the funds available for international exchanges, a worldwide tendency also asserting itself in Hungary. The older generation in charge of the scientific establishment must struggle to maintain its own relationships in the circumstances, so that the chances of the young researchers lower on the rungs of the professional ladder are even smaller.[10]

Women: Doctoral Degrees; Few Long Trips Abroad

The international contacts of women researchers in our model show the same tendencies (Table 5). The dimension of the foreign experience differs according to the sex of the researcher, yet not as much as our prejudices would lead us to expect. Specifically, families might be reluctant to send daughters to study in foreign universities, and the girls themselves might not be able to break away from the family environment. Later, the division of labor within the family shifts the burden of raising children overwhelmingly to the women; this is the case even in intellectual families. Thus the social environment outside the world of science makes the acquisition of experience abroad, *a priori*, difficult for female scientists. The findings in our sample show, however, that this is only moderately true, that the average performance of women in this respect is only a few points below the sample's average.

Still, the index numbers for conference participation and Western study tours are considerably lower for females. These are the points where, throughout the network of international scientific relations, the economic constraints manifest themselves most strongly. Hence, the struggle between various elements in the scientific establishment is the fiercest at these same points. The disadvantage of women in this respect is not, therefore, a consequence of their perceived role; rather, it is the result of women's particular place in the power hierarchy of science.

According to our data (Table 6), the possession or absence of a higher scientific degree is the major dividing line among the basic parameters determining staff in the research establishments.[11] Whereas one-third of those without such higher degrees are involved in some kind of cooperation with foreign countries and two-thirds take part in some non-formal international cooperation, six-sevenths of those holding an academic doctor's degree have such relations. The picture is more balanced in regard to relations with socialist countries—especially

Table 5. Scientific experience abroad, by sexes of respondents.

Experience	Male	Female	Total (percent)
Higher education in socialist country	75.53	22.34	almost 100.00
Higher education in non-socialist country	83.33	16.67	100.00
Graduate studies (first, second degree) in socialist country	61.54	38.46	100.00
Long scientific trip to non-socialist country	84.24	14.55	almost 100.00
Long residence for scientific and other purposes in non-socialist country	76.36	23.64	100.00
Regular participation in international scientific meetings	83.28	15.11	almost 100.00
No significant international experience	69.14	29.90	almost 100.00
Sample structure	71.92	26.69	almost 100.00

Number of persons asked = 1300   No answer: 1.38 percent of respondents.

because of the massive Comecon affiliations of the computer and petroleum experts reflected in the sample. In the case of non-socialist relations, holders of higher scientific degrees have every advantage. The index is 2.6 for candidates of science over persons without degrees, and 5.7 for academic doctors over those without degrees.

Another remarkable fact is that more than twice as many persons holding a candidate's or academic doctor's degree have studied at a

Table 6. Scientific experience abroad, according to academic degree.

Experience	None	Ph.D. (first degree)	Candidate of sciences (second degree)	Doctor of sciences (third degree)	Totals
Higher education in socialist country	6.70	5.19	14.29	14.29	7.23
Higher education in non-socialist country	0.70	2.60	0.90	0.00	0.92
Graduate studies (first, second degree) in socialist country	0.40	1.95	14.75	7.10	2.00
Long scientific trip to non-socialist country	8.85	17.53	36.61	64.29	12.69
Long residence for scientific and other purposes in non-socialist country	3.81	3.90	8.40	7.10	4.23
Regular participation in international scientific meetings	18.62	31.17	59.82	71.43	23.92
No significant international experience	63.17	51.30	21.43	14.30	57.08

Number of persons asked = 1300.

Comecon university outside Hungary (mainly in the U.S.S.R.). There may be two reasons for this: first, the overwhelming majority has acquired the first scientific degree abroad; secondly, the ratio may reflect, to some extent, policies prevailing in an earlier period. During the 1950s and 1960s, many of our graduates of Soviet universities worked in research as a matter of policy.

Long study tours and conference participation taking place in non-socialist countries are linked, as we have seen, to an individual's place and promotion within the scientific hierarchy. The major rates of opportunity therefore are as follows (computed from Table 7):

Table 7. International cooperation, according to academic degree.

Type	None	Ph.D. (first degree)	Candidate of sciences (second degree)	Doctor of sciences (third degree)	Totals
No answer	6.38	8.44	5.36	0.00	7.00
Only socialist contacts	26.03	22.08	38.39	57.14	26.69
Additional, non-socialist, contacts	3.70	6.49	13.4	28.57	5.00
No contacts	63.9	62.99	42.9	14.29	61.31
Totals	100.00	100.00	100.00	100.00	100.00

Number of persons asked = 1300

Activity / Type of applicant	Long study tours (compared to)		Conference participation (compared to)	
Candidate of sciences	2.9	4.1	2.5	3.2
Academic doctor	5.1	7.3	3	3.8

The reader will see that Table 8 groups the foreign travel of researchers during a recent five-year period according to types of research. Long trips are so rare that our data are not, statistically, significant. A work assignment in a foreign country (the most fruitful type of relationship for Hungarian science) may occur at both ends of the scale: in theoretical basic research and in development and design.

Functional Goals of Travel Abroad

One-third of the short-voyages for basic research include occasional visits or exploratory meetings in order to build future contacts.

One-fourth is for deliberations, regardless of eventual future cooperation. There is much less of both of these in applied research; here, regular meetings and planned cooperation carry significant weight.

Tables 9 and 10 show our findings as to the various organizational forms of cooperation. Table 9 demonstrates the connection between previous international experience and current, formalized relationships. There is marked correlation between the Comecon specialization of some groups of researchers, their university studies, scientific degrees, and subsequent forms of Eastern European cooperation. The formalization of relations with the West results partly from the researcher's position, partly from his scientific experience and other relationships. Table 10 portrays the connections between various types of research and the kinds of cooperation.

It is clear that intensity of cooperation diminishes along the "theoretical basic research/application" axis but that its technological structure does not change fundamentally. The overwhelming majority of all relations belongs, then, to four types:

Table 8. Typology of scientific trips, according to purpose.

	Theoretical fundamental research		Strategic fundamental research		Goal-oriented fundamental research		Applied research	
	(1)	(2)	(1)	(2)	(1)	(2)	(1)	(2)
a	38.46	0.0	33.64	2.58	36.17	1.21	34.80	1.37
b	7.14	0.0	12.72	5.54	11.36	3.38	10.05	1.91
c	5.63	4.11	3.88	4.26	3.40	2.41	5.26	3.29
d	5.56	2.74	6.16	2.14	9.20	1.69	8.68	1.64
e	2.90	0.0	3.98	0.43	6.72	0.48	6.00	0.27
f	8.82	0.0	7.11	0.43	8.14	0.24	10.69	0.0
g	4.17	0.0	4.39	0.0	7.02	0.0	8.10	0.0
h	24.62	0.0	22.49	0.85	13.42	0.08	14.37	0.24
i	2.74	0.0	2.98	0.85	1.93	0.48	1.99	0.55
j	4.11	4.11	0.86	1.28	4.63	1.69	3.07	2.46
k	4.11	0.0	2.14	0.0	5.10	0.0	3.32	0.0
l	8.33	1.37	3.93	1.28	5.99	0.96	7.61	1.10

Table 8.   (Cont'd).

	Development		Construction		Totals	
	(1)	(2)	(1)	(2)	(1)	(2)
a	31.78	1.17	27.87	1.46	22.3	0.1
b	7.14	1.88	6.07	2.92	7.2	0.3
c	4.98	2.11	5.15	2.19	3.9	0.2
d	8.85	1.41	6.82	0.73	5.1	0.1
e	6.38	0.23	0.76	0.0	3.1	0.0
f	13.16	0.23	10.85	0.0	6.4	0.2
g	8.89	0.0	4.42	0.0	4.5	0.1
h	16.42	0.0	10.85	0.0	8.8	0.1
i	2.34	1.17	0.0	0.73	2.3	0.2
j	2.15	1.17	3.06	2.19	2.3	0.1
k	7.14	0.23	4.48	0.0	3.0	0.0
l	6.48	1.87	6.62	2.19	4.6	0.1

Notes: (1) -- less than 3 months
          (2) -- more than 3 months

   a -- Irregular visit by other research units for exchange of information
   b -- Further professional/educational visit for existing research cooperation
   c -- Further professional visit outside context of existing research
          cooperation
   d -- Planned exchange of personnel
   e -- Meetings for R & D management
   f -- Special seminars and meetings in context of existing research
          cooperation
   g -- Discussions concerning results of common research
   h -- Meetings outside context of cooperation
   i -- Language courses
   j -- Employed abroad
   k -- Concerning foreign trade
   l -- Miscellaneous

   N.B.   Trips, rather than individual researchers, are counted.

- random exchange of information (27.2 percent)

- exchange of reports, chemicals and equipment, as determined by agreements (16.0 percent)

- planned partial research in international projects (9.3 percent)

- permanent correspondence, regular meetings without formalized relations (7.6 percent).

Table 9. International cooperation, scientific experience according to respondents' experience abroad.

Experience	Only socialist contacts	Additional, non-socialist, contacts	No contacts	No reply	Totals
Higher education in socialist country	37.2	8.5	46.8	7.4	almost 100.00
Higher education in non-socialist country	33.3	0.0	66.7	0.0	100.00
Graduate studies (first, second degree) in socialist country	38.5	19.2	34.6	7.7	100.00
Long Scientific trip to non-socialist country	34.5	14.5	46.1	4.8	almost 100.00
Long residence for scientific and other purposes in non-socialist country	34.5	3.6	54.5	7.3	100.00
Regular participation in international scientific meetings	43.1	10.6	42.4	3.9	almost 100.00
No significant international international experience	21.4	2.7	72.1	3.8	almost 100.00
Total sample	26.7	5.0	61.3	7.0	100.00

Table 10. Typologies of international cooperation, by types of research.

Co-operation typology / Research typology	Theoretical fundamental research	Strategic fundamental research	Goal oriented fundamental research	Applied research	Development	Construction	Totals
a	34.25	35.74	30.92	34.52	29.27	27.74	27.2
b	16.44	16.17	11.35	7.67	6.56	4.38	7.6
c	17.81	17.02	19.08	22.74	21.55	11.68	16.0
d	2.74	3.83	4.11	2.47	3.04	4.38	2.9
e	10.96	12.77	10.63	9.04	10.77	10.22	9.3
f	6.85	6.38	5.80	5.75	6.32	4.38	4.5
g	1.37	2.98	1.69	0.55	1.64	0.73	1.2
h	2.74	4.68	2.66	2.74	1.17	6.57	2.3
i	4.11	3.83	1.93	1.64	3.28	2.19	2.7
j	5.49	6.81	6.76	4.93	8.43	7.30	0.0
k	5.48	4.68	7.97	9.86	8.20	8.76	0.0

Notes: a = Irregular exchange of reports and information
   b = Permanent correspondence and regular meetings (informal)
   c = Contract-based exchange of reports concerning chemicals, equipment, etc.
   d = Common use of research equipment in joint program
   e = Planned national distribution of program elements in international research project
   f = Parallel use of different research techniques
   g = Establishment of common, basic laboratories
   h = Routine work in international research or education centers
   i = Regular or irregular activities related to bilateral or multilateral research
   j = Participation in special, goal-oriented international projects
   k = No significant data.

Some Conclusions

Science is an international and, indeed, a supranational enterprise. Hence questions regarding international cooperation are, ubiquitously, at the center of science policy.

These questions are of special importance in countries where science, or the major segments of current research and the production of knowledge, are relatively peripheral when compared to where the forefront of world science can be found.

Yet special measures in behalf of science policy, in respect to co-operation abroad, may push things in unexpected directions if the internal power structures of research organizations are not taken into account during the planning and regulation of international scientific relations.

Short-term solutions for optimizing international cooperation could lie in careful analysis of the social mechanisms viable in international scientific contacts. Long-term solutions might require institutionalized regulatory mechanisms.

Notwithstanding the remarks above, systematic study of the particularities of the scientific periphery should prove to be a more important task than might have been thought possible before the existence of social studies of science. If we wish to accomplish the task, we need to hurdle certain methodological traps which students of scientific production itself have already overcome successfully.   □

FOOTNOTES

[1] Our survey covered all three organized segments of Hungarian science: the Academy of Sciences which, as in other socialist countries, operates independently, isolated from the establishments of higher education, and is a network concerned chiefly with basic research; industrial research; and the universities. Owing to the particularities of the sample, our data are representative of the first two segments, but not of the third. It is also to be noted that high-technology fields (computers, petroleum, etc.) are over-represented.

[2] At any given time, about 1500 young people are abroad for study; of these, about 1100 attend Soviet universities.

[3] Before the Second World War, deliberate study in other Eastern European universities was rare in Hungary. Studying "abroad" meant studying in the West, with one exception: the German-speaking higher engineering schools of contemporaneous Czechoslovakia.

[4] Scholarships granted to university students in Hungary do not cover subsistence. The majority of students are supported by their parents, while the rest do part-time or casual work. State scholarships granted to those studying abroad, however, satisfy students' needs based on the living standards of the average worker.

[5] Applicants are usually older than their western counterparts, averaging about 30 years of age. In Hungary, these have subsistence, an apartment and, very often, also a family. Candidates in the U.S.S.R. and most other socialist countries are younger and their living conditions more like those of an undergraduate. They are accommodated in colleges and, given what they receive as scholarships, cannot afford to rent a flat in order to live with their families; they must live apart, and in conditions more severe than in the recent past.

[6] Under the impact of different factors, these differences diminish or disappear; later, the differences will be replaced by other inequalities (to be investigated in a future study).

[7] The Hungarian school system prescribes the learning of two foreign languages. The first, Russian, is compulsory in grades 5 through 12 and during the first years of university. The second, optional as to language but obligatory, is a Western language taught in grades 9 through 12 and at university. (It is realized that the self-evaluation of language knowledge used in our survey may give rise to distortions as to real ability.) But the knowledge of English has more prestige among most researchers than the knowledge of Russian. Thus, in reality, the true difference in degree of knowledge of the two languages may be less than indicated; our respondents may thus have credited themselves with more points for English than for Russian.

[8] The need for knowledge of Russian is manifest in two aspects of daily practice in research establishments: in certain domains within the technical literature (but not on the entire thematic front), and in the broad relations with Comecon (in which Hungary's share grows steadily).

[9] Current experience indicates that the average age is 30-34 years.

[10] Science policy, as well as the scientific community, tends to counter this obvious trend—although the general situation is not likely to change.

[11] In Hungarian practice, we distinguish the so-called university doctors (whose degree is received two to four years after the first university degree) from candidates, who average 33-38 years of age and whose degree corresponds to the German *Dozent*, or senior lecturer. An "academic doctor" is the equivalent of professor.

The generation of descriptive and prescriptive models of various aspects of social organization finds widespread currency. These models are of two types: system models relate to a system's internal components and their influence on the behavior of the system as a whole, whereas process models relate to flows through a system. Here are given examples of such systems taken from ecology, communication, demography and education, and their functions and strictures are explained.

Chapter 15

USES AND LIMITATIONS OF MODELS IN POLICY PLANNING AND EVALUATION

Rahat Nabi Khan

Systems and Process Models

The use of models is becoming more and more widespread in the policy sciences. Models are generally of two kinds: systems models and process models. A systems model shows the phenomenon under study as a whole having interconnected parts, whereas a process model shows the flow of a process along a path or set of connected parts.

This chapter was written by Rahat N. Kahn, an Indian graduate of the London School of Economics who holds a post-graduate diploma in European studies from the University of Strasbourg and a doctorate from the University of Paris I. Since 1965, he has served intermittently as consultant to both the Organization for Economic Co-operation and Development and Unesco. He has contributed articles to *Politique Etrangère, France-Asie,* and *impact of science on society.*

In a systems model, all the elements or parts are interrelated, so that a change in one part brings about a change in all the others. Generally, the system is able to accommodate these changes and thus the system as a whole comes to a new equilibrium or balance. If a change in some crucial element is of such a magnitude or nature that the other parts cannot adjust through appropriate changes, then the system is unable to establish a new equilibrium and we would say the system suffers a breakdown. At what point this breakdown occurs is a question of degree of blockage or maladjustment to change and the importance of the elements or parts affected by changes.

A system has a definite structure. The various parts are related to each other in some specific manner and their role in the functioning of

Figure 1. Simplified systems model of a hypothetical research project on land transformation and population migration in a largely undisturbed tropical forest region. (After F. di Castri and M. Hadley, MAB in the Humid Tropics, *impact of science on society*, Vol. 30, No. 4, 1980.)

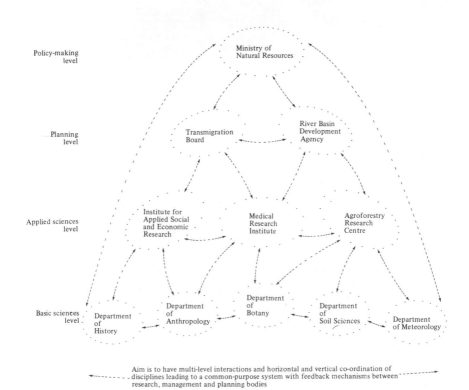

the structure as a whole is well determined. The analogy is with a mechanical model of a machine, which is a functioning whole with all parts related to each other. This interconnectedness of various elements and their interactions are represented graphically in Figure 1, which shows a very simple systems model.

The process model is generally linear, having a beginning, a middle, and an end. Shannon's model was extremely useful in the development of modern communication technology. A modified version of his model is shown in Figure 2.

The linear model in Figure 2 shows the flow of a process through the system connecting sender and receiver of a message. The model shows what characteristics are specific to a communication system as well as the various parts constituting the system as a whole.

Figure 2. A communications process model. (After Sidney W. Head. *Broadcasting in America*, p. 23, Boston, Houghton Mifflin, 1976.)

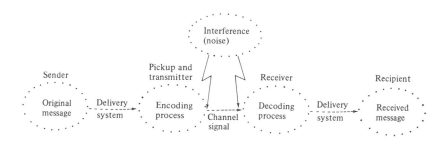

In the process model the emphasis is put on the "flow process," the various stages through which it passes and what happens to it between the first and terminal stages. The system, the constituent elements and their role in this process are shown, but only as a supporting structure or framework for the process.

Sometimes a systems model can be combined with a process model. This combined model then illustrates the characteristics of the system as well as the process and its many and varied effects. This can be the case when the model is concerned with a circular-flow process as shown in Figure 3.

Here the combined model shows the subsystems in the larger system together with the effects of various processes on the system as a whole. This same combined model could also embody the system change caused by the combined effects of various processes occurring in the system and their impact on its structure. The change is both qualitative and quantitative, for various quantifiable changes lead to certain muta-tion within the elements comprising the system.

Both the process model and the systems model are "static," since they assume the system to be fixed or stable. Our combined model in Figure 3, combining elements of these two types of models, illustrates both the "static" and "dynamic" characteristics of the phenomenon with which it deals. The ecological system is undergoing changes but the system of natural laws known to man through science remains

Figure 3.   Web of complexity in the conversion of tropical forest to cattle pasture.
N = Nitrogen; P = Phosphorus; S = Sulfur (Illustration courtesy of R.J. Goodland, World Bank. Reprinted from *impact of science on society*, Vol. 30, No. 4, 1980.)

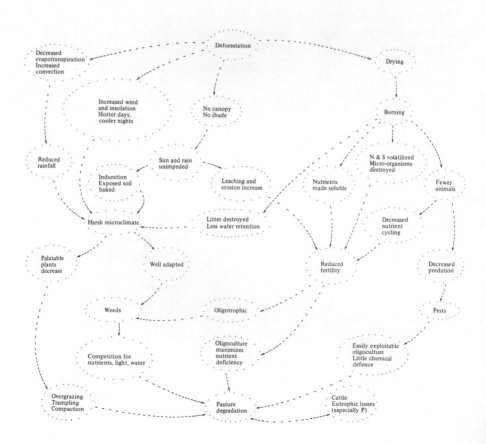

stable. It is through the functioning of this stable system of natural laws that changes in its ecological subsystem can be understood and explained. The nature of this explanation consists of putting the part into the whole—a subsystem within the system, an element within its subsystem—and seeing the resulting effects in the context of the totality of the larger system. We can therefore define a model as a conceptual framework for explaining a set of interrelated observable phenomena. The model can be represented in visual terms through a diagram or can be expressed in some other terms, such as a mathematical formula. This is often done by both mathematical and graphical means.

Modeling Economic Changes

Models are widespread in economics and demography. Economists use models of the national economy for purposes of planning. Economic development plans are necessarily based on such models.

In Table 1 three numerical models of the Indian economy are shown for the period of the Third Five-Year Plan, 1960-66.

The three numerical models (a), (b) and (c) are based on two fundamental hypotheses. The capital-output ratio and the marginal rate of saving. The first is a technical factor: at a given state of technical knowledge, a given input of capital will increase output by a given amount. The second is social: in the aggregate a given increase in income would lead to a proportion of it being used to raise the level of consumption, the rest being saved.

These basic assumptions are crucial to the growth models, which are generally constructed by economists as far as possible on hard empirical data; sometimes when data are ambiguous or hard to get, they must necessarily rely on hunches or inspired guesses. The fundamental characteristics of a model are present in these three numerical examples.

If changes occur in the two elements of the model, i.e., capital-output ratio and the marginal rate of savings, then a set of changes follow in A, B, C, D, and E, which are the subsystems composed of elements designated by 1, 2, 3, etc. Thus the path of the system's growth and change is traced through the changes in the numerical values of the cells, constituted by each row and column of the table. These changes in the cells indicate the differences between models (a), (b), and (c), which are of the the same type. The system accommodates changes in some elements by subsequent changes in other elements, thus maintaining its equilibrium and containing growth. The growth of the system is a quantitative phenomenon, a change represented by balancing various elements in a framework that remains stable. We thus see

Table 1. Three numerical models of Indian development, 1960-66 (in crores of rupees; 10 million rupees = 1 crore.)

			Captial-output ratio 2.2:1 Marginal rate of savings 28%		Captial-output ratio 3:1 Marginal rate of savings 38%		Capital-output ratio 3:1 Marginal rate of savings 23%
			(a)		(b)		(c)
A	1.	National income, 1st year	12,500		12,500		12,500
	2.	National income, 5th year	17,000		15,800		15,800
	3.	Increase in national incomes over 5 years	4,500		3,300		3,300
	4.	Rate of growth	6%		4.8%		4.8%
B	1.	Domestic savings, 1st year (% of national income)	1,050	(8.4%)	1,050		1,050
	2.	Domestic savings, 5th year (% of national income)	2,300	(13.4%)	2,300	(15%)	1,800 (11.4%)
	3.	Domestic savings over 5 years	9,000		9,000		7,500
C	1.	Increase in consumption over 5 years	27%		18%		22%
	2.	Rate of increase	5%		3.5%		4.1%
	3.	Rate of increase per capita	3%		1.5%		2.1%
D	1.	Increase in agricultural production (assumption of income elasticity of demand (*not* consumers' expenditure elasticity) equal to 0.75)	5%		4.1%		4.1%
E	1.	Taxation yields	9,600	(9,568)	9,600	(9,581)	8,500
	2.	Existing taxes	6,600	(6,568)	6,300	(6,270)	6,350[2]
	3.	New taxes	3,000		3,300[3]	(3,311)	2,150[4]
	4.	Share of taxes in national income, 1st year	9.8%		9.8%		9.8%
		Share of taxes in national income, 5th year	14.4%		16%		12.5%

Table 1 (Cont'd.).

	Captial-output ratio 2.2:1 Marginal rate of savings 28%		Capital-output ratio 3:1 Marginal rate of savings 38%		Capital-output ratio 3:1 Marginal rate of savings 23%
5. Government enterprise surplus	2,400	(2,419)	2,400[1,3]	(2,419)	2,300[4]
6. Government borrowing	2,600		2,600[1,3]		2,400[4]
7. Foreign aid	1,100		1,100		2,500[5]
8. Total government expenditure	15,700		15,700		15,700

[1.] More difficult to achieve if income increase is smaller (4.8% instead of 6% p.a.).

[2.] Existing taxes yield 50 crores more than under (b) because consumption increases at the rate of 4% p.a. instead of 3.5%.

[3.] The sum total of E_3 + 5 + 6 must amount to 8.300 crores. How it is to be distributed among the three items is a matter of policy decision.

[4.] The sum total of E_3 + 5 + 6 must amount to 6,850 crores. How it is to be distributed among the three items is a matter of policy decision.

[5.] We assume foreign aid of 3,000 crores out of which 2,500 are available for investment and 1,500 used for converting short- and medium-term credits to a long-run basis.

Source: P.N. Rosenstein-Rodin (ed.). *Capital Formation and Indian Economic Development*, pp. 24-5. Cambridge, MA: MIT Press.

that all three models are of the same type. There is no mutation of the elements constituting the system nor is there any fundamental change in the stable framework of the system such as would require a change in the classification or taxonomy of the observable phenomenon. What the model represents is change *within* the system of the national economy rather than change *of* the system.

Models of Population Change

The science of demography could be said without exaggeration to be based almost wholly on model-building. Demography is concerned with the measurement of population and changes in population and thus provides basic data to the policy-makers and policy planners. It is concerned with the interrelationships among births, *B*, deaths, *D*, and net migration, *M*, over a given period of time defined in advance: a year, ten years, or a century or more; it is also concerned with the results of these events, referred to as vital events.

Population growth can be measured in various ways. We can measure it as change in population between two points in time. Demographers use varying mathematical models from very simple to highly complex, all with the same fundamental basis. We give below some of the simplest models to show their fundamental characteristics and uses.

Measuring Demographic Variation

First method: compares population counts at two successive points in time. These figures have to be of the same quality and standard to be comparable in terms of scope, geographical area and completeness of enumeration. An example of such comparable figures is the decennial census enumerations. These allow us to express population growth in a formula or "model" as : $(P_2 - P_1)$, where P_2 represents the later census and P_1 the earlier.

Second method: the relative size of the two census counts is expressed by their ratio:

$$\left(\frac{P_2}{P_1}\right)$$

Third method: population growth can also be expressed as percentage growth:

$$\left(\frac{P_2}{P_1} - 1\right) \times 100$$

These are examples of the simplest "generalized mathematical models." To apply them to a concrete case would involve substituting numerical data for algebraical expression as follows: suppose a census, taken in 1931 indicates a total population of 347,959 and a later census, in

1946, indicates a total population of 450,114. This means a growth of 102,155 in roughly fifteen years, a ratio of 1.29358, or a 29 percent growth.[1]

Population growth can also be projected by use of the following model: $P_2 = P_1 + B - D + M$ where B, D and M are as defined above. The projection into the future is generally based on already registered vital statistics. Models that measure population changes are called population "growth models." A decrease in population is technically called "negative growth."

Apart from population growth models demographers also use "stationary" population and "stable" population models. A stationary population model is a hypothetical model in which the number of births and deaths are assumed to be exactly equal giving a stationary population. Its main use is to make the effects of some other phenomenon on a given population more clearly apparent for policy-makers by neutralizing the effects of births and deaths such as, for example, the effects of net migration, M, or some other factor which it is desired to study. Indeed a stationary population model serves the same function as zero in mathematics: it provides a useful baseline or starting-point to build logical structures (models) that are comparable with each other and thus permit rigorous analysis of the effect of their various components.

The stable population model is a more ambitious model. It does not assume, as does the stationary population model, that the number of births equals the number of deaths leaving the age structure of the population unchanged. Instead, it assumes that fertility (birth rate) and mortality (death rate) will not alter over a given span of time, which could be anything from ten years to several centuries. A projection of the population on this hypothesis (which is not unrealistic) shows the changing age structure of the population and suggests well in advance what policy matters have to be considered in the fields of health, education, housing, employment. The model used by demographers to show the age structure of a population is called the "age pyramid" (Figure 4).

The word "pyramid" applies to the historical pattern where, owing to high fertility, the younger age-groups are the largest in the population. This pattern still prevails in the developing countries as shown in Figure 4 for India. However, when fertility declines as in the developed countries during the course of the last 100 years, the shape of the pyramid undergoes a change. The base of the pyramid, the youngest age-groups, shrinks relative to the middle of the pyramid, the older age-groups, as seen in the case of Sweden (Figure 4).

Figure 4.   Population pyramids for India and Sweden. Beyond age 70, data are unavailable in five-year age intervals for India. (After G. Barclay, *Techniques of Population Analysis*, p. 224, New York, John Wiley, 1958.)

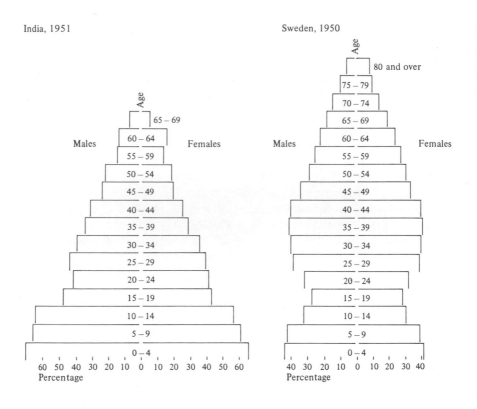

A further refinement of the stable population model is to assume that age-specific fertility and mortality rates remain stable. These rates could be projected separately for each age-group and their effect in the overall population trends for a given period can be seen. This could reveal a cyclical pattern if projected for a long-term period and show the period in which population rises rapidly, and periods in which the population curve tends to flatten out or even to decline on condition that the basic hypothesis continues to apply. This cyclical pattern is usually shown as a "logistic" curve (Figure 5).

Figure 5.   **Logistic curve of growth.** (After J. Janer, "Population Growth in Puerto Rico and its Relation to Time Changes in Vital Statistics," *Human Biology*, Vol. 17, December 1945. Cited by Barclay, *op. cit.*, p. 205.)

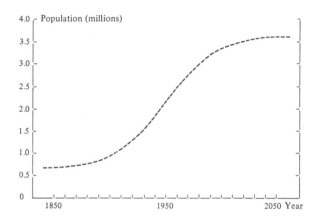

Modeling an Educational System

Models are increasingly being used in educational and manpower planning and are being integrated into the economic development plans of most countries. The reasons for this are well known. A changing or growing economy requires forecasts of its manpower needs and the education and training of manpower well in advance to fill these needs. The various paths that can be followed in an educational system to obtain the certificates, diplomas or degrees called for by various professions, vocations or trades are shown in Figure 6, a model of the post-compulsory education system (age 15 and above) in the United Kingdom. The heavy arrows indicate full-time study courses and the light arrows part-time or evening courses. A more sophisticated process model of the British educational system is shown in Table 2. This process model divides the whole pattern of life into 22 steps or stages, 18 of which are concerned with education, three with employment and the remaining two with infancy and retirement. At each stage some leave the educational system while others proceed to the next stage.

The process model shows the policy-makers what flows are operating in the educational system and whether they are compatible with

Table 2. Matrices of gross flows. Male population of England and Wales, 1966 (in thousands).

Final state	Initial state 0	1	2	3	4	5	6	7	8
0. Outside world		10.7	1.1		0.7	0.1	0.1	0.1	
1. Pre-school	435.6	1,602.2							
2. Nursery and primary schools	− 4.0	411.8	2,055.9						
3. Special schools		5.8	0.8	35.7					
4. Secondary schools: 1st level	−1.5	2.5	324.6	0.1	896.1				
5. Secondary schools: 2nd level					64.6	16.7			
6. Final school year: no certificate				5.1	187.3				
7. Final school year: O-levels					70.6				
8. Final school year: one A-level						8.8			
9. Final school year: two or more A-levels						42.9			
10. Further education: GCEO/OND/ONC							2.5	3.3	
11. Further education: GCEA/HND/HNC								2.7	1.0
12. Further education: external 1st degree	0.1								0.1
13. Further education: external 2nd degree	0.1								
14. Further education: other courses							4.8	3.1	0.8
15. Teacher-training colleges								0.9	1.5
16. University 1st degree: medicine	0.1								
17. University 1st degree: other									
18. University 2nd degree	1.4								
19. School teachers									
20. Other teachers									
21. Other employment	18.2						197.8	62.2	5.3
22. Home and retirement				0.1					
Total	450.0	2,033.0	2,382.4	41.0	1,219.3	68.5	205.2	72.3	8.7

Source: M.A. King. Primary and Secondary Indicators of Education, in A. Schonfield and S. Shaw (eds.), *Social Indicators and Social Policy*, p. 57, London: Heinemann Educational Books, 1972.

9	10	11	12	13	14	15	16	17	18	19	20	21	22	Total
0.1					0.1			0.1		0.7	0.2	100.2	174.4	288.6
														2,037.8
														2,463.7
														42.3
														1,221.8
														81.3
														192.4
														70.6
														8.8
														42.9
	5.8											5.9		17.5
1.3	5.0	6.7												16.7
3.2		0.3	4.9									0.5		9.1
				0.4				0.9						1.4
1.9					20.6							37.2		68.4
2.0		0.7				13.5		0.2		1.3	0.1	5.5		25.7
1.8		0.2					7.7	0.3				0.4		10.5
22.0	0.3	1.4	0.3					51.5				5.1		80.6
							0.5	6.2	9.6			6.8		24.5
					0.3	6.9	0.1	0.4	2.0	134.3		0.5		144.5
						0.7		0.2	1.4	1.3	54.2	0.1		57.9
9.5	6.4	4.8	2.8	0.4	42.3	1.2	1.5	14.5	7.5	0.5	0.1	14,414.5		14,789.5
										1.5	0.6	162.4	2,079.8	2,244.4
41.8	17.5	14.1	8.0	0.8	63.3	22.3	9.8	74.3	20.5	139.6	55.2	14,739.1	2,254.2	

Figure 6. A model of the British educational system. (After Mark Blaug, *An Introduction to the Economics of Education,* p. 328. London, Allen Lane, Penguin Press, 1970.)

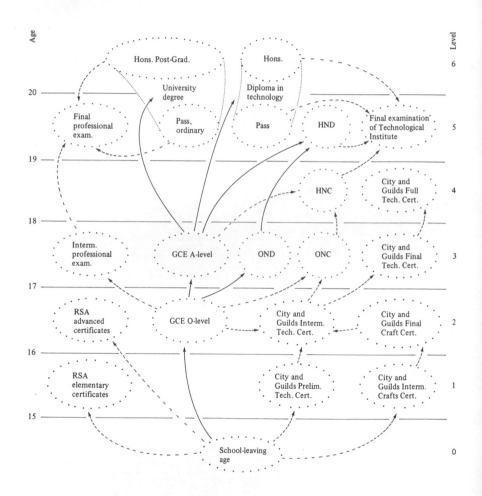

public policy such as manpower requirements of the economy, or some consideration of social justice such as equality of opportunity irrespective of social-class origin. If they are not compatible with public policy, then the policy-makers and planners will have to decide what elements in the social situation have to be manipulated to bring social reality in line with what is socially desirable.

Conclusion

To conclude the above discussion we can say that models are essential tools which make abstract concepts operational and help policy-makers manipulate reality in the light of social options. They are thus essential instruments. They are necessarily based on certain assumptions and operate within the limitations or restrictions of such assumptions. The assumptions or restrictions have to be kept in mind if models are to serve as useful instruments in policy formulation and implementation. Assumptions have to be changed and refined in the face of evolving situations. Unless these limitations are clearly observed, models, no matter how sophisticated, will not adequately serve their purpose as necessary tools in social engineering.   □

FOOTNOTES

[1] The actual figures are for Cyprus. From G. Barclay. *Techniques of Population Analysis,* New York: John Wiley, 1958.

To delve more deeply

BUSSIÈRE, R. and T. STOVALL. *Systèmes évolutifs urbains et régionaux à l'état d'équilibre,* Paris: Centre de Recherche d'Urbanisme, 1980.
EARLE, T. and A. CHRISTENSON, (eds.). *Modelling Change in Prehistoric Subsistence Economics,* New York: Academic Press, 1980.
NAJIN, M. and Y. ABDEL-FATTAH. *System Approach for Development,* Oxford: Pergamon Press, 1980.

See also

Any issue of the following journals: *J. Policy Modeling* (North-Holland), *Modeling, Simplification and Control* (Royal Norwegian Council for Scientific and Industrial Research), and *Omega, the International Journal of Management Science* (Pergamon).

By being content with less than optimal solutions—a relatively small price to pay—the micro approach employs simple heuristic models to put the average manager in touch with his own experiences in such a way that he can build upon his admittedly subjective rules of thumb. The gain is considerable, the author contends, especially in the consistency of the manager's behavior and his new ability to handle complex problems. A concluding case-study gives the reader opportunity to judge this matter for himself.

Chapter 16

MICRO-OPERATIONAL RESEARCH: A SIMPLE MODELING TOOL FOR MANAGERS

James Clayson

Models are formal expressions of the essential elements of a problem in either physical or mathematical terms.

J.N.R. Jeffers, 1979

Introduction

Because modeling in Western industry has long been associated with large-scale computers and techniques for seeking optimal solutions, there is a tendency to assume that this approach to modeling is equally appropriate for developing countries. A closer look, however, at the

James Clayson is an American engineer who resides at 42 rue de Bruxelles, 75009 Paris, France. He has examined managerial methodologies, at the small- and medium-levels, in both developing and industrialized countries.

history of operational research (OR)—the discipline that encourages mathematical modeling in government and industry—reveals that these large complex systems have a very limited applicability since their great cost can be borne by only the largest and richest organizations. An even greater disadvantage, especially in developing countries where managerial skills are at such a premium, is the fact that OR models must be formulated and interpreted by highly skilled technicians to be useful. Because they cannot be manipulated by the shop-floor manager himself, they cannot help improve his own problem-solving skills.

I will propose an alternative approach which I believe is better suited to the needs of most smaller firms and for nations with very limited resources. This micro-approach is based on the building of simple, heuristic[1] models which are not necessarily expressed in mathematical terms, and are derived from the user's own experience.

Because this micro-approach does not seek optimal solutions, its models can be expressed in a wide variety of physical, rather than wholly abstract, terms which make them easier for the average manager to grasp. The manager can do his own modeling, based on his own personal view of the problem he faces.

The Traditional OR Approach

The traditional OR approach aims at improving overall industrial efficiency by supplanting the manager's traditional and "unscientific" methods with mathematical models designed and built by OR "scientists." Advocates of this kind of OR also believe that the uncertainty of the future can be resolved by building ever larger predictive models based on ever growing data bases. Unfortunately, most managers do not have the mathematical ability to structure these large models, nor do they generally have the motivation or time to do so. Consequently, whenever OR techniques have been used, they were introduced by OR specialists drawn mainly from the physical sciences, mathematics and engineering.

These OR people have formed an intellectual and organizational elite. They have held advanced degrees in the hard sciences and have reported to top officers in their organizations, and they have been paid large salaries. Their privileged position in the hierarchy has given them authority to build models reflecting the complexities of a total firm. This kind of OR is very expensive.

When a mathematical model is built to encompass many different organizational goals, for example, profit, rate of return on capital, growth, job creation, environmental impact, political influence, risk aversion, etc., along with a description of how each of these goals is affected by the variables that describe the interrelationships and dynamics of the organization, it must include an enormous number of equations. The collection of specialized data needed to support these models and the time necessary to verify their appropriateness make heavy demands on computers and computer staff, thus contributing to their cost before they are even applied. Obviously, unless the savings generated by their applications are substantial, the entire exercise is not justifiable financially. And since, characteristically, large models of this type generally produce savings of less than 10 percent, it is only in the largest industries that these savings are enough to cover their costs.

In short, conventional OR has been most effective in large firms where it could be applied to well-defined problems of a technical or logistical nature. But this kind of macro-OR does little to improve the problem-solving skills of the average manager upon whom the ultimate success of most firms will continue to rest.

Micro-OR: An Alternative Approach

Fortunately, there is another, much more simple, approach to operational research whose modeling and problem-solving techniques can be made available to any manager. Micro-OR, as I call this approach, makes it possible for managers to design their own models for solving the routine tactical problems that occur each day.

Micro-OR uses small models based directly on a manager's own rules of thumb, or his heuristics. It welcomes more physical forms of expression, such as symbols, words, charts, worksheets, diagrams, and maps, in place of mathematics. In this way, the very "quirky" aspects of a real operational environment can be accommodated with a manner and ease that more formal systems-modeling techniques do not permit.

As already noted, the conventional OR approach claims that a manager's heuristics are suspect because they are too subjective and should be modified or replaced by "objective" mathematics. But the nice thing about the micro-approach is that the person using it does not have to try to be objective, which as everyone knows is an exceedingly difficult task anyway. The micro-approach encourages the manager to build models using his own idiom. By articulating his admittedly subjective heuristics in this explicit way he begins to see just what the rules are, and then he is able to apply them more consistently and objectively in his work. Thanks to micro-OR, the manager models his own view of the world and is not obliged to accept a model constructed by someone else. The distinction is, I believe, a critical one.

Improved Managerial Consistency

Some recent research on managerial problem-solving seems to support my own point of view: modeling a manager's subjective model of the world may be a more realistic path towards improving overall firm effectiveness than by having non-managers try "objectively" to model the total firm in strictly mathematical terms. The evidence shows that the manager's biggest problem is not that he does not have ways of handling his responsibilities, but that he does not know how to apply his own heuristics consistently.

In the management literature, Bowman (1936) has shown that if the inconsistency of a manager's decisions were to be removed by enabling him to base future decisions on the average of his past decisions, performances could be improved. This finding has been verified by a number of other researchers (Remus, 1978).

In the psychology literature, Goldberg (1970, 1976) has shown that a model based on a manager's past decisions and rules of thumb will out-perform the manager himself in a test situation, because the man is inconsistent and the model is not. The analyses made by both Bowman and Goldberg apply to recurrent decision-making activities in relatively stable, non-competitive environments. This kind of environment is typical of much middle-level management to which micro-OR activity is best directed.

Obviously, not all problem-solving environments can be characterized as stable and non-competitive. Certainly in situations where the world is changing rapidly, consistency for its own sake might very well be a disadvantage. However, other research (Hogarth and Makridakis, 1981) on managerial consistency in a rapidly changing environment indicates that there are strong arguments for a consistent application of common sense rules even when the world is changing rapidly and the decision-maker is under a great deal of stress. Micro-OR modeling can help a manager better formulate rules based on common sense so that he can apply them more widely and consistently.

Encouraging the Manager to Experiment

There are other attractive features to this micro-approach. Because it links the manager directly to computer terminals or micro-computers, the manager has more personal space—more freedom and privacy—in which to find his own answers. He no longer has to define and defend his own methods for solving problems in a public and competitive environment: a daunting and often impossible task for a host of obvious psychological reasons. He can "describe" his subjective models to an impersonal machine in the privacy of his own office. This inter-active approach between manager and computer can not only produce good, workable solutions to problems quickly, but it seems also to provide an incentive for the manager to experiment with and improve upon his own heuristics on a continuing basis.

Research carried out by economic historians (Hollander, 1965; Rosenberg, 1976; Usher, 1954) into the sources of productivity gains in the West points to the importance of incremental improvements in bringing about economic growth. These studies emphasize that the accumulation of relatively minor, but continuing improvements in industrial technology are every bit as important as the more dramatic technological breakthroughs. Obviously, there are limits as to how many minor improvements can be made in a system once it approaches its point of obsolescence. But in the meantime a major industrial inno-vation cannot be fully exploited unless there exists an institutionalized capacity for incorporating and extending minor improvements.

These studies also make it plain that minor improvements are usually as much managerial in nature as they are technical. Indeed, the secret seems to be to combine these two aspects in such a way that improvements in one lead inevitably to improvements in the other. The middle manager, whose operational responsibility spans these two func-tions, is a key figure. Obviously, techniques like micro-OR that can assist the middle manager to improve his skills are critical for institu-tionalizing the process of overall industrial innovation.

The idea that simple models may be more efficient than complex ones is already gaining ground. Many large American firms are closing their centralized OR departments and dispersing OR activity and OR personnel throughout their operating divisions (Hall and Hess, 1978; Tobin, 1980). The same trend may be seen in universities and profes-sional associations which are beginning to integrate OR techniques into their training programs in the traditional disciplines of accounting, marketing and production, rather than treating them as worthy of special disciplinary status.

Micro-OR in the Developing World

I think this rather subtle shift of viewpoint in Western industry has important—and perhaps even radical—implications for developing nations: simple computer models based on heuristics are not only more cost-effective, but they provide the opportunity for many people in a given country to improve their own skills. Skills that are self-taught and self-learned tend to have a more lasting impact than those which are imposed; and the possibility for continuous, incremental improvement becomes institutionalized. This is one key to industrial development.

I think the lesson for countries with limited resources is obvious: an investment in simple and heuristic models, which are applicable throughout the industrial sector on a grass-roots management level, may be better value for money than investment in fancy models, which will, at the very best, be relevant to the activities of only a limited number of people in only the largest organizations.

The Model as Tool

The reader will recall that in the title of this article I describe models as a tool for managers. My use of the word "tool" is deliberate, for it contains a very specific definition which has important implications for industrial development.

A tool, in its simplest sense, is an amplifier of either manual or intellectual skills. The history of technology has shown that whenever new tools are created which are easy to use, rely on existing skills and are applicable to a wide variety of situations, new technologies are likely to arise. To illustrate this point, let me cite two well-documented cases of such catalyst tools from the history of technology: the brace and bit, invented in the 1420s by an unknown Flemish carpenter or shipwright (White, 1962), and the steam engine, invented by Thomas Newcomen in 1712 (Rolt and Allen, 1977). Both of these tool/machines had spread throughout Europe and were applied to a wide spectrum of industries within a matter of years. And this without benefit of modern communications.

The invention of the brace and bit was revolutionary in so far as its usefulness was recognized simultaneously in sectors ranging from shipbuilding, to millwrighting and the construction trades. In the same fashion the atmospheric steam engine was diffused from the mining sector, where it was first used to pump water, to such diverse industries as textiles, brewing, and municipal sewage disposal. In both cases, and following my rule of thumb for the rapid diffusion of technology, these tools were successful because they required few new skills to operate, while the same tool itself created its own demand for an environment in which change and development were self-generating.

Today's equivalent of these revolutionary, historical tools is the ubiquitous pocket calculator. Like its antecedents, the pocket calculator is relatively cheap, simple and fast, and fun to use. In addition, like other successful tools, it encourages the new user to experiment and adapt it to other situations. This constant experimentation creates its own demand for incremental improvements in the technology itself. Thus the simple hand calculator lays the groundwork for the spread of more advanced calculators with built-in memories and additional mathematical functions, which in turn leads to programmable calculators and, more recently, to micro-computers.

These micro-computers are tools that have the same potential for mobilizing skills useful to industrial development as the historical examples given. But the potential will not be exploited until such time as their utility becomes self-evident. What is needed to bring this about is the creation of micro-OR programs of the sort I described at the start of this article. If they are sufficiently versatile and easy to use their diffusion is assured. Most of the software for micro-computers on the market today is specific to such applications as payrolls, stock-control, and invoicing procedures. These are specialized routines requiring specialized skills for their application, and which do nothing, consequently, to improve general management skills.

Managerial Creativity

I have been experimenting with the design of programs which will encourage the manager to build his own models for problem-solving. The manager's "problem," as I see it, is to assemble and to present relatively limited amounts of data in a meaningful way. But the most meaningful way is rarely obvious. For a manager to find it he must be able to manipulate his data in a variety of ways to see if a pattern emerges and what alternative courses of action may be followed. The manager's facility in experimenting with different ways of finding relationships in data is, I believe, at the heart of managerial creativity.

One of the most effective ways of seeing relationships in data is in laying out the different elements side by side in a tabular format so that they can be compared at a glance. In this case, the data picture is worth, literally, a thousand words because it combines the temporal and the spatial dimensions of the problem in one display. Double-entry bookkeeping is the classic illustration of this.

Obviously, most managers already have rules—or heuristics—on how they like to visualize problems through the tabulation of data. The spread-sheets that are used to illustrate the cash-flow effects of an addition to a firm's product line are good example of tabulation. Worksheets used for production scheduling are another. Worksheets are found in firms of all sizes and each worksheet has it own associated format, symbols, and rules on how it is to be used for finding the answer to a specific problem. If we look back to the definition of models given at the start of this article—"models are the formal expression of the essential elements of a problem either in physical or mathematical terms"—we will see that the rules governing the use of worksheets are the result of managerial model-building.

By introducing at this stage a tool like the micro-computer, with its potential for creative graphics,[2] the simple worksheet can be transformed into a much more revealing display. Besides the conventional row-and-column format, micro-OR routines can transform the same data into other graphic modes such as curves, histograms or maps, thus providing the user with a choice of modeling aids. Good graphical displays can also suggest alternative heuristics.

Because these routines are not dependent for their effectiveness on either the size or the wealth of the organization in which they are used, they have maximum applicability. And they should be just as cost-effective in either developed or developing nations. I will end this chapter by describing a study in which a micro-OR model was used to solve a distribution problem. While the material comes from France, it seems nevertheless to illustrate the principles set forth. Thus I hope it is evident that these techniques should be useful in many industrial situations.

A Case-Study in Micro-OR Modeling

Problem: Where to Locate Warehouses?

A medium-sized French company manufactures consumer items that are sold to shops throughout France. The products are produced at a number of scattered locations in France. The firm currently uses five warehouses. Each of these warehouses receives full truck-loads of product from the manufacturing points and then delivers truck-loads of mixed product to individual customers. Problem: the distribution manager wants to know if he can lower the total cost of distribution by changing either the number or the locations of his warehouses. How does he find out?

The manager already knows a great deal about his distribution system; now he wants to put these ideas together in a formal way so that he can predict how his distribution system would look if he changed the geometry of it. He knows that the cost of storage will decrease as the number of warehouses decreases because it is easier to control inventories when they are concentrated in a few rather than many locations. He also knows that the cost of transportation from warehouses to customers will increase as the number of warehouses decrease because the average distance traveled per customer will increase. Finally, he knows that the cost of serving warehouses from the plant may or may not be affected by changing their number because the distance traveled will depend more upon the shape of the configuration than on the absolute number of warehouses. The manager also knows how he would calculate all these cost elements for any particular warehouse's configuration; but he does not know which configuration to pick.

The first thing the manager must do is to look hard at the data he already has to see if there are any patterns that suggest ways of attacking the problem. These patterns may suggest heuristics that can be used to manipulate the data towards solving the distribution problem. Later he can use the tabulation and data-manipulation programs to evaluate the relative efficiency—in the total distribution cost sense—of each of the heuristics as the manager moves progressively towards finding a solution that he "likes".

Building the Model

Note that although no equations have been written down during this initial exercise, a model is none the less being built using word definitions, diagrams, and already available sales and transportation cost information. Models of this kind can be every bit as formal as mathematical equations and can be much easier to use by non-mathematicians.

Let us go back and look at the data as the manager first arranged it. Figure 1 shows the sales data for France in weight units by *département*. Figure 2 shows the ninety-some departments into which France is divided, as rendered by a computer. Now go back to Figure 1, and note how the company's sales are distributed among the various departments. The manager sorted the departments—by sales weight—from largest to smallest. The vertical scale of Figure 1 indicates the sales volume per department and the top horizontal scale gives the position of the four quartiles and the running number of departments represented from left to right. The bottom horizontal scale—read downwards—gives the department number. Thus Department 13 has the largest sales of 91 units; and the first seven largest departments fall into the first quartile (25 percent of total sales). Note further that 19 departments represent 50 percent of total sales, and that 39 departments represent 75 percent.

Figure 1. Sales data for France by department (ordinate: department
number; abscissa: magnitude of sales [arbitrary unit]).

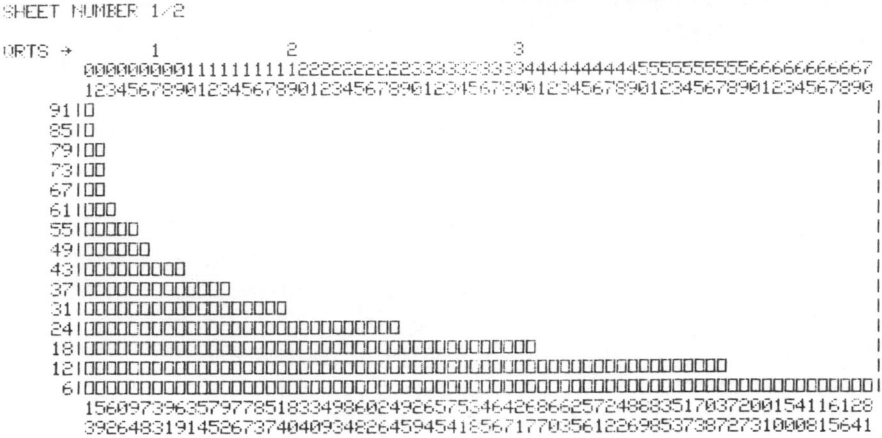

```
SHEET NUMBER 1/2

ORTS →         1                  2                  3
       00000000001111111111222222222223333333333344444444444555555555556666666666 7
       1234567890123456789012345678901234567890123456789012345678901234567890
    91 |□
    85 |□
    79 |□□
    73 |□□
    67 |□□
    61 |□□□
    55 |□□□□□
    49 |□□□□□□
    43 |□□□□□□□□
    37 |□□□□□□□□□□□□
    31 |□□□□□□□□□□□□□□□□□□
    24 |□□□□□□□□□□□□□□□□□□□□□□□□□□□□□
    18 |□□□□□□□□□□□□□□□□□□□□□□□□□□□□□□□□□□□□□□□□□□□
    12 |□□□□□□□□□□□□□□□□□□□□□□□□□□□□□□□□□□□□□□□□□□□□□□□□□□□□□□□□□□
     6 |□□□□□□□□□□□□□□□□□□□□□□□□□□□□□□□□□□□□□□□□□□□□□□□□□□□□□□□□□□□□□□□□□□□□□□□□□□□|
       15609739635797785183349860249265753464268662572488835170372001541161 28
       39264831914526737404093482645945418567177035612269853738727310008156 41
```

Figure 2.   Computer map of France.

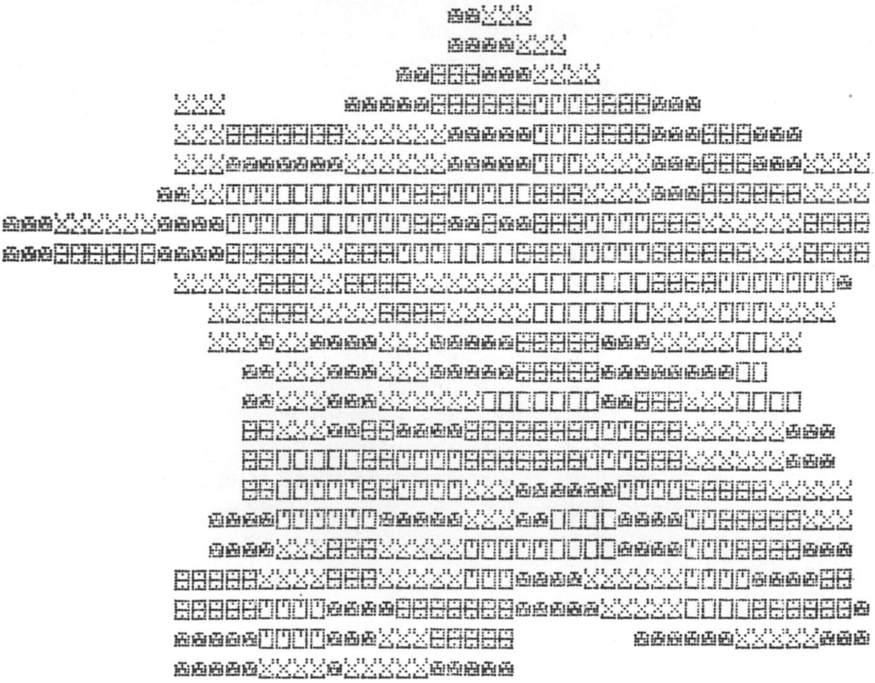

Figure 3.   Quartile map 1: four suggested warehouse locations.

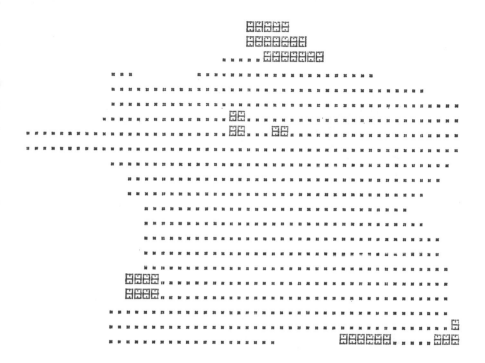

While one can learn a great deal from these figures—such as that sales are skewed into a few areas rather than being smoothly distributed across the entire country—the display does not yet suggest potential warehouse sites to the manager nor does it suggest some appropriate number of warehouses to evaluate. What is needed, since this is a spatial problem, is a way to represent the information of Figure 1 in a spatial idiom: that is, on a map of France.

Figures 3, 4, and 5 provide the spatial dimension. Looking at these three figures, we can now learn what was lacking from Figure 1. We can see clearly where sales are concentrated. On seeing these three displays, the manager was able to suggest what turned out to be a good heuristic: to locate warehouses within the zones of greatest sales concentration for each of the three quartile maps. Thus in Figure 3, four warehouse locations were suggested. In Figure 4, eight locations were indicated and about 14 were suggested by Figure 5. Then by evaluating the cost differences between the three different warehouse configurations suggested by these three maps, he could determine roughly how total costs would be affected by the differing numbers of warehouses. Having established three basic alternatives, the manager was able to experiment with other possibilities as well. This eventually led to his minimizing total transportation costs by selecting the best number and location of warehouses in France.

Figure 4. Quartile map 2: eight suggested warehouse locations.

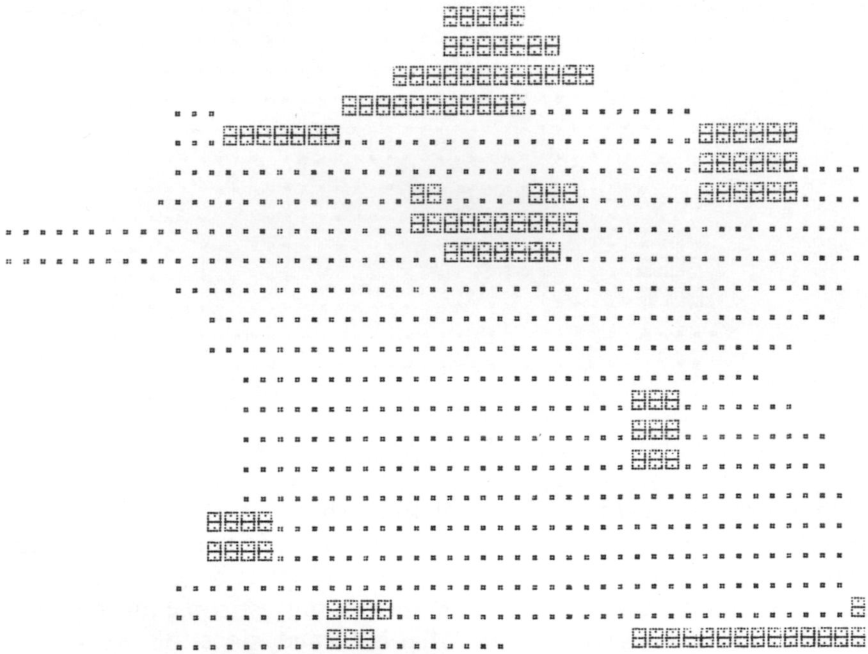

How did he do his calculations? First, he gathered transportation costs for every warehouse-to-market area. Then he calculated the cost of serving every department from every warehouse and then selected the cheapest source of each department. Finally, the approximation for the cost of carrying inventory was made based on the calculated volume per warehouse. Obviously, all of these calculations were done with the aid of a micro-computer.

Figure 5.   Quartile map 3: fourteen suggested warehouse locations.

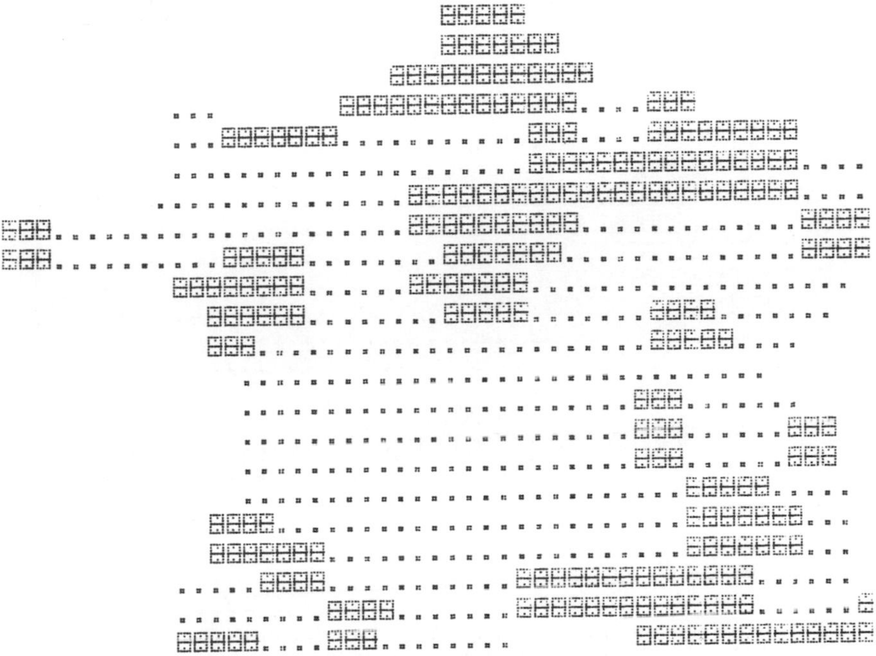

Beyond Mere Cost Considerations

The visual display may be helpful in considering other aspects of the distribution problem. For example, although cost considerations may dictate certain distribution patterns, other considerations such as weather and road conditions, labor conflicts, or unacceptably long distances may require that these be modified. Figure 6 shows some distribution patterns as they exist prior to taking these other considerations into account.

Having looked at distribution patterns, it may be of interest also to look carefully at some of the distribution costs associated with any particular configuration of warehouses. Figure 7 shows graphically those departments whose delivery costs from warehouse to customer—on a per-unit-weight basis—are more than twice the national average, suggesting areas where the manager might work out better solutions. He might wish to re-negotiate these high rates, change truckers, make slight

Figure 6.   Unmodified distribution patterns.

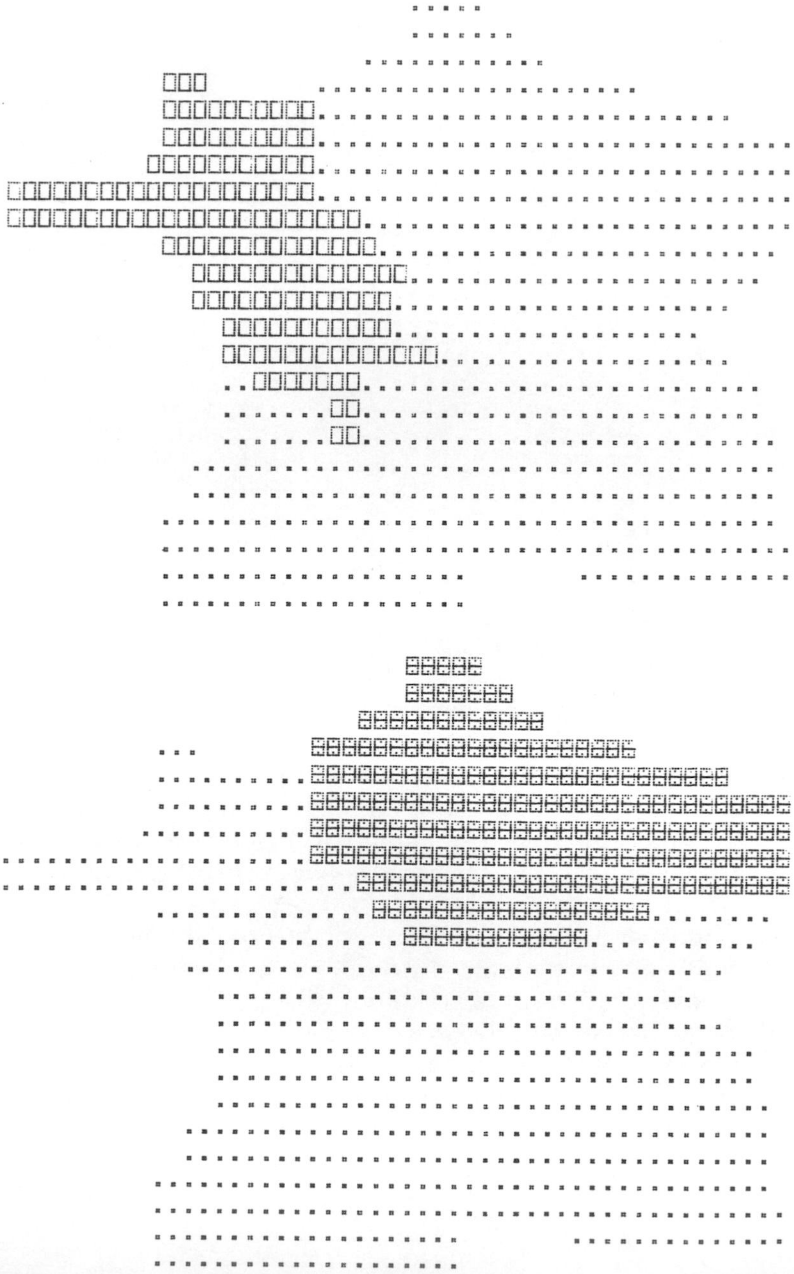

Figure 7. Pattern showing where delivery costs are above national average.

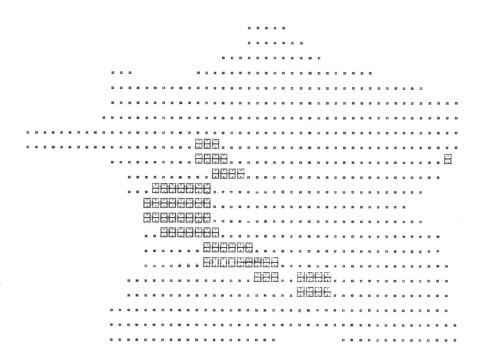

changes in warehouse sites, or add new sites, for example. To simulate the effects of these changes the manager re-runs the earlier routines using substitute information.

Summary

The case-study described above gives the gist of how micro-OR can be a tool for managers. This technique does not necessarily produce or guarantee that the final solution is a "mathematically optimal" one. But it has the advantage of being easy and cheap to use because it is derived from the manager's own heuristics. It allows the user to assess the worth of his own common-sense rules and experience, while producing a means to extend these to other areas.   □

FOOTNOTES

[1] The word heuristics comes from the Greek *heuriskein*, to discover. It was coined in the nineteenth century to describe any hint or rule of thumb that helps a person discover, for himself, a solution to a problem. Sometimes heuristics are very specific, as, for example, when we know that by hitting the side of a jar lid we will probably loosen the lid. In other situations, heuristics provide our knowledge of the "correct" way to do a particular job. We just "know" how to do the job, based on experience or intuition, even though we are not conscious of following any particular rules.

[2] The study of the effective use of graphics in heuristic model-building has hardly begun apart from two important and basic books (Tukey, 1977; Newman and Sproull, 1979).

References

BOWMAN, E. "Consistency and Optimality in Managerial Decision Making," *Management Science*, Vol. 9, 1963.

GOLDBERG, L. "Man versus Model of Man," *Psychological Bulletin*, Vol. 73, 1970.

―――― . "Man versus Model of Man: Just How Conflicting is the Evidence?" *Organizational Behaviour and Human Performance*, Vol. 16, 1976.

HALL, J. and S. HESS. "OR/MS: Dead or Dying? RX for Survival," *Interfaces*, May 1978.

HOGARTH, R. and S. MAKRIDAKIS. "The Value of Decision Making in a Complex Environment: An Experimental Approach," *Management Science*, Vol. 27, 1981.

HOLLANDER, S. *The Sources of Increased Efficiency*, Cambridge, MA: MIT Press, 1965.

JEFFERS, J. "The Development of Models in Urban and Regional Planning," paper presented at the International Meeting on the Development and Application of Ecological Models in Urban and Regional Planning, Bad Homburg, Federal Republic of Germany, 13-16 March 1979.

NEWMAN, W. and R. SPROULL. *Principles of Interactive Graphics*, 2nd edition, New York: McGraw-Hill, 1979.

REMUS, W. "Testing Bowman's Managerial Coefficient Theory Using a Competitive Gaming Environment," *Management Science*, Vol. 24, 1978.

ROLT, L. and J. ALLEN. *The Steam Engine of Thomas Newcomen*, Moorland Publishing, 1977.

ROSENBERG, N. *Perspectives on Technology*, Cambridge: Cambridge University Press, 1976.

TOBIN, N. "The Changing Role of OR," *Journal of the Operational Research Society*, April 1980.

TUKEY, J. *Exploratory Data Analysis*, Reading, MA: Addison-Wesley, 1977.

USHER, A. *A History of Mechanical Inventions*, Cambridge, MA: Harvard University Press. 1954.

WHITE, L. *Medieval Technology and Social Change*, Oxford: Oxford University Press, 1962.

To delve more deeply

TRADITIONAL OPERATIONAL RESEARCH

CHURCHMAN, C.; R. ACKOFF and E. ARNOFF. *Introduction to Operations Research*, New York: John Wiley, 1957. (A classic text.)

WOOLSEY, R. and H. SWANSON. *Operations Research for Immediate Application*, New York: Harper & Row, 1975. (A newer and livelier presentation.)

THE FAILURE OF TRADITIONAL OR IN DEVELOPING COUNTRIES

CLAYSON, J. "How Relevant is Operational Research to Development: The Case of Kenyan Industry," *Journal of the Operational Research Society*, April 1980.

A literature survey of OR articles in a Third World context has been produced by the Developing World OR Group, University of Sussex, Falmer, Brighton, Sussex BN1 9RF, United Kingdom.

HEURISTICS IN THE SENSE USED IN THIS CHAPTER

GRAHAM, N. *Artificial Intelligence*, Blue Ridge Summit, PA: Tab Books, 1979.

SILVER, E.; R. VIDAL and D. DeWERRA. "A Tutorial on Heuristic Methods," *European Journal of Operational Research*, Vol. 5, 1980.

GENERAL HISTORY AND CRITIQUE OF SYSTEMS MODELING IN OR AND OTHER DISCIPLINES

LILIENFELD, R. *The Rise of Systems Theory, An Ideological Analysis*, New York: John Wiley, 1978.

MICRO-COMPUTERS

By far the best source of up-to-date information on the world of micro-computing is found in magazines devoted to machines, programs and applications. A selection: *BYTE* and *Creative Computing* (United States); *Personal Computer World* (United Kingdom); *L'Ordinateur individuel* (France).

Two experienced science educators make a convincing case for school science that transcends mere rote memorization of textbook statements. The key lies in putting students into creative contact with nature itself—through use of models. For the sceptical reader, the authors provide (see appendix) the rules of some model games he can play in order better to understand nature—a strategy these educators would urge teachers not to be ashamed to use in the classroom.

Chapter 17

MODELS IN SCIENCE EDUCATION

George Marx and Esther Tóth

A good model is worth a thousand facts.

Mircea Malitza, mathematician,
currently Rumanian ambassador to the
United States of America

Man and His Models

Man is a model-making animal. The animal nervous system has a modeling function, processing incoming stimuli, anticipating coming events, and by this means guiding the organism. The use of models has

George Marx and Esther Tóth are both teachers of science. Professor Marx is head of the Department of Atomic Physics at the Eötvös University in Budapest. His research lies in high-energy physics and theoretical astrophysics. He has been president of the Hungarian Physical Society, chairman of the High Energy Division of the European Physical Society and vice-president of the International Astronautical Federation. He is a member of the Hungarian Academy of Sciences and of the International Academy of Astronautics, and is currently vice-president of the Groupe International pour l'Enseignement de la Physique. (Continued on page 266.)

reached its highest level in the case of man. His outstanding predictive power gives him a selective advantage over his physically stronger rivals.

This child likes to play. Reptiles never play, but young birds and mammals do. Games are very varied in the case of the intelligent species like young chimpanzees. Play is a modeling exercise. The toys of the man-child are material models for the objects of the adults' world. What counts in girls' dolls and boys' matchbox-cars is not the correct coloring—only the toy-industry and aunts think this—but how functional they are. Every child knows that matchbox-cars are not real autos, that dolls are not real infants, but the child still enjoys playing with them; he is getting ready for behavioral patterns required of adults.

Science makes extended use of models. The history of science could not be told without mentioning celestrial spheres, rigid bodies, indivisible atoms, elastic lines of force, the vibrating ether, the atomic planetary system, the valance-hook, the double helix, corpuscle-wave dualism. World-consciousness and self-consciousness are efficient evolutionary achievements; for this model-like splitting of reality it is worth accepting the logical traps of the quantum mechanical theory of measurement. Pierre Aigrain stated at a recent international physics education conference:

> The aim of the physicist is to make quantitative predictions about the behavior of simple models. The models have to be realistic enough to reflect the considered aspect of reality. At the same time the model has to be simple enough to make its quantitative understanding possible.

If a model fits reality well, its predictions will be fulfilled to a great extent. Because it is easy to mistake the successful model for reality, success is often the mother of dogmatism. The geocentric world-order, action at a distance, the light-carrying ether, electron orbits—all looked so convincing that academic judgment, public opinion and even our

Esther Tóth teaches physics in the József Attila Grammar School in Budapest. After receiving a Ph.D. in 1976 from the Eötvös University, she took part in creating the new activity-oriented Hungarian physics curriculum and has written chapters on modern physics in secondary-school textbooks. In 1981, Dr. Tóth was awarded the Mikola Prize of the Hungarian Physics Teachers for the excellent achievements of her pupils. Correspondence to both authors can be addressed as follows: Roland Eötvös University, Department of Atomic Physics, Poskin utca 5-7, 1088 Budapest, Hungary.

minds remained their slaves far too long. The scientific revolutions fought to overthrow outdated ideas belong to the most brilliant pages of human history.

The universe, even a single atom, possesses potentially an infinite number of degrees of freedom. On the other hand, the number of neurons in the human brain is finite. With this limited brain, with computers that are also limited, man can only cope with a finite number of variables. For his purposes of prediction, then, man cannot use the inexhaustible universe but instead must resort to models of that universe, which can be grasped by his brain or used in a computer. Models vary, evolve, multiply and by selecting among this growing and varying number, and modifying what we select, our ability to understand the world, to anticipate events, to shape our environment improves accordingly. While research is never-ending, it does converge through its successive approximations. Through thesis-antithesis-synthesis man rises higher and higher in the realm of knowledge.

Models in the School

According to Piaget, school-aged children think in a concrete operational way. If the teacher refutes one of two alternatives, his pupils will not accept the other until they can visualize it much as a motion picture. What they imagine, they would also like to catch, to build and to take apart. Abstract logic matures in them only at the end of the secondary school, even then not for all, so models play at least as important a role in science education as in the groping of research.

The school curriculum presents science through a variety of models: the mass point, the rigid body, the incompressible fluid, the ideal gas, indivisible atoms, integer valency, the carbon cycle of the ecosphere and invariable species. We have learned to like these models, using them in our teaching of theorems and letting them serve other educational purposes. In the end, our pupils accept these models as ultimate reality.

A pedagogical problem is created by the way we let a variety of incoherent models fill the heads of our pupils. Secondary-school chemistry treats the periodic table and the chemical bond on the basis of the structure of atoms. At the same time, physics teaches the corpuscular model of a gas, in which rigid balls fly around. In the iconography of our posters the electron is shown as an ellipse drawn around the nucleus. In one school book the electron is presented as a marble, another depicts it as wave, while the ambitious author treats it as a probability cloud. Are all these valid 'scientific truths' at the same time? If one asks a pupil what an atom is, he may ask in return: "In which course—physics, chemistry or philosophy?" We as teachers know, of course, that sometimes this model applies, at other times that model, depending on the occasion. We understand that these are alternative models and that behind them there is the abstract conceptual system of the Schrödinger or Dirac equations as the best models we possess at present.

A real conflict arises when for pedagogical convenience the model has been solidified to "ultimate truth." Our pupils are then unable to reason dialectically and thereby revise their world picture. In centuries past when the astronomical and social universe seemed to stand still, dogmas might have had practical advantages. Nowadays we live in a changing world where an unbroken link to changing conditions and an elastic variation in our models is required. Social and technological progress owes much to political and scientific revolutions. Why, then, are Hooke's law and Ohm's law not presented in the school as first approximations rather than as fundamental theorems? If the definition of force and resistance is based upon linear dependence, any deviation from linearity appears as a logical impossibility. Yet linear extrapolation breaks down in microelectronics and also in world economy. In 1980, at the Conference of the International Union for Pure and Applied Physics on Physics Teacher Education in Trieste, Goery Delacote pointed out that the trivial picture of a linear and reversible world is offered by the school instead of the interwoven degrees of freedom of matter, instead of the expanding and evolving universe. Scholastically educated young people are shocked by this conflict of school and reality. Instead of the canonization of models, young people need to be taught the art of model creation.

Modeling Exercises

"Pour cool water into a glass, hot water into another one! Drop a cube of sugar in each of them! Watch carefully what happens!"—This is the beginning of the Hungarian physics course for Grade 9. After observation and description of the phenomena, the next question put to the pupil is: "Why does the cube of sugar dissolve differently in hot and cold water?" A number of answers can be obtained: "It may be that the glue holding the cube together melts away in the heat." Or: "Perhaps the hot water hits the cube more frequently, like artillery shells hitting the castle." And so on. The teacher may be inclined to suggest the expected answer: "In warm water the speed of the molecular motion is larger"—but he knows the joy of play and discovery would soon be lost. An enforced early convergence would act to paralyze fantasy and curiosity. Creative thinking needs divergence as well, because only by seeing the alternative of the various models can one raise the next question: which model should be selected?

The ninth-grade school book tells the tale of a curious Martian who is interested in learning about terrestrial people but because of the danger of infection he cannot meet them. One of them, a tailor, sends a tailor's dummy, while another, a pharmacist, sends a white mouse as the instructive model of man. The poor Martian does not find anything in common between the two models except whiskers. The discussion in the class following the tale leads to the conclusion: if someone is interested in shape, he will choose the tailor's dummy as a substitute for man while someone concentrating on metabolism would prefer the white mouse. In this way a pupil is introduced to the complementarity of different models of the same object. This will be very useful later when presenting the dual nature of the electron. The teaching of the structure of matter offers some of the most appropriate opportunities for education in modeling. Here the dialectics of experience and logic guides us from the simplest ball model of molecules to better and better concepts of atoms. It should be evident that discovery does not end in school; it can continue throughout a person's lifetime.

But it is a long way to the electron. At the beginning, the teacher may ask: *"What kind of child is modeled by the following animals: donkey, pig, snail, sloth?"* Then the school-books may include questions of increasing difficulty, such as: In what respects are the following objects similar: a dragonfly and a helicopter; a little girl and a doll; a camera and an eye; a horse and a car? Which needs more data to be understood? Which can be explained most easily by the other?

Later a problem is assigned from the excellent book of Wenhem et al., *Physics—Concepts and Models:*

> *Descartes proposed a very simple model to explain the phenomenon of seeing. He suggested that the eyes shot out rays which, on touching an object, gave rise to the sensation of light. Suggest experiments or observations you could make which could support or refute this model!*

The recognition strategy of modeling can start with simple situations. In the black-box experiment introduced by Robert Karplus, students must infer the shape of barriers in the box that restrict the rolling of pebbles it contains by shaking the box but never opening it. A similar experiment is performed with the "electric black box." Metal contacts on the outside of the box are connected by wires hidden inside. Students must infer these connections using only battery and bulb. They are often surprised to find that several different models of the wiring can be given for the same box. Pupils at the higher secondary school level are provided more sophisticated black boxes for these exercises. For example, the box may contain condensers that transmit only alternating current, or diodes that conduct direct current in only one direction.

In discussing these experiences and findings with his pupils, a traditional Hungarian teacher will praise the child who gets the same results as that found in the teacher's notebook. He will say benevolently: "Although your model would work, the actual connections in the box are different from what you show." Such a teacher leads a pupil to respect only him and not reality.

Our pupils learn through these exercises not only about observation and reasoning but also about respect for reality even in contest with adult authority. In the interplay between teacher, pupil and nature, the teacher should see to it that the pupil and nature become the main actors—with models mediating effectively between these two.

Models as Teachers

The far-away sweetheart is brought to mind by a look at her picture. In the search for a criminal, his picture may perform a considerable service to the police.

School-books on atomic structure will frequently picture the s, p, . . . electron states. One can even build expensive statues of these electron states, paying scrupulous attention to the exact reproduction of the quantum, mechanically calculated, density profiles. This representation is informative but it does not say too much about the way nature works. A pupil is likely to learn far more by dipping a wire circle into a soap solution, removing it carefully and shaking it with the frequency required to form standing waves; or he can manipulate a steel loop that allows him to feel directly how nature spontaneously sets up a regular circular pattern or "8" shape characteristic of the s and p quantum states. Such active modeling teaches abstract concepts more efficiently than all the words of a teacher.

The appendix to this article describes several different model games as examples of ways to present some of the rather abstract faces of nature. The essence of playing and modeling are very similar. The teacher should not be ashamed to bring such games to the classroom because these educative models help in understanding nature.

Our children will enter a new fast-changing era. The facts of this brave new world—energy sources, technology, genetic engineering and all of their social implications—cannot be memorized in advance because they are not yet known. Their teachers can offer them a strategy for orienting themselves in unknown territory, one that is used effectively by scientists: (a) respect for and observation of reality; (b) selection of relevant aspects and important data; (c) creation of a model, which interprets the variation of these data, has a restricted number of degrees of freedom, and is simple enough to be easily grasped by the mind; (d) use of the model to predict coming events; (e) submission of the model to experimental check and exploration of its limits of validity; (f) practical application of the model within the limits of its validity; and (g) modification of the model to fit the region that lies beyond its limits and, when finally necessary, search for a new model, that is, re-enter this sequence at step (c). These are not just text-book steps to be memorized in school, but an educational goal leading to a behavior pattern that can be useful even for those who are not going to become scientists.

Looking at reality in an unbiased way stimulates explanation. If a model is working well it is used to explain more and more observations until it finally reaches its explanatory limits. At the first sign of these limits, the response should not be regret but excitement, a sense of fresh challenge. This is the intellectual adventure that keeps science alive and young—witness the Michelson experiment or the strange spectrum of black body radiation. Such shock treatment prevents rigor mortis from setting into one's thinking!

In the lower grades pupils have seen that rubbing a glass rod causes it to attract a plastic ruler that has been similarly rubbed but to repel another glass rod that has been rubbed. They also have witnessed the way a glass rod that has been rubbed will, when brought near a water jet, pull the jet towards the glass rod. "The water certainly contains negative ions" guessed one pupil bravely who then went on routinely to the conclusion: "I expect that the ruler will push the water away." To his great surprise, on carrying out the experiment, he saw that the jet of water was *attracted* to the ruler. In this most unforgettable fashion the pupil learned for himself about the dipole character of water molecules.

It is worth organizing as many such shock situations in the class as possible as a way of inducing pupils to take more initiative.

In a Finnish-Swedish-Hungarian student competition the Finnish organizers gave synthetic fishing line to the pupils, asking them to investigate its elastic properties as accurately as possible. Weights and a measuring ruler were provided.

The competitors measured the stretching of the sting caused by different weights. They divided the force by the extension and the mean value obtained was recorded as the "spring constant" of the meter-long line. But some of the pupils plotted the force versus extension on a diagram and recognized that as the pull increases, the length of the string does not increase beyond a certain limit. The matted synthetic molecular chains become straightened but they do not tear. It was interesting to watch the reaction of pupils to the conflict created by the collision of the memorized linearity of Hooke's law with the empirical evidence of nonlinearity. Their reactions were rather characteristic for the style of their teachers. Some of them "corrected" the evidence in the interest of Hooke's law. Others "discovered" even the phenomenon of irreversible deformation (or hysteresis).

In another competition, we asked the pupils to find the resultant of two parallel and two series-coupled resistances. We provided bulbs (or lamps) as the resistances.

Pupils have memorized the formula for the resultant of parallel and series resistances but the bulbs have not. With the bulbs in parallel the current was stronger and they became hotter than with the bulbs in series (the more vehement thermal motion of the ions increasing the resistance of the tungsten fiber). The pupils tried hard but simply could not get measured values to agree with the calculated results. A number of diligent pupils "succeeded" in obtaining the "correct" value, in spite of the facts.

At the end of secondary school, a humanistic-oriented pupil decided to choose a career as a physicist. To our surprised question he replied: "The laws of physics are valid in the widest circle. In spite of this, it was only the physics teacher who spoke about the limits of the laws."

APPENDIX

Statistical Model Games: Equilibrium

1. Ehrenfest invented a game to show how a large number of random events may lead to a well-defined final state. Two dogs meet each other. One of them, the white dog, is an orderly clean dog just coming from the bath. The other comes from a country kennel which has not been cleaned for years. This black dog is covered with fleas. The dogs are happy with each other, they smell and rub each other. The fleas are happy too about the increased *Lebensraum*. They jump randomly from one dog to the other. After a lasting friendship, which dog will scratch itself more strongly?

For simulation, let us draw two tangent circles (the two dogs). Let us shade one of them. Six counters are numbered 1 to 6 representing the fleas. In the initial state let us put all the fleas on the black dog. Let us throw dice many times. Each throw indicates a flea with that number and this flea jumps over to the other dog.

One observes that at the beginning more fleas flow to the white dog than the opposite way. The number of the fleas decreases on the black dog. After a number of throws the number of the fleas are becoming about equal on the two dogs, the flow in one direction being as intensive as the backflow. The number of fleas on the black dog fluctuates around a constant equilibrium value. The final equilibrium number does not depend on the choice of the initial state. The game illustrates why air is distributed with equal density in two connected rooms, or why raspberry juice mixes with water spontaneously.

2. Six children are sitting on the wide steps of a stairway. Let us draw ten horizontal straight lines on a piece of paper and let us put the six numbered counters on these lines in arbitrary distribution. Two dice are thrown simultaneously. The counter selected by the number on the black die moves one step lower, the counter selected by the number on the white die moves one step higher. In this way the total "elevation energy" remains constant. Since from the lowest step one cannot move lower, a throw giving this instruction is invalid. After a number of throws, what will be the distribution of children on the stairway? One reaches an equilibrium distribution that becomes thinner upwards, in principle, as a geometrical sequence. The average "height" of the counter distribution depends on the value of the initial energy, i.e., on the sum of the heights of the counters in the initial distribution.

The counters stand for the molecules, the throws of the dice model the energy transfers in the random collisions. Compared to the first game, the only difference is the condition of energy conservation. This game illustrates the barometric distribution of air molecules or, in a more abstract way, following Gurney, Black and Ogborn, the equilibrium Boltzmann-distribution of energy quanta in an Einstein crystal. The model becomes more instructive if the die thrown has twenty faces, i.e., it is an icosahedron instead of a cube, representing twenty children, atoms, molecules, etc., moving up and down. Fortunate people may make use of computer simulation, using a hundred-odd counters instead of six.

3. Let us draw a series of six squares indicating the six hunting territories in a jungle. Each territory gets a number 1 to 6. In the jungle there live wolves and panthers of equal strength, one on each territory. If any of them succeeds in making a surprise attack upon the other, it will kill the competitor and the territory of the victim will be given to the offspring of the killer.

Let us put three wolves (grey counters) and three panthers (pink buttons) on the six territories of the jungle and then toss a pair of dice simultaneously. The number on the black die indicates the victim, which is then removed. The number on the white die indicates the killer, so a new beast of the species of the killer (a new counter with the appropriate color) takes the territory of the victim.

In the first phase of the game, the population numbers of the two species show random fluctuations. But once all the territories are taken by the representatives of one species, the extinction of the other species is final. This game, invented by Eigen and Winkler, offers a model for the spontaneous breakdown of a symmetry. The initial state and the rules of the game are completely symmetric with respect to wolves and panthers. The ecosystem, however, is unstable and one is unable to predict which species will survive. Even if one takes five wolves and only one panther as initial state, it may turn out that the panthers become the surviving species. In the classroom the game can produce an excitement similar to the atmosphere of a casino!

This game relaxes the rigidity of the conclusion of the two previous games. Indeed, history plays a role in shaping the flora and the fauna of a given region. This may be how right-handed amino acids were eliminated in biochemical evolution. Now all living beings use only left-handed amino-acid molecules.

Behavioral Model Game: Research

A group of players take their seats around a table. One of them, designated as Nature, shuffles a deck of cards and distributes them among the players, who are designated Scientists. Each Scientist is dealt about a half-dozen cards by Nature. The game now begins. Nature lays a card face up at the center of the table and asks each Scientist to place his card on top in such a way that all earlier cards remain clearly visible. After each play of a card by a Scientist, Nature will call out "O.K." if the card put down by the Scientist is in accord with the particular "law" that Nature has selected but is keeping to Herself, or will say "Wrong" if the card played is not in accord with this law. In this latter case, the Scientist must take his card back. The Scientist who gets rid of all his cards first—i.e., who has acted in accordance with the law of Nature—will be proclaimed the winner. He then takes the role of Nature in the next game.

The game is made interesting by the fact that at the beginning the law is known only by Nature since, of course, Nature invented it before play started. As the game gets under way the Scientists pay close attention to the right and wrong plays and begin to make their private hunches as to what the law might be. As the empirical evidence, i.e., the sequence of the "right" cards, begins to pile up, each Scientist tries to make use of various analogies to guide him in his choice of cards to play. A failure forces a modification to his working hypothesis. When an experiment—playing a particular card—confirms the prediction, the Scientist tries to generalize the rule. Once a player discovers the law, each of his subsequent plays will be correct and the number of cards in his hand diminishes rapidly.

The law selected by Nature must, of course, be unambiguous. Moreover, should Nature be inconsistent at some point, she will be punished, for at the end of each game the players discuss the law that Nature selected and review the plays each of them made. True Nature never cheats! This game is more exciting if the law selected is relatively simple but not trivial. Thus, the law "Red card, black card, red card, black card. . ." is simple but too transparent. Everyone playing discovers the rule the first time around, and the excitement vanishes. On the other hand, if the law is so complicated that no one succeeds in figuring it out, the game also ceases to hold interest.

This game simulates scientific research in the same way chess simulates war. It introduces young people to the scientific attitude held in research. It also offers an excellent opportunity for the teacher to observe the different patterns of thinking among his pupils, identifying the conventional and the creative minds. Teenagers are usually better at this game than adults. Many of them dislike the game—they would prefer to watch football on their television! ☐

Bibliography

BAKANYI, FODOR, MARX, SARKADI, TÓTH, UJJ. *Fizika tankönyv és munkafüzet a gimnáziumok I. osztálya részére*, Tankönyvkiadó, Budapest, 1981. (Physics school book in Hungarian.)
BLACK, P. and J. OGBORN, *Nuffield Advanced Physics, Unit 10*, London: Longman, 1970.
EBISON, M. "Models in Science," *Physics Education*, Vol. 13, 1978, p. 267.
EIGEN, M. and R. WINKLER, *Das Spiel*, München: Piper, 1975.
GARDNER, M. "Mathematical Games," *Scientific American*, June 1959, October 1970, November 1970, February 1971, October 1977.
GEE, B. "Models as a Pedagogical Tool," *Physics Education*, Vol. 13, 1978, p. 287.
GURNEY, R.W. *Introduction to Statistical Physics*, New York: McGraw-Hill, 1949.
HAKEN, H. *Synergetics*, Berlin: Spinger, 1978.
HARRE, R. "Models in Science," *Physics Education*, Vol. 13, 1978, p. 275.
HESSE, M.B. "Models in Physics," *Brit. F. Phil. Sci.*, Vol. 4, 1956, p. 202.
KARPLUS, R. *Introductory Physics—a Model Approach*, New York: W.A. Benjamin, 1969.
———— *Models*, Berkeley, California: Rand McNally, 1971.
MARX, G. "Some Simulations of Science I–II," *Physics Education*, Vol. 15, 1981, p. 152.
MARX, G. and E. TÓTH, "Energie und Ordnung," In: G. Schaeffer (ed.), *Information und Ordnung*, Kiel: Inst. für Ped. der Naturw., 1981.
MAYNARD-SMITH, J. *Models in Ecology*, Cambridge: Cambridge University Press, 1978.
SAUER, G. "Playing the Quantum Shuffling Game," *Physics Education*, Vol. 16, 1981, p. 108.
STACHOWIAK, H. "Models," *Scientific Thought*, Paris: Unesco, 1972.
WENHAM, SNELL, TAYLOR. *Physics—Concepts and Models*, London: Addison-Wesley, 1972.

To delve more deeply

HEBENSTREIT, J. "Microcomputers in Secondary Education," In: E. Tagg (ed.), *Microcomputers in Secondary Education*, Amsterdam: North-Holland Publishing Company, 1980.
OSBORNE, A. *Models for Learning Mathematics*, Columbus: Ohio State University, 1976.

The neuroscientists who designed 2 million brain cells in a computer are making a revolutionary model of the mind and the world. A science journalist describes the work of Rodolfo Llinás and András Pellionisz at New York University and Donald Perkel at Stanford University.

Chapter 18

THE BRAIN BUILDERS*

Alissa Swerdloff

Nine years ago, a team of brain researchers decided that the best way to explore the function of the body's most complex organ was to try to "grow" a portion of the brain in a computer. That experiment, and the novel theory of brain function it spawned, may revolutionize neuroscience as thoroughly as the theory of relativity revolutionized physics. Scientists have produced plastic hearts and grown muscle cells in petri dishes, but could a simulated portion of the brain be grown in a computer? And would the brain's complex inner workings be better understood as a result? The task was gargantuan.

Two years and 2 million computer-generated "brain-cells" later, Drs. Rodolfo Llinás and András Pellionisz and their collaborator, Dr. Donald Perkel of Stanford University, succeeded in simulating a cerebellum, the part of the brain responsible for coordinating voluntary

---

Before turning to specialized journalism, Ms. Swerdloff worked at the neurobiological laboratory of Cornell University. She can be reached c/o Editor, *Science Digest*, 888 Seventh Avenue, New York, NY 10106.

movement. When the two New York University Medical Center scientists activated their creation, it responded with the kind of electrical patterns characteristic of the real thing. Remarked Llinás: "It's like building a bird out of bits of straw and saying, 'O.K., you look like a bird. Can you fly like a bird?' If it does fly like a bird, you have a very good model."

By studying the electrical activity of single brain cells in anesthetized animals or in brain slices or in isolated brains, scientists have become familiar with the structure of the cerebellum. They know that the cells in each cerebellar cortex lie stacked like plates. Researchers have also studied the way the cells communicate with one another across countless tiny junctions called synapses.

At the outset of their experiment, Llinás and Pellionisz—both experts on the cerebellum—knew all the parts of the region and felt they knew the properties of the parts. They also understood the range of services performed by this region of the brain. Just because you are familiar with the wheels and springs inside your watch and know the device tells time, however, doesn't mean you can build a working timepiece. The important thing is understanding the relationship between structure and function.

The human cerebellum is made up of 100 billion nerve cells, the neurons, or as many cells as there are stars in the Milky Way. These cells communicate via a network of a million billion internerve connections, or synapses.

The central neurons of the cerebellum are slender in one dimension, thick in the other two and are about 400 millionths of a meter in diameter. They look a bit like microscopic trees, with numerous branchlike projections called dendrites that grow from one end of the cell. At the other end, a single branch emanates from the cell's body. This long central stem, or axon, transmits the signals gathered by the dendrites to other nerve cells.

Each neuron is capable of receiving chemical signals through the synapse and transmitting them electrically along its axon to the synapse at the other end. There the signal is reconverted into packets of chemical messenger that move across to the next cell and trigger it.

Without the cerebellum, animals are unable to perform coordinated movements. Humans who suffer cerebellar damage develop tremors and have difficulty performing the simplest motor tasks, such as touching the nose.

Whereas real brains are made of nerve cells, blood vessels and supporting tissue, computer brains need a different sort of building material. To program neurons into the computer, Pellionisz and Llinás equipped their machine with both a microscope and a TV camera and instructed it to examine and memorize the forms of hundreds of real neurons from various locations in the cerebellum.

The computer recorded the exact shape of each cell: the length of its axon, the number of branches, the interbranch distance, the angles of branching. It compiled information about what a computer-generated nerve cell might look like and compounded the data into a neuron-shaped probability cloud that could serve as a template for generating hypothetical neurons.

As instructed by Llinás, Pellionisz and Perkel, the computer then created hundreds of thousands of neurons, each slightly different from the next. Governed by the knowledge that certain types of cells occur in certain layers of the cerebellum and that each part of the cerebellum has its parallel neurons oriented in a particular direction, each cell was assigned to an appropriate layer and oriented.

Neuron Stimulation

To make the computer cerebellum complete, the researchers programmed each neuron with the ability to stimulate any other neuron it touched. Thus, when the computer laid down the cells, each point of intercellular contact became a synapse.

In a real brain, there is simply not enough information in the genes to tell each neuron exactly where to send its fibers and exactly where synapses should be. Instead Pellionisz and Llinás believe brain cells grow toward a neighborhood rather than an exact address and simply synapse with the cells they happen to touch. They feel, therefore, that their method of computer brain construction probably mimics real neuron growth.

The uniqueness of the experiments becomes apparent when one realizes that all the computer synapses were determined by randomly generated variations in the cells' branching fibers. Other points of synapse would have presumably served as well. The simulation suggests that our wonderfully capable cerebellum—which enables us to walk, to ski or to write—depends on millions of locally *random* connections. *Exact* connectivity is not necessary.

When their computer cerebellum was completed, it was the largest simulation of a brain ever made, containing nearly 2 million nerve cells, roughly the same number as in a frog cerebellum. In an additional experiment, the two scientists attached a computer simulation of a human arm to another computer version of a cerebellum and instructed it to copy the letters *OK*.

When the command was channeled through the cerebellum, the arm wrote *OK* in nice, neat script. If the same instructions were sent directly to the arm without benefit of transformation by the cerebellum, the arm developed a tremor and produced a jerky, disorganized version of the letters—just the kind of *OK* that a person with cerebellar damage would construct.

Throughout the twentieth century, the brain has been compared to a sophisticated machine. People now say the brain is like a living computer, remarks Pellionisz. Before computers, they said it was like a radio—or a telegraph—or whatever was the top technology at the time. In all machines, the sequence of connections is vital. To draw an analogy between brain and machine function, researchers have proposed that the nervous system transmits encoded information along linked chains of nerves to a point in the brain where it is received and decoded. You see an orange, and its code signal travels down your neural pathways.

The success of the Llinás-Pellionisz simulation militates against the brain-as-machine theory. If the brain mimics a machine, its specific wiring pattern would be crucial; an improperly wired computer is no computer at all. But the brain simulation demonstrates that parallel neurons can be wired together with a great deal of variation—nothing like a mechanical device. If a machine could work on this principle, the transistors, capacitors and resistors of a stereo could be wired up in a sloppy fashion—and music would flow.

Triggering Images

But if the brain does not work like a machine, how does it work? Based on their simulation, Llinás and Pellionisz propose that information reaches the brain as the result not of a chain of transmission but of the *pattern* of nerve activity created by hundreds of thousands of parallel fibers firing simultaneously. Because each neuron is slightly different from the next, it experiences its own version of an object or event. Each fiber therefore fires off nerve impulses at its own particular frequency. The pattern of transmission—that is, which cells are firing and at what rate—produces the internal image we call a thought.

The situation is a little like having a large number of witnesses to a car crash. Each viewer sees the event from his own perspective, but the incident can be reconstructed fairly accurately from the consensus of all the witnesses.

Our perception of a jet plane, for example—its size, color, shape, sound, number of engines, etc.—sets off certain neurons at certain rates.

The entire array of stimulation means *jet* to the brain. And since there are millions of neurons, an almost infinite variety of patterns is possible, each corresponding to a unique object or situation in the outside world.

Llinás uses the analogy of a color TV screen to demonstrate that the mind routinely resolves discrete signals into the perception of a whole object. A color TV screen is composed of thousands of little dots—some red, some blue, some green, some brighter than others—and each fires differently from its neighbors. But when you look at the *Tonight Show,* you don't see the dots—you see Johnny Carson.

If you hold an apple in your hand, you know its position, size, shape, color, texture, hardness, aroma and temperature simultaneously. These dimensions are perceived all at once and seem to mix together; the experience has a unity to it that we call *apple.*

In scientific terms, Pellionisz and Llinás would say that every human being has inside his head an n-dimensional hyperspace, that is, a nerve network that can accommodate an almost infinite variety of different patterns, each corresponding to unique objects or events in the world. This rather cosmic-sounding entity has given the researchers a tool for organizing the thousands of simultaneous nerve firings that accompany perception.

Einstein postulated a four-dimensional hyperspace, a model of the universe that consisted of the three dimensions of physical space—length, width and height—plus a fourth, time. But hyperspace can have any number of dimensions above three. Indeed, if time can be considered a dimension, why not redness? Or hardness? Or temperature? Or any of an infinite number of other qualities?

Why not? Probably because we are trapped by our own preconceptions. We have always thought of dimension in terms of length, width and height. When we want to graph something, we think of three axes: x (left and right), y (up and down), and z (front and back).

Now, try to free yourself from the constraints of three or even four dimensions. Imagine hundreds, even thousands of axes on the graph paper—one for redness, one for suppleness, one for fluffiness and so on. Along each axis, a particular quality can be described on a scale of 1 through 10. An orange juggler's ball at the top of its trajectory will have position values—x, y, z—but it will also have values for orangeness (say 10), hardness (say, 4), temperature (say, 5) and a host of other qualities. Somewhere in n-dimensional hyperspace is a point whose coordinates are these numbers—and that point represents precisely this ball.

Theory Outruns Experiment

In simplified fashion, the concept of a hyperspace—the so-called Tensor Network theory of brain function—works like this: each neuron is considered a dimension, and the number of times it fires is thought of as units along that dimension. Just as the theoretical values associated with a juggler's ball can be made to correspond to a single point in hyperspace, so too can the neuron-firing values produced by any stimulus.

With a little abstract geometry, the activity in hundreds of thousands of parallel nerve fibers can be reduced to one point, called a vector. An apple would create a unique firing pattern, which would reduce to a different point in n-dimensional space—an apple vector. An orange would create an orange vector.

Actions as well as perceptions can be explained in terms of neuron-firing patterns. You want to sneeze and you also want to scratch. The sneeze, of course, takes precedence. According to Llinás and Pellionisz, your choice depends on the fact that the sneeze involves so many neurons firing simultaneously that it's almost like a small epileptic discharge.

By far the most elegant and useful aspect of the hyperspace brain model is that it proposes a method for converting intention into action. Leonardo da Vinci sees Mona Lisa and decides to paint her. But how can he organize the thousands of muscle cells in his arms and hands to reproduce the image of his model? Vectors in brain hyperspace may hold the key.

Vectors are geometrical entities that can be mathematically translated from one frame of reference to another. The process is called transformation. Llinás and Pellionisz feel that the brain may be adept at such calculation and could readily transform Leonardo's perception vectors into the action vectors required to paint the portrait. Signals come in, informing the brain of Mona Lisa's appearance; signals go out, telling the joints and muscles of Leonardo's arm and hands how to reproduce her face.

But does the brain actually read nerve-firing patterns and translate them into action? The best test of the theory would be to record real nerve impulses in hundreds of fibers entering the cerebellum and then record the impulses in another set of nerve cells leaving the cerebellum. The computer could then combine these values so that a mathematician could tell whether the outgoing signals represented a transformed version of the incoming data. Here, unfortunately, we are approaching the limits of modern technology: Pellionisz and Llinás have already completed designs for a device capable of simultaneously recording large numbers of individual neurons, but for the moment, theory has outrun the possibility of experimental validation.

Undoubtedly, the proof (or disproof) will come someday. If this new model of brain function is validated, it will be of interest to philosophers as well as scientists. We may have to alter the way we view ourselves, our consciousness—our very being.

Internal Universe

According to Llinás, the ability to close our eyes and construct a perfect image of an orange suggests the existence of an internal universe. We create at will the firing pattern that means *orange*.

In fact, the two scientists feel that we may be born with a tentative model of the world already programmed into our brains. Other animals, they note, seem to be wired to recognize those structures of the universe that will be important for their survival. The nerve-firing patterns caused by various objects—apples, oranges or sports cars—merely turn on the appropriate portions of the internal world. In a strict sense, no fundamental information passes into the brain, and very deeply, we learn only what we already know, says Llinás.

At least some of man's knowledge and ability is probably preprogrammed as well. Human infants are born with the ability to pronounce all phonemes, the sound components of language. They can even pronounce the phonemes of languages foreign to their place of birth. German babies can easily pronounce the *th* sound of English, and English infants can pronounce the rolled *r* of Spanish. (A child starts to lose this ability at about six months, when it begins to specialize in a particular language.)

Perceptual Wiring

How extensive is this innate wiring? It depends on the creature. A chick's perceptual abilities are largely predetermined, with some small ability to learn. Human preprogramming is much less extensive—but we seem to be wired to some extent. Says Llinás: You will recognize those patterns that form part of your perceptual library; you will recognize the colors that you have evolved to be able to recognize.

We utilize this inner universe to great advantage. By mentally mobilizing our props, we can monitor or experiment with behavior and predict the outcome of our actions. As Llinás puts it: You hunt your bear many times before actually trying it on the outside. In this way you can find out what you need. You can even project yourself into the bear. . . . The hunter can become his prey. The brain is a most versatile part of man.

But is the brain simply a part of man? Or is man, perhaps, part of the brain? If the brain contains a model of the universe, then in a sense it must be far more than the self. The *I* is only one pattern that the brain generates.

The *I* is an important pattern, no doubt. In order to survive, you know that you are a particular kind of beast with particular competitors and certain nutritional needs. Nevertheless, the *I* disappears when you sleep—but the brain hums on. It is busy producing the many other patterns of which the conscious *I* is unaware, patterns that lie outside the small portion of reality we inhabit on this Earth.

Ironically, the metaphysical speculation that grew out of the computer cerebellum experiment suggests that a full computer brain may be an impossibility. A computer can utilize only the information that man can arrange to have programmed in.

According to Llinás, we are the music that the brain's instruments, the neurons, create. Each neuron plays it own notes, and together they play the tune called man. When they die, we die. Even in life, they do not always perform the symphony of consciousness. At night we dream, and they move on to other songs.   □

This is a chapter for the brave. Quantum theory explains the power-house of the sun, the explosive power of the atom and the workings of modern electronics. It remains, for most people, a closed book—because it is a difficult theory to understand. This is an attempt to make it comprehensible.

Chapter 19

QUANTUM PHYSICS: THE POWER AND MYSTERY

OF THE SUBATOMIC WORLD

the Editors of *The Economist*

Fifty years ago a revolution shook the foundations of physical science. Under the cryptic name of "quantum mechanics," it swept away many cherished beliefs about the nature of space, time and matter and put in their place concepts that were profoundly baffling, even disturbing. However odd, the new ideas worked.

Today, quantum mechanics is the foundation stone of modern physics; scarcely a topic is left untouched by it. On an understanding of quantum mechanics are based lasers, the electron microscope and the frontiers of microelectronics. Yet few people outside the world of the professional scientist know of the quantum revolution, or appreciate the huge impact it has had on science and technology.

The original text of this chapter appeared in the science and technology columns of *The Economist* of London, 3 April 1982. As in the case of almost all material appearing in this distinguished weekly journal, the authors remain anonymous. Reproduction by permission of The Economist Newspaper Limited, 25 St. James's Street, London SW1A 1HG, United Kingdom.

This utter ignorance is curious. After all, most people have heard of Einstein's theory of relativity—even if their conception of it may be very hazy. And the two revolutions—relativity and quantum mechanics—happened much at the same time. Einstein himself was involved in both. Probably there are two explanations of why quantum mechanics has remained locked away from laymen. One is simply that it deals with the subatomic world; quantum effects rarely obtrude in any significant way into the everyday, macroscopic world people inhabit. The second reason is more fundamental. Quantum physics is hard to grasp.

All theories of physics tend to be expressed in mathematical equations rather than in words or pictures. For physicists, that precision is part of their beauty. As it happens, quantum mechanics is a mathematical theory par excellence. As one American physicist has put it, quantum mechanics has no "imaginative conception." Indeed, most quantum physicists would argue that the theory simply cannot be understood without its math; the concepts and the mathematical rules 'are one and inseparable. Try to explain the concepts without the math and you will distort the theory.

We have decided to ignore that warning. It seems wrong that a theory that has already become an ordinary working tool for people who work on things like micro-electronics and superfast computers should remain a closed book to the laymen whose lives are already being transformed by its products. So the rest of this article will attempt to open the book—to explain how the quantum revolution happened, what its basic concepts say, and how it is being applied. Finally, it will have the temerity to point out some of the weaknesses of the theory.

The Beginning

Quantum mechanics is a twentieth-century science largely because the world it was born to explain, the subatomic world, was not discovered much before; the electron was discovered only in the 1890s. Confronted with the structure of an atom—a heavy nucleus with light-weight electrons whirling about it—scientists set out to describe how such a structure worked.

Their first instinct, naturally enough, was to assume that an atom differed from other matter only in scale, and to try to apply to the atom the same physical rules that worked so well in the macroscopic world. The obvious analogy to the structure of an atom was that of the solar system—with the sun playing the role of the atom's nucleus, and the planets the role of its electrons.

It seemed neat. The electrons were attracted to the nucleus by electrical forces; they escaped being sucked right into it by circling around very fast, so balancing the electrical attraction with their outward centrifugal force.

Unfortunately, it soon became apparent that this tidy model did not work, The stumbling block was light. As physicists of the time were aware, an electron whirling around in an atom gives off light. This fact threw two wrenches into the mini-solar-system model of the atom.

As anybody who has ever played with a prism knows, light waves of different wavelengths (or frequencies) have different characteristic colors. (The prism separates the jumble of waves that make up white light into its component frequencies, to yield the rainbow.) Now, an electron whirling around a nucleus will emit light of a certain frequency, the frequency depending on how close it is to the nucleus.

Suppose you had a quantity of hot, hydrogen gas, each atom of which has only a single electron orbiting its nucleus. The atoms in a hot gas are all rushing around and banging into each other. With all that knocking about, you would expect some atoms to pick up energy, and in these atoms the electrons would be able to whirl out to larger orbits around the nuclei. In others, the electrons would lose energy and spiral in closer to the nuclei.

In short, you would expect to find electrons in a whole range of orbits, emitting light in a whole range of frequencies. So, if you passed the light being emitted by your collection of atoms through a spectroscope (a prism device), you would expect to see a smear of rainbow colors. Right?

Wrong, as it turns out. Instead of a continuous range of frequencies (colors), certain sharply defined frequencies appear. (In the diagram they look like sharp lines.) Classical physicists could not work out why.

■■ ■■■■■■■■■ ■■■■■ ■■ ■■ ■ ▮▮▮ ▮▮▮▮ ■■

The second problem was even worse. If electrons whirling around a nucleus emit light, that means they are constantly losing energy. (Light is a form of electromagnetic energy.) If an electron is losing energy, it spirals closer to the nucleus, so begins to rotate faster. But if it rotates faster, the light it emits will be more energetic (with a higher frequency)—so it will be losing even more energy and so have to rotate still faster. And so on.

Classical phyicists soon realized that their mini-solar-system version of the atom had problems. It could not explain how electrons avoided spiraling inexorably inwards, causing the atom to collapse on itself.

In 1913, the Danish physicist, Niels Bohr, proposed an ingenious solution to the problem. He suggested that the electrons orbiting a nucleus operated under certain constraints: they were confined to a certain number of orbits and could "jump" from one allowed orbit to another only by emitting (or absorbing) a discrete lump of energy. The classical idea that energy was a continuum—and could always be divided into smaller and smaller amounts—would not do. As had been suggested by the German physicist Max Planck (and demonstrated by Einstein in explaining the photo-electric effect), energy was lumpy.

Once in an allowed orbit, the electron would not radiate energy at all. It would do so only when it jumped from one orbit to a lower one. And then it would not emit just any amount of light but discrete packages containing a certain quantity of energy. The packages are called "quanta," and the quanta of light are known as photons.

The energy a photon of light packs is proportional to the frequency of the light. (Red light, which is a low-frequency light, has less energetic photons than blue, high-frequency light.) Every time an electron jumped from one orbit to another, it would emit a photon of a particular energy (light of a particular frequency). Bohr's picture of the atom neatly explained the puzzling light spectrum of hydrogen. That lent it credence.

Still, the Bohr picture was hard to accept. As we have seen, the notion that electromagnetic waves of energy (heat, light) are "grainy," that the energy in the waves comes in discrete packages, had already been proposed. But Bohr was the first successfully to ascribe quantum behavior to subatomic particles of matter.

Many physicists at the time were uneasy. The way in which Bohr assigned the allowed orbits of electrons appeared essentially ad hoc. Bohr's theory was not a mechanical theory: it had no rules of mechanics, no laws of motion as does Newtonian mechanics. It gave no explanation for why electrons were fixed in certain orbits.

Bohr's picture of the atom was clearly better than the classical one. It worked better; it explained more. However, it became increasingly clear that there was a lot that it did not explain. Many physicists felt that it could not be the last word.

And so it proved. Bohr was only halfway there. The ad hoc rules Bohr (and others) used to assign quantum values to various physical parameters, like energy, came to be known as the "old quantum physics." It merely set the stage for modern quantum mechanics.

The New Era

Modern quantum mechanics burst upon the scientific world in the mid-1920s. It was largely the brainchild of two men, initially working quite independently: the Austrian physicist Erwin Schrödinger and the German physicist Werner Heisenberg. It appeared in the form of abstruse equations: an American physicist, who early on tackled a Schrödinger equation, called it "hostile-looking." From the math flowed weird new notions.

The guts of the theory can be summarized in three propositions:

- *In the subatomic world, few things can be predicted with 100 percent precision.* Accurate predictions can, however, be made about the probability of any particular outcome. The decay of radioactive particles illustrates the point. Just as an insurance actuary can tell you the average expected lifetime of a child born in Britain today, so a quantum physicist can tell you what the average lifetime of a group of radioactive particles will be. But just as the actuary cannot say when any particular person will die, nor can the physicist tell you when one particular radioactive particle will decay.

- You have to work with probabilities rather than certainties in the subatomic world because *you can never accurately describe all aspects of a subatomic particle at once.* You can measure, say, the location of an electron at a certain instant; or you can decide instead to measure its motion; you cannot do both at the same time. (Why, we shall see later.)

  This means that you cannot, as you can for a billiard ball, describe the exact pathway a subatomic particle will take. In fact, it is meaningless to think of a subatomic particle following a precise pathway at all. It is not just a scaled-down billiard ball. It behaves very differently. The entire conceptual structure used by quantum mechanics to describe its behavior is quite alien to that of Newtonian mechanics.

- As we have seen, scientists had already realized that electromagnetic energy (light, heat) does not always behave like a continuous wave. Instead, it is "grainy"; energy can be transfered only in quantum packages. Light therefore has a dual character. Although it may display wavelike aspects under some circumstances, it may also have some of the characteristics of particles. Quantum mechanics maintains that this duality is true of matter too. *Just as lightwaves have certain particle-like characteristics, so particles have certain wave-like characteristics.*

It is important to be clear about this last point. Quantum mechanics does not say that particles are waves nor even that they bob up and down on some sort of physical wave, like a cork on water. It says that particles can behave like waves—they move according to wavelike principles.

The waves are not waves of any substance, but are probability waves. They can be described in an abstract way by a mathematical equation, the solution of which enables precise predictions of relative probabilities to be made. (A rough analogy is a crime wave; if you say a crime wave has hit a neighborhood, what you are really saying is that the probability of a crime being committed is now higher in that area.)

The quantum-mechanical description of an atom is therefore different from Bohr's. Using the principles of quantum mechanics, you can work out a wave equation for each electron orbiting the nucleus. The points of greatest amplitude (or strength) of the waves tell you where your electrons are most likely to be found. As it turned out, for the hydrogen atom, these points of maximum probability roughly coincided with the locations of Bohr's allowed orbits. Which is why Bohr's approximate picture worked reasonably well.

The notion of particles behaving like waves seems bizarre. Yet an electron microscope depends on the fact. It operates just like an ordinary microscope but uses electrons rather than lightwaves.

Important effects flow from the wavelike behavior of particles. For one thing, the waves can interfere with one another. They can experience the same behavior as do criss-crossing waves of light or water. Find that hard to believe? Consider the following experiment.

Suppose you had a screen with two small slits in it and on one side of the screen, an electron gun and, on the other side, some sort of detector that would register the arrival of any electrons that passed through either of the slits. Electrons that did manage to pass through one of the slits would spread out on the other side, like pellets from a shotgun.

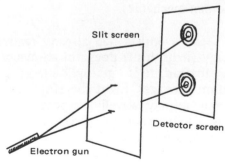

Suppose that you first closed one of the slits, shot electrons at it and recorded where they turned up on your detector. Most of the electrons that got through would wind up more or less opposite the open slit (bang on target) but some would stray further afield. If you took a piece of graph paper and plotted the distribution of electrons, you would get a curve that looked something like line (a) our chart:

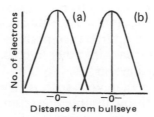

Distance from bullseye

If you then closed the first slit, opened the second and repeated the procedure, you would get a plot like line (b) our chart. If you had both slits open at once, you might expect to get a result that was the sum of the two previous ones—a plot that looked like this:

In fact, you would get something that looked completely different. It would look like this:

It is a pattern that scientists see often enough. It arises from the wave-like behavior of the electrons, and is the typical pattern thrown up by waves that interfere with one another.

To understand, envisage a quiet pond into which two stones are thrown simultaneously. Each stone will set up a radiating ring of ripples around it. And, where the ripples from the two stones meet, you will see a distinct pattern of peaks and troughs on the surface of the pond.

The pattern arises because where the peaks of the ripples from one stone coincide with the peaks of the ripples from the other, the disturbance of the water is enhanced while, where peaks and troughs meet, the disturbance is dampened. In the experiment described above, the two slits are the equivalent of the two stones. And the beams of electrons passing through them create the same pattern of wave interference as do the ripples of the water on the pond.

Of course, any individual electron can pass only through one slit of the experimental apparatus and arrive only at one point on the detector screen. You see the wave interference pattern by recording the arrival of many different electrons—in other words, by superimposing the results of many individual events.

The curious point is that you do not have to shoot off a lot of electrons all at once to throw up the interference pattern. You can turn your electron gun right down—so that it releases only one electron at a time. So long as both slits are open—and only if both slits are open—you will still get the pattern showing up. This implies that each electron, proceeding—on its own towards the slits, does not have a well-defined path—and somehow manages to probe both slits at once.

This is an uncomfortable way of looking at things. Quantum physics is full of such uncomfortable concepts. Yet—as in the two-slits instance—the ideas are consistent with the results of experiments.

Intrinsic Uncertainty

The notion that particles behave in a wave-like manner is hard enough to get used to. Many scientists (among them Einstein) were more upset by the assertion of quantum mechanics that there is an intrinsic uncertainty in nature—that it is meaningless to try to ascribe a precise path that a particle will follow in the way that you can say what path the earth will follow around the sun. The notion that a particle had to be viewed as following a number of potential paths was abhorrent.

Surely, these scientists argued, uncertainty does not have to be intrinsic. It could merely be the result of ignorance about all the relevant factors involved. In practice, you cannot usually predict the winner of a horse race. But, in theory, if you had all the necessary data (on the course, the metabolism of the horses and so on), you could predict the outcome of the race.

Pie in the sky, retort the quantum men. There are fundamental limits on what you can ever know about a subatomic particle. These limits will not go away, however clever your technology becomes. The key to the problem is very simple. It is size.

If you look at a billiard ball on a table you can "see" exactly where it is, because its presence disturbs the pattern of lightwaves impinging on it—and your retina and brain register the disturbance. The ball disturbs the waves because it is big enough to do so. The distance between two troughs in a lightwave is minuscule by comparison. So the lightwave cannot just lap right over the ball.

Furthermore, although light packs energy and so gives the ball a "kick" when it hits it, the amount of energy is so small compared with the mass of the ball that it is utterly insignificant. It can be ignored.

It is quite otherwise with an electron, which is so tiny as to be literally next to nothing. Light, which has a relatively long wavelength (a big gap between succeeding thoughts), could lap over a collection of electrons without much disturbance.

Of course, one could use a probe with a shorter wavelength—e.g., gamma rays—to try to "see" the electron. Snag: a wave with a shorter wavelength has a higher frequency and, as we noted above, that means it is more energetic. It packs a bigger punch—indeed, one that is thousands of times greater than that of light.

Hit an electron with a gamma ray and you will learn where it is at that instant. But, in the process, you will knock the particle wildly off course in an unpredictable way. So once you measure the location of the electron, you are not able to say what its motion is. You could decide to measure its initial momentum instead (using a different technique) but the same sort of problems would ensue. In measuring its motion, you would lose information about its location.

There are other trade-offs. Suppose you wanted to measure the energy of a photon. As we have seen, photons of a certain energy correspond to light of a certain frequency. So you can measure the energy of a photon by counting the number of peaks and troughs of the lightwave with which it is associated. This takes time—at a minimum, time enough for two peaks (or two troughs) to pass through your detector.

This imposes a fundamental limitation on the accuracy with which you can measure the energy of a photon in a given interval of time. If the time interval is less than one cycle of the wave, the energy is indeterminate. Only if the time interval allows you to record several cycles, will the energy measurement be accurate.

If you wanted to know, say, the precise moment when a photon of a certain energy was emitted, you would be stuck. There is a trade-off between the accuracy with which you can determine the energy involved in an event and the precise time at which the event occurs. This is more important than it sounds. It lies at the root of an effect that would never be predicted by classical physics, but which is very important to modern electronics, tunneling.

Quantum physics tells you that, confronted with a barrier (e.g., a thin film of insulation), some electrons will manage to pop up on the other side of it—even though, according to classical calculations, they do not have sufficient energy to do so.

There is a fuzziness about the subatomic world quite unparalleled in daily experience.

The Golden Age

Physicists look back on the late 1920s and early 1930s with a mixture of awe and nostalgia, for that was truly the golden age of physics. Discoveries flowed from the new quantum mechanics like water from a burst dam.

The British physicist, Professor Paul Dirac, made refinements to the maths to bring quantum mechanics into line with certain aspects of Einstein's theory of relativity, providing a description of electrons moving at close to the speed of light. Dirac's work showed that electrons possess an intrinsic "spin," an idea which helped to explain their behavior when immersed in electric or magnetic fields. Most exciting of all, Dirac was able to predict the existence of antimatter.

Increasingly, experimental evidence confirmed the correctness of quantum assumptions. New particles were predicted—and found—that demonstrated the same duality as electrons, having wave-like behavior. Many new properties of atoms were shown to display quantum characteristics. The nature of the forces that bind atoms into molecules—the basis of chemistry—was explained.

As the rules of quantum mechanics began to be applied to the very heart of atoms, to their nuclei as well as their electrons, scientists began to unravel the secrets of nuclear reactions. Applications of the theory came thick and fast. The conduction of electricity in solids, radioactivity, the behavior of materials cooled to close to absolute zero, the energy source of stars—all began to yield to the powerful new tool. Above all, the huge energies locked up in nuclear power were revealed.

Clearly, quantum mechanics can be applied in ways that have a big impact on the macro-world—destructive in the case of a nuclear bomb, constructive in the case of nuclear power. Yet, unharnessed, quantum effects do not seem to obtrude in the everyday world at all. Objects are well-defined, not fuzzy, and behave in apparently predictable ways.

At first blush, this seems odd. After all, macro-objects are made up of micro ones, atoms and their constituent particles. If the subatomic world is jerky and discontinuous, how is it that the macro-world seems smooth and continuous?

In fact, quantum effects do operate at the macro-level. You could apply quantum-mechanical rules to the motion of a billiard ball. It is just that it is not worth the bother. The answers you would get from the quantum equations would be virtually the same as those yielded by simpler, classical rules.

This is because the discontinuities—the quanta—that modulate matter are extraordinarily small. They are rather like the dots that you could envisage as making up a newspaper picture. Work out the photons emitted per second by a domestic lightbulb and you would come up with a number on the order of 100 billion billion. Small wonder that, if you are working with domestic lighting, you can treat the lightwave as continuous—rather than, so to speak, counting the dots in the picture. Scaled up, quantum effects are submerged.

Not always, however. There is one macro-window onto quantum effects. It is a temperature window. When cooled to temperatures just above absolute zero (-273°C), certain materials become superconductors—an elecric current can flow through them, undiminished, virtually forever, meeting no resistance.

This is a quantum effect writ large. And it is at the frontiers of R and D now being done into superfast computers by companies like IBM and AT&T. Central to this work is a device that is known as a squid—which is short for superconducting quantum interference device.

Quantum Electronics

Just as vacuum tubes were the basis of yesterday's computers while transistors and other semiconductor devices are the basis of today's, so superconducting squids could be the basis of tomorrow's. The aim is to produce computers capable of operating at least 10-25 times faster than now. Or capable of doing 10-25 times as much work in the same amount of time. That means reducing the time they will take to do one operation from a range of 12 to 50 nanoseconds to just one. That is phenomenally fast: a nanosecond is a mere billionth of a second.

How to get such speeds? Two basic factors determine the rapidity with which a computer can crunch numbers. One is how quickly its switches—the circuits that handle the noughts and ones of machine language—can be flipped on and off. The other is how long it takes a signal to travel from one circuit to another.

If you want your computer to be able to handle a bit of data within a nanosecond, no signal path can be much longer than 15 centimetres, because that is roughly the distance an electrical signal can travel in a billionth of a second. So your computer will have to be tiny. Snag: it may need a few million circuit elements to do its job. How can you get that many circuits into a glorified shoebox?

Getting them small enough is the least of the problems. The real headache is that high-speed semiconductor devices give off a lot of heat. Crowd a few million of them into a small space and your computer could literally melt.

Squids—and the so-called Josephson junctions they link together— are one possible solution to the problems. They are by no means the only possible solution. Using chips based on gallium arsenide instead of silicon, the Japanese electronics company Fujitsu thinks it can develop a rival computer that would work as fast—and at higher temperatures— than one based on superconducting devices. Yet another approach would be to use, e.g., a laser beam to make ultra-fast optical switches.

At present, however, work on computers based on superconducting devices is farther ahead. There are problems. Josephson junctions are fragile and a computer based on them would itself have to be kept at temperatures close to minus 273°C. But IBM is undaunted.

Why? Computer switches based on superconducting devices are not only fast—they can flick on and off in just 13 trillionths of a second. They also consume little power—so little that a computer using several million such circuit elements would give off only a few watts of heat.

The ability of squids and Josephson junctions to operate speedily with little power depends on two phenomena of quantum mechanics: the ability of some materials to lose all resistance to a flow of electrons (to become superconductors) and the "tunneling" of electrons through an insulating barrier. A Josephson junction comprises two superconductors linked by a thin insulating barrier. A standard squid is a circuit linking two or more such junctions.

The phenomenon of superconductivity was first observed back in 1911, but remained an unsolved mystery until 1957, when three American physicists worked out its quantum-mechanical nature. The work that opened the door to its exploitation in microelectronics came only with the 1960s. And, even now, the phenomenon is not completely understood.

For example, it remains impossible to predict theoretically which materials will act as superconductors at achievable temperatures (copper will not.) Nor is there any explanation of the fact that certain elements are superconductors only when under high pressures or in thin films. Still, quantum physicists have come up with a useful explanation of what happens when a material does become superconducting.

An ordinary electric current in, e.g., a copper wire, is simply a stream of individual electrons. And resistance to the current arises from collisions between the electrons and metal atoms in the wire. According to quantum theory, the electrons propagate through the metal in the fashion of a wave, scattering round the metal atoms like an ocean swell meeting an oil rig. A well-ordered metal (one whose atoms are arranged in a neat lattice) will be a better conductor than a disordered one. Even so, the agitation of the atoms of the lattice caused by heat and, also, the presence of impurities will impede the electrons' flow.

Now, to the extent that the problem is caused by heat, you would expect electrical resistance to decline with temperature. And, generally, this is so. But the phenomenon of superconductivity is by no means so simple. A superconductor differs from an ordinary conductor in the very mechanism of current flow.

A clue to the quantum nature of superconductivity lies in its onset. Cool a material like lead or niobium and its electrical resistance will fall off gradually—until a certain threshold temperature is reached (typically a few degrees above minus 273°C). At that point, all its remaining resistance will disappear quite suddenly. It will make a sort of quantum "jump" from a state of having a small resistance to one of having none. Why should this happen? The answer given by quantum mechanics is a surprising one—and needs a bit of explanation. In understanding the picture that emerges, it may help to keep a military analogy in mind. Electrons trying to barge through an ordinary conductor are rather like an undisciplined rabble of troops, operating with little intelligence of the enemy (the atoms in the lattice fortress of the conductor.) Electrons moving through a superconductor are, by contrast, highly disciplined. Moreover, they get some active co-operation from the lattice atoms. At extremely low temperatures, it seems, electrons and lattice atoms fraternize.

Begin with the electrons. Below the threshold temperature at which a material suddenly becomes superconducting, it turns out that electrons flowing through it no longer act only singly. Instead, they act in pairs. And the motion of these pairs is highly coherent. If you considered each pair as a single entity, you would find that each marched at exactly the same pace as all the others. (Physicists say that the centre of mass of each pair has exactly the same momentum.)

Now, according to quantum theory, the advancing electron pairs move along like waves. And, in this, too, they show discipline. Because the momentum of each pair is the same as that of every other, the waves all have the same velocity, the same wavelength and are in phase (their peaks and troughs rising and falling together.) The electron waves of a supercurrent march to step, coherently, like the light waves produced by a laser.

Nor is that all. The advancing electron pairs seem to know exactly how to avoid confrontations with the atoms in the lattice of the superconductor. In fact, this apparent "sixth sense" is not so odd. The "glue" that binds the electron pairs together is itself a result of subtle interactions between the charges of the electrons and those of the atoms of the lattice: the passing electrons produce an electric distortion of the lattice's shape.

A good analogy is a ball rolling on a rubber sheet, slightly depressing it. The depression will tend to pull another ball into the dip and so "bind" the two balls loosely together. In the case of the sheet, the distortion is produced by the gravitational force of the balls. Replace the sheet by the lattice and gravity by electricity and you can understand what is happening in the superconductor.

The upshot is that the electron waves move through the lattice without colliding with it. Presto: there is no resistance to their flow. Set up a small current in a superconducting loop, take the initial source away and the current already in the loop will continue to flow.

These paired-electron waves have two other interesting quantum properties. First, they can pass right through a thin insulating barrier: they show the "tunneling" behavior mentioned earlier. Second, because the "glue" binding each electron pair together is weak, a supercurrent can readily be switched off.

If you had a device consisting of two superconductors linked together by a thin film of insulation, set up a supercurrent that tunneled through the insulating junction and then applied a sufficient magnetic field at the junction, you would switch off the supercurrent. Your junction would no longer have zero resistance—and a voltage would suddenly appear across it. As the diagram shows, the superconducting state could be made to represent a binary "0" and the resistive state a binary "1". (Still more bizarre effects—the conversion of your initial direct current into a high-frequency alternating one—can be achieved by applying a weaker magnetic field at the junction.)

The way such a device would behave was first predicted by Professor Brian Josephson in 1962, when he was still a graduate student at Cambridge in England. His predictions were confirmed a year later by workers at Bell Labs in America. Now Josephson junctions form the guts of what IBM hopes will be the first of tomorrow's superfast computers.

Devices based on Josephson junctions can not only make switches but can also be used for computer memory functions. As IBM's Dr. Juri Matisoo put it in the journal *Scientific American:*

The quantum-mechanical nature of superconductivity provides a natural mechanism for the storage of digital information. If a current is established in a loop of a superconductor, it generates a magnetic field that passes through the center of the loop. . . . The magnitude of the field and of the current are quantized—that is, they can assume only certain discrete values and if they change, they do so only by jumping from one allowed value to another. What is more, both the current and the field are persistent. . . . Information can be stored in such loops by letting one quantized state correspond to a binary 1 and letting a different state represent a 0.

Figure 1.   A simple Josephson switch.

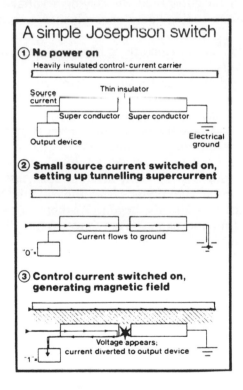

Nor are computers the only application of superconducting electronics. Exquisitely sensitive divices for detecting tiny changes in magnetic fields are already on the market. Based on squids, they are so sensitive they can register changes caused by the beat of a heart or a signal in the brain. Many other applications are in the laboratory.

One promising substitute for radar is a device known as a passive millimeter-wave imager. This detects a target not by bouncing a signal off an object but by picking up weak electromagnetic radiation emitted naturally by the object itself. Josephson junctions promise to make these imagers more sensitive and faster than radar.

Researchers are hard at work at telecommunications applications of superconducting electronics too. Crowding of satellite frequency bands and the increased use of wider bandwidths both place a premium on equipment that can exploit higher frequencies. At high frequencies, conventional telecom devices can run into a variety of problems: increased noise, power losses and so on. Josephson junctions can operate directly at nearly any frequency up to 1,000 GHz, or even beyond. And the frequency can be controlled by varying a voltage across the junction. Applications being developed include: radiometers; high-frequency, low noise mixers and amplifiers for space communications; and resonators that could operate as frequency-stabilizing devices, filters and multiplexers.

The American defense and space systems group, TRW, points out that it is even possible to conceive of a complete communication-satellite electronics package using superconducting devices and circuitry for all its components save the final power amplification of its transmitter output. The whole thing could be about the size of a soccer ball.

Something like a soccer ball-sized communications satellite is still a long way off, although, with luck, the first superfast Josephson computer could appear by the 1990s. Nonetheless, the age of superconducting electronics has already begun. Workers in the field are keen students of quantum mechanics. They have to be. For them, it is not exotic fare but their bread and butter.

Puzzles

As we have seen, quantum mechanics cannot answer all the questions posed by the phenomenon of superconductivity, useful though its partial explanation is proving. In other areas, too, quantum theory runs into difficulties.

One problem is gravity. As yet, quantum theorists have been unable to come up with a convincing quantum-mechanical way of handling gravity. In a practical sense, this is not too important. Gravity is such a weak force that it is felt only when massive bodies are involved—bodies like the earth and its moon. In the subatomic world, it hardly counts. Still, for quantum theorists, this gap is worrying. A universal theory of matter should be able to cope with gravity.

Another problem is mathematical. Try to solve certain of the equations of quantum mechanics and you tend to come up with infinite, instead of finite, numbers. Mathematicians have developed cunning tricks to by-pass most of these disconcerting results. (The procedure is known as renormalization.) But many physicists are not at all happy with this. Interviewed in the 1970s, Professor Dirac had this to say of renormalization:

> It's just a stop-gap procedure. There must be some fundamental change in our ideas, probably a change just as fundamental as the passage from Bohr's orbit theory to quantum mechanics. When you get a number turning out to be infinite which ought to be finite, you should admit that there is something wrong with your equations, and not hope that you can get a good theory just by doctoring up that number.

Perhaps. By no means all physicists would agree that quantum mechanics is so far out as that judgment seems to imply. Certainly, so far, it has stood up to the test of all the experiments designed to verify it. Its compelling power has grown, not diminished, over the decades.

It does remain a disturbing theory. This brief introduction has turned only a few pages of the book of quantum mechanics. There is much else in it that is even stranger than the phenomena that we have discussed: particles which lead such a fleeting existence that physicists call them "virtual" rather than real; an insistence that the observer and the object he observes cannot be regarded as independent of one another; even, in some way-out interpretations of the theory, that there are multiple realities, multiple worlds, that coexist with one another.

For readers who would like to delve deeper, we include a reading list. For those who feel they have had enough—and feel that even now they find it hard to feel at home with the theory—we have a word of consolation. Here is how a top American physicist, Dr. David Bohm, described the way he felt about quantum mechanics after years of working with it. Talking about the difficulty of visualizing what is actually happening in quantum mechanics, he recalled:

> When I studied quantum mechanics I was fascinated with it. I felt it was a very deep, important study, but I didn't really understand it. Eventually I taught a course on the subject and wrote a book about it, to try to understand it. After finishing my book, I considered the matter again and I felt that I still did not understand it.

If you feel you at least have some idea of what the theory is about—and why it matters—you get full marks.   □

References

BERNSTEIN, J. *Experiencing Science,* Burnett Books (Andre Deutsch), Burnett Books, 1979; see Chapter 2 on Professor Isaac Rabi.
BUCKLEY, P. and F.D. PEAT (conducted by), *A Question of Physics: Conversations in Physics and Biology,* London: Routledge & Kegan Paul, 1979; the source of the quotes from Professor Dirac and Dr. David Bohm.
DAVIES, P. *The Forces of Nature,* Cambridge: Cambridge University Press, 1979.
_____*Other Worlds,* London: J.M. Dent, 1980.

See also

WEISSKOPF, V. "New Insights into the Basic Structure of Matter," In: *New Horizons of Human Knowledge,* Paris: The Unesco Press, 1981.

The evolutionary process undergone by physics during the twen-tieth century has severely altered our basic concepts of the unitary nature of matter, of its interaction at the level of organismic bodies, and of the relationship between physics and the other classical disci-plines. We are beginning to have a clearer understanding of the models we call reversible and irreversible processes. The absolutes tend to appear less absolute, and physics is seen as a human (social) science.

Chapter 20

A NEW MODEL OF TIME, A NEW VIEW OF PHYSICS

Ilya Prigogine and Isabelle Stengers

1

For some years, physics has been undergoing profound change. We are not referring so much to the things of physics as we are to the motivation of interest in these. Physics, long fascinated by the quest for the ultimate (whether microscopic or galactic, but at any rate alien to our world), is currently rediscovering a rich and diversified universe—one involving intermeshed evolutive processes and producing qualitative

Ilya Prigogine, born at Moscow in 1917, directs the Service de Chimie Physique II at the University of Brussels as well as the Department of Statistical Mechanics at the University of Texas (Austin). Prof. Prigogine was awarded the Nobel Prize for physics in 1977. Ms Stengers, born in Brussels in 1949, holds bachelor's degrees in chemistry and philosophy. She is completing her doctor's thesis in philosophy on the historical evolution of the various approaches to theoretical physics. Her ad-dress is 6 rue du Zodiaque, 1180 Bruxelles, Belgium.

differences. Multiple theoretical and conceptual developments are supplying us with new means to state problems as we unearth their difficulty and relevance.

Furthermore, this repositioning of physics on the world in which we live is accompanied, or should be, by changes in the relationships with other fields of knowledge. As long as the goal of physics was to unravel the secret of the world and reduce the diversity of phenomena to a universal legality, each of physics' achievements succeeded in putting further distance between man and nature, in denying to nature all that connects us with it, thus emphasizing the strangeness of the human species.

During this period, the universality of scientific rationality has thus been associated with the commonality of a negation extracting from the world all that which lends sense to life and human endeavor; this reduced our world to blind automatism, to an array of laws corresponding to an intelligible environment—where we should be able to deduce everything that exists, but an inhuman world where man and everything else living have no place. Classical science thus seemed to impose a tragic opposition between human subjectivity, to which the totality of our experience led, and an objective truth excluding the very ones who discover it.

To be sure, philosophers such as Bergson, James and Peirce have underlined that it is precisely because physics is human that it has led to objective verity which seems to exclude man. Because our interests and our habits are centered on problems of forecasting and experimentation, we have selected preferentially as objects of knowledge those phenomena which we judge to be the most regular. It was Peirce who predicted, "The further physical studies depart from phenomena which have directly influenced the growth of the mind, the less we can expect to find the laws which govern them 'simple,' that is, composed of a few conceptions natural to our minds."[1]

Contemporary developments have partially confirmed this prediction. Twentieth-century physics is no longer the knowledge of certainties; it is one of interrogation. The physical universe open to research has burst wide open. We have discovered the world of elementary particles, the size of which is typically 10^{-15} cm, and we receive signals from the boundaries of the universe 10^{28} cm distant. And everywhere, instead of uncovering the permanence and immutability that classical science had taught us to seek out in nature, we have encountered change, instability and evolution. But the surprises do not end here; from the universe's boundaries and from the microscopic core of matter, the complex, manifold and evolutionary properties are now flowing back to the world at our scale, the one we had once thought to respond to classical laws.

The story of this "re-enchantment" of the world in which we live can be told as the abandonment of mechanical determinism, of the progressive integration of an irreducibly random dimension within our theoretical description of the behavior of matter. This story is also, inseparably, that of the gradual rediscovery of the bonds between physics and the temporal world it explores.

2

Today the question of time takes on particular resonance. Population growth is taking on proportions heretofore unknown. We learn, sometimes tragically, that the decisions we take now can result in unforeseeable consequences tomorrow, results which we cannot always control. In this unstable world where causalities are intermixed and reinforcing, we know that we are responsible for our present actions as well as for a future in which these acts will have both implications and a thrust for which we are responsible—without having in the least been able to foresee them fully.

And yet, even while we are intensely aware of the evidence of the irreversible nature of the story in which we are involved, the idea of a basic difference between reversible and irreversible processes remains a controversial matter among physicists. Those who remain fond of the classical determinist idea are steadfast in concluding that the symmetry between past and future (typifying the determinist fundamental laws of physics) must remain a foundation of our concept of nature. According to this view, the fact that we ought to characterize certain change as irreversible would be a consequence of the fact that we do not have access to the level of reality corresponding to these basic laws. (Fig. 1 describes tersely the laws of thermodynamics.) The whole point would be that we are capable of manipulating only populations of molecules rather than individual molecules. But for Maxwell's demon, sorting individual molecules one by one as he observes their reversible and determinist trajectories, there is no irreversible change. A judicious sorting can help a mixture to separate itself, a homogeneous thermal environment to dissociate itself into different temperature groups. Consequently scientific concepts such as entropy (typifying the irreversibility of physico-chemical change) are, in the words of Max Born for example, a "consequence of the explicit introduction of our ignorance into the fundamental laws."[2]

Figure 1. Understanding the three laws of thermodynamics, as they evolved during the nineteenth and early twentieth centuries. It is these laws which the authors wish to elaborate further.

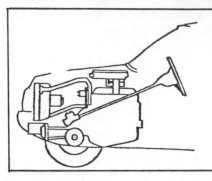

First
Conservation of energy

This principle observes the basic equivalence of different forms of energy (mechanical, electrical, chemical energy of fuels, heat). In transactions converting energy from one form to another (as in the automobile's internal combustion engine), there is total conservation. The work done to propel the vehicle when added to the heat lost (through the radiator, for example) equals the chemical energy consumed in combustion of the fuel.

Transfer of heat   ## Second

It takes work to produce order in a system. Left on its own, the system evolves so that disorder increases. The quantity measuring this disorder is called entropy.

 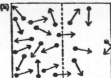 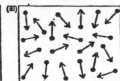

Gas is trapped within a definite space (i). As the size of the space available to the gas is increased, gas molecules fill the supplementary empty space (ii). The system evolves towards state (iii), a state of maximal disorder, because the molecules are evenly distributed throughout the whole space. As randomness of molecular distribution increases, entropy increases too. Evolution towards state (iii) is irreversible; the initial state where all the molecules are in the left part of the system can never again be attained by a spontaneous change of the system.

Crystalline structure   ## Third

Absolute zero of temperature

Heat experienced on macroscopic (observable) levels is matter in motion on microscopic level. Temperature 0 ($-273, 16°$ C) at the macroscopic level means that, at the microscopic level, all molecular motion is stopped and all molecules have assumed an unchanging position. Consequently, at temperature zero, entropy is nil which is its absolute minimal value. In reality however, absolute zero can never be attained.

The totality of these subjectivist ideas, in which irreversibility simply reflects man's own limitations, imbeds itself in the work of Boltzmann, manifesting at one and the same time its novelty and its limitations. Novelty, because Boltzmann was the first to undertake the interpretation of a physical concept—entropy—as the translation of an irreducibly collective process, the behavior of a large number of particles. Limitation, because Boltzmann did not succeed in imposing the notion that this number, as such, is not an artifact which we introduce because of our inability to observe individual molecules, thereby avoiding that entropy too be reduced to a simple matter of approximation.

Towards the end of his life, Boltzmann was obliged to recognize that, within his own interpretation, the difference between past and future is nothing more than relative, bound to the human point of view, that this difference makes no more sense basically than that between top and bottom. As Karl Popper has written, such a conclusion "is quite untenable, at least for a realist. It brands unidirectional change as an illusion. This makes the catastrophe of Hiroshima an illusion."[3]

3

Still, the situation was far from being so clear, and today we can understand both the reasons for Boltzmann's failure and the means to overcome this. The relation established by Boltzmann between entropy and probability does not allow, indeed, introduction of the essential dimension of irreversibility, "time's arrow." But we realize now that this could not be otherwise. Boltzmann's model studies the behavior of a group of spheres which interact only upon collision. We know today that it is the taking into account of the dynamics of interaction which permits us to understand the significance of physical irreversibility.

Let us take a simple example, a population of particles in mutual interaction. We can conduct an experiment in which, after a more or less long evolution, the different particles will stabilize themselves in regular configuration corresponding to how the different interactions stabilize. The interactions create coherence, the order of the final state. And yet, there is certainly question here of an irreversible change similar to one in which (on the contrary) a population of molecules, unified by negligible interactions, evolve towards a disorganized state.

The concept of entropy, when it transcends Boltzmann's simplification and integrates the taking into account of interactions between particles, no longer allows the opposition simply of order (the improbable) and disorder (the probable). Order and disorder can appear to be not contradictory but complementary, relating to different definitions of a single object; a homogeneous mixture of molecules is in disorder, but it is constituted of units internally in order—molecules with their nuclei and electrons.

As to the "orderly" state in which molecules stabilize themselves at regular distances, there exists a description of this whereby the units are no longer molecules; instead, the units are redefined so as to "integrate" their interactions, such that this state appears as maximally incoherent. Order and disorder are no longer opposed in an absolute fashion (or else they no longer bring our ignorance to the fore); they characterize dual descriptions concerning the same physical situation.

We begin to find, moreover, the conceptual structure pertinent to development of the project which Boltzmann was unable to do, that is, finding an objective criterion which allows us to define which physical systems are equipped with "time's arrow." In the specific case, let us say only that this is a matter of expressing—contary to what is presupposed in classical dynamics—that all changes are not similar in value (they are not equivalent) because, as soon as we deal with complex systems, all the initial conditions (from which "legal" trajectories take form) are not similar in value. We are free to organize some of these conditions, or to imagine that a demon wiser and more powerful than we could develop these conditions. Other conditions cannot be prepared at will; the only way for these to come into existence is to be produced by change itself in a system.

From this point, the statistical character presupposed by Boltzmann is not one of approximation. The idea of a determinist trajectory in complex systems, which assumes equivalence of all initial conditions, must give way to a description whereby the first and irreducible terms relate to groups of trajectories and thus is, irreducibly, of statistical nature.

4

We thus find, but this time at the level of dynamics, an indication of the limits constraining our possibilities of action. These limits do not reflect on our imperfection, however; they are a reflection of the objective microscopic structures whose inherent properties invalidate the extrapolations of classical dynamics. Hereafter, confronted by irreversibility, Maxwell's demon is as powerless as we. Omniscience is as much of a lure as omnipotence; the latter translates, for the one manipulating it, the indifference and submission falsely postulated by classical science about the object being manipulated. Here physics can call itself a *human science* because physics recognizes explicitly the constraints determining our activity, all the while embracing the origins of these constraints in nature.

After Boltzmann, incorporation of an irreducibly random dimension in the description of material behavior passed through a second stage with quantum mechanics. Here, too, the question of time is in the foreground. Quantum description articulates in indissociable fashion the reversible and determinist change in wave function, as well as the measurement interaction which is irreversible and the result of which we can know only in a statistical manner.

Seen retrospectively, the two great conceptual revolutions which shook physics at the beginning of the century—relativity and quantum mechanics—both, in this sense, tell us the same story. Each is rooted in the discovery of what the existence of the universal constants, c representing the speed of light and h Planck's constant, imply: insurmountable obstacles to certain manipulations, to certain ways of "taking knowledge" that we had believed conceivable. It is impossible for us to define absolutely two distant events as simultaneous. It is impossible to know both the position and velocity of a quantum being.

And in both cases, the development of these theories (which had at their origin given special place, following the classical model, to the search for non-temporal laws) brought to the fore once again the problems of time and randomness. The universe pursued by cosmological theories is no longer Einstein's static geometric universe; it is a temporal universe, one subject to instabilities, whose future we try to foresee and whose thermal history we seek to rebuild (a history fundamentally irreversible).

By the same token, quantum mechanics is now concerned with unstable particles and their mutual transformation. Furthermore, these new developments in research on the infinitely large and the infinitely small are now deeply in consonance with science dealing with the world on our scale—macroscopic knowledge—where the problem of time, the problem of the relation between laws and history, has emerged too.

This third stage of the incorporation of the random dimension in our descriptions of the material universe demonstrates in a decisive way that the world of irreversible processes, rebelling against omniscience and mechanical determinism, should not be associated with the ideas of loss or insufficient control.

5

Indeed, since its origins in the 19th century, the concept of irreversibility was associated with the idea of the limits to the possibilities of manipulation: that in thermal machines producing motion on the basis of heat certain changes occur irreversibly—this meant that such changes had partially escaped our control. This translated itself into wasted energy, or an output lower than the ideal output possible if everything had been perfectly regulated.

This association of irreversible time, loss of control and waste coincides with an impenetrable human experience often expressed by philosophers: Time is what opposes our projects, it is the basic opacity which prevents us from conceiving the world in which we live as one responsive to our plans and decisions. Jankelevitch has written, in this vein, that we learn quickly "that time is not to be manipulated as we wish. . .we cannot seize time haphazardly at one end or the other, that time does not even have 'ends,' that time dictates the direction we shall take. The sense of future-ness is the basic impediment imposed on our manipulations."4

Yet this irreversible world which, in itself, imposes limits upon our control and experiment, is equally a world of self-organization. The irreversible processes, which we have termed "dissipative" because of the waste they produce, are also those whence the active and organized structures comprising nature are produced. The world which resists our manipulation, which does not accept indifferently what we impose upon it, is just as much the world whence order emerges—where develop breaks in symmetry, differences, rhythms, where diverging changes take place, where we can see evolving the dialectic between chance and necessity characterizing the history of living populations and their environment.

We have said that physics today has the characteristics of a human science, in the sense that physics no longer is grounded on a truly objective world, but on an illusory world reflecting our own opposition of approximations and imperfections. Yet this opposition is transcended not only because physics gives us access to a world where we *understand* the constraints to which we are subject, the intrinsic obstacles to any model of an omniscient and all-powerful ideal knowledge. There is another reason: physics is no longer totally alien to the most anguishing problems of our times, especially that of the overwhelming historical responsibility which today is ours in terms of the total evolution of the world.

Perhaps, from this point of view, the most profound novelty is that of the end of the traditional priority given by physics to units as opposed to their interactions. This priority was far-reaching. Thus systems with precisely calculable trajectories (the model of classical dynamics) are typified by the fact that there is a mathematical way to describe them by "eliminating" their interactions. Units corresponding to the description behave as if each were isolated. Conversely, we owe the emergence of coherent collective behaviors to interactions between chemical molecules—implying billions of billions of molecules.

Furthermore, as soon as there is question of animal or human societies, or of interactions between living populations and their environment, it is still the interactions that count. Thus it can be thought that for these cases the conclusion we come to in chemistry prevails here as well. That is, as we shall now see, the search for a general law by which a behavior can be deduced deterministically is a poor model of intelligibility for such systems.

6

In certain cases in chemistry, theory allows foreseeing that, however delicate might be our control of a group of interactions, we cannot prevent an inherent unforeseeability; experience even confirms this. The system is subject to assuming a number of possible ways of functioning and its evolution can lead it, through a series of "bifurcation points" (points at which a necessary choice is made between two divergent possibilities), to adopt a unique behavior. Such behavior is, simultaneously and inseparably, the product of its definition as system as well as of the particular history giving it rise (See Figure 2).

The very necessity, implied by the bifurcal nature of evolution, of taking into account the system's history, the internal structures "accumulated" by the sum of the "choices" it has made, the diversity of the possible development paths offered, leads us back to the historical problem now acutely evident on a planetary scale. By the same token, the necessity we face at the level of chemistry—that of distinguishing between regimes functioning stably or not, or of "small" disturbances capable of provoking global change—underscores the naivete of accepting the great projects embodying plans which fail to explore the possibilities intrinsic to a given situation, projects tending to impose on a system a deterministically pre-ordained behavior (much in the way a clockmaker would adjust an automaton.)

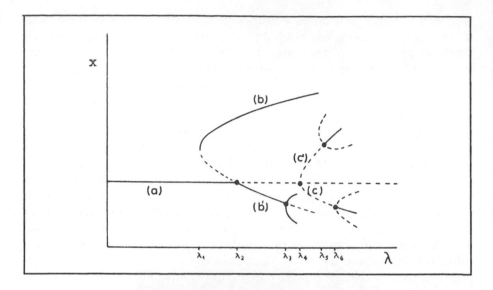

Figure 2. The divergence or bifurcation parameter, λ , measures the distance of a system's normal operation in relation to equilibrium. The value x represents a concentration allowing us to characterize the normal operation in question. When $\lambda \langle \lambda_1$, a single stationary states exists for each value of λ, and this family of states is depicted as (a). When $\lambda = \lambda_1$, two additional families of states become possible, (b) and (b'), the states depicted as (b'), being unstable. When $\lambda = \lambda_2$, the (b') states become stable and those depicted as (a) become unstable. When $\lambda = \lambda_3$, the (b') states are again unstable, whereas two stable situations appear. If $\lambda = \lambda_4$, unstable (a) arrives at a new point of bifurcation where two new families of states become possible; these are unstable until $\lambda = \lambda_5$ and $\lambda = \lambda_6$, respectively. (After a diagram originally prepared for Prigogine and Stengers, *La nouvelle alliance, métamorphose de la science,* Paris, Gallimard, 1979.)

If we now recognize the distance separating the problem of describing human populations from that of describing chemical populations, the richness of the changing behaviors that chemical populations already offer is all the more interesting. Indeed, as soon as we take leave of physico-chemical systems, we need also to take into account that the unit/interaction dialectic becomes as much more complicated and subtle as the units themselves with which we are dealing. Contrary to the physico-chemical elements, these are the products of both history and individual and collective learning.

Chemical molecules are characterized by a fixed number of possibilities of interaction; one can even say that the molecules remain the "same" regardless of the interaction in which they may be involved.

But man is not a well defined unit in this sense; he cannot be isolated from the interactions in which he is involved with other groups (and which help make him what he is.) Thenceforth the perspective cannot be that of a universal theory deducible from an exact definition of elementary units; it cannot avoid the problem of searching for the link between (a) how units which are part of such-and-such a collectivity interact and (b) the global behavior of the collective.

7

The kind of science born in Europe around the early 17th century has been, from its beginnings, one of the most fascinating dialogues that man has ever held with the world to which he belongs. What is new and rich in hope if we can learn the lesson is that, hereafter, this dialogue will no longer leave us as strangers—neither to our world nor to the questions and praxis germane to other cultural traditions. The universality of science is no longer the commonality of negation, of an *a priori* discrimination between "the right way of formulating a problem" and all the others rejected as illusory or irrational. This universality makes it possible, on the contrary, to respect and incorporate problem analysis alien to the ones in which its origins are rooted.

Henceforth, too, we can better appreciate the accomplishments of our heritage in classical science. This knowledge exposed us, indeed with peerless exactitude and force, to a great number of phenomena and enabled us to unify the seemingly disparate. Who, before Newton, would have thought that the fall of an object towards the ground, the motions of planets and the flight of comets depend on the same law? How, before the days of molecular biology, could we have imagined the subtly regulated interdependence of the chemical transformations in human metabolism, or the infinite complexity of the most insignificant bacterium? But there was also a heavy price to pay. Anything that failed to correspond to the classical model of intelligibility was reduced, *ipso facto*, to the level of those things we believed only because of sloth or irrationality.

Classical theory can assume universal validity. We have no doubt that wherever we will encounter what physics describes as mass we shall find that its laws are the same governing the masses with which we are familiar. But our predecessors had proceeded further, they had also tried to extrapolate the intelligibility model that these laws comprise. They came thus to be a denial of the world or, more precisely, of anything which allows to recognize the world we occupy: a world of events, a world diversified, evolving, and producing order and disorder. They achieved the denial of time having direction, they were even able to affirm a basic equivalence between the processes we know—the growth of plants, the mixing of liquids, the uniformization of temperatures—and the inverse processes "undoing" the work of the former.

8

With the theoretical development of physics, we can now understand to what degree had been limited our understanding of the natural processes as long as we stayed in the realm of classical physics. The simple phenomena which classical physics held up as models enabling us to differentiate objective truth from illusory appearance are not, despite what Peirce might have said, simple only because our intelligence has adapted itself to them. Today, in a larger framework, we can describe these phenomena as *objectively simple* and, in this sense, *exceptional*. Physics can now precisely define why an automaton or a pendulum cannot be a model for our understanding. These constitute only limiting cases, where some of their most important properties are lost.

Classical physics laid the stress on universality, on the search for an underlying simplicity, on necessity. Because we feel bound today to jettison this ideal form does not mean the end of science. Quite to the contrary, we realize that we are only at the beginning. New outlines of theories are emerging that could make numerous aspects of the world we are exploring more intelligible. In order to accomplish this, it is vital that knowledge transfer develop between the different cultural traditions, between the physical and human sciences, and between science and philosophy. No one can arrogate to himself a monopoly on truth or certitude.

The transformation of physics which we have described bears witness, moreover, to the fertility of the interrelations connecting the different forms of knowledge and diverse habits. This transformation has not happened in isolation. The new questions and problems commanding the attention of physicists have largely been induced by questions and interests coming from outside (or from other sciences.) It is thus not surprising that they are consonant with new questions in other disciplines, whether these deal with philosophy, anthropology, biology, psychology, or even art. The dynamic, elective, and constructive dimension of time is again coming forth; the proliferating diversity of problems arising as soon as a field concentrating on relationships, instead of stable entities, becomes clearer.

Physics, having become the science of relationships and processes, is aware of the illusory nature of some of its former pretensions about attaining encompassing truth, one which would allow physics to stand in judgment in other disciplines. Physicists now comprehend that the truths they establish can and should be in cross-communication with truths reached along other rational paths. Now immersed in a world it long considered itself capable of dominating, physics has still to learn the exacting fecundity of exchange and mutual apprenticeship.   □

FOOTNOTES

[1] C.S. Peirce, "The Architecture of Theories," in *Selected Writings (Values in a Universe of Chance)*, New York: Dover, 1958, p.146.

[2] M. Born, *Natural Philosophy of Causes and Chance*, Oxford: Clarendon Press, 1949.

[3] K. Popper, *Unended Quest*, LaSalle, IL: Open Court Publications, 1976, p. 160.

[4] V. Jankelevitch, *L'Irréversibilité et la Nostalgie*, Paris: Flammarion, 1974.

To delve more deeply

HOLYE, F. and N. WICKRAMASINGHE. *Evolution From Space*, Letchworth: J.M. Dent, 1981.
PRIGOGINE, I., *et al.*, "Can Thermodynamics Explain Biological Order?" *impact of science on society*, Vol. XXIII, No. 3, 1973.
TEMPERLEY, H. "Could Life Have Happened by Accident?" *New Scientist*, 19 August 1982. The author is an applied mathematician who has calculated that life on earth could have begun without intervention from space.

As is true of all models, words simplify to some degree the reality which they represent. In this lies their usefulness: human beings can function effectively in a complex world only by mentally imposing some form of simplifying order. In science, this modeling procedure is at the heart of what is called "the scientific method."

Chapter 21

MODELS OF REALITY

Geoffrey S. Holister

The structure of the fact consists of the atomic facts. We make to ourselves pictures of facts. The picture is a model of reality.

Ludwig J. Wittgenstein,
Tractatus Logico-Philosophicus

To paraphrase a rather well-known work: "In the beginning was the word—and the word was a model." To be more exact, the word is a sound we utter or a symbol we inscribe to *represent* some object or concept: or rather our mental image of that object or concept. Thus the words we use are, in a very real sense, models.

If a model gives a faithful representation of some aspect of reality then it is a good model. The procedure used in science is to use the model to make a prediction about the behavior of reality and then to compare this prediction with actual behavior in an experiment. Then, if the model is faulty, a better model can be sought.

A biographical note concerning Geoffrey Holister, who conducted the interview with Dennis Meadows, will be found accompanying Chapter 11 (see p. 161).

Because all models misrepresent reality to some extent, the observed behavior or reality seldom corresponds exactly with the predictions even of a very good model. Often a model is very good under some conditions and very bad under others. For example, the model of the relationship between the pressure, volume and temperature of a mass of gas is very good if the temperature is high enough. At temperatures approaching those at which the gas could condense as a liquid, the model is less accurate, its accuracy deteriorating with decreasing temperature until, rather than calling the model inaccurate, we would call it invalid and look for a different one.

Scientists build up their picture of the cosmos through such models, which does not mean to say that they "believe" in their models in the sense that a religious person uses the word belief. Indeed, it is the essentially provisional nature of the scientific view that is so difficult to transmit to the non-scientist, particularly one holding a view of the universe as "an article of faith." It is a prevalent misunderstanding which is at the heart of much unnecessary conflict between science and religion.

Models and a World View

In primitive societies, the models of reality adhered to often result in the imposition of codes of behavior that must be strictly complied with if the gods are not to be angered. For example, some hunter-gatherer tribes worship a god who is "Keeper of the Animals"—a god who becomes angry and will punish the tribe if they kill too many of one species. While we may reject the concepts inherent in this model of the world, we must admit that it is an admirably functional one. Like all good models, it works, in the sense that it helps preserve the well-being of the group that believes in it.

As I implied at the beginning, words are the most basic models of all, and there is little doubt in my mind that the language we use cannot help but influence the way we think about the world. I am told that there is a tribe of Indians whose word for time and distance is the same. Some Eastern languages use the same symbol for energy and matter. But we should not jump to the conclusion that such examples represent startling pre-Einsteinian insights by the groups that use them: it is simply that, in the context of their environments, the distinction between the concepts is not worth making. So if language can, in addition to other environmental factors, influence our view of the world in a profound manner, it should not surprise us if such differing world views produce conflicting ideological and psycho-cultural states.

An example of such conflict is the recent furor surrounding the book *Third World Calamity* by Brian May, in which the author asserts that some Third World countries possess psycho-cultural traits (such as preoccupation with the occult, the caste system and a conviction that an individual cannot control his own destiny) that ensure the stagnation of its peoples and virtually bars them from industrial development. Not unnaturally, this assertion has caused a storm of protest, including personal attacks on the integrity of the author. But such attacks are foolish: if my doctor tells me I have a terminal illness, should I denounce him as an anti-intellectual with a pathological dislike of university professors, or should I call for a second opinion from a specialist? If, as May asserts, real psycho-cultural barriers to development do exist in parts of the Third World, then it is the duty of organizations like Unesco, which are committed to endogenous development, to study such cultural barriers dispassionately so as to ascertain the true nature of the problem.

Development, after all, has many faces other than the industrial one, and it seems to me unlikely that societies cannot be helped towards a better standard of living and quality of life whatever their cultural beliefs and social customs—provided we remember that what is important is what they tell us they need—not what we tell them. That would be cultural arrogance of the worst sort: "My world model is better than your world model."

Disagreement on World Models

Speaking of world models, readers have found two sources of information on these in this book: a concise review of the "state of the art" with respect to global modeling in an article by John M. Richardson, Jr., and my interview with Dennis Meadows (p. 161). In this interview, I have tried to pose the sort of questions about the computer modeling of socio-economic problems that I think readers would want me to ask.

The attempts by Dennis Meadows and others to develop computer models of the world's economic and environmental condition for descriptive and (perhaps eventually) predictive purposes, as described in *The Limits to Growth* and *Mankind at the Turning Point,* have caused a storm of outraged reaction from social scientists in general and economists in particular. The assertions of the anti-Meadows camp can be summarized as follows:

1. The model neglects to examine and use the relevant theory and empirical evidence generated by the discipline of economics and, as a consequence, it also neglects technical progress.

2. Others (Ricardo, Malthus) have concluded that growth could not continue indefinitely because of physical limits and they have turned out to be wrong (i.e., "Why do I need insurance, I haven't died up to now!").

3. Arguments that growth in the industrialized countries should stop are unwarranted; ". . .we should also consider the possibility that we should go on working, not to increase our own consumption, but to better the lot of the poor majority of the world" (Keith Pavitt).

4. Assumptions made in formulating the models are gross over-simplifications, and in particular the aggregation (in *The Limits to Growth*) is hopelessly unrealistic.

Of these objections, only (4) has any real substance. The rest are petulant (1), silly (2) and almost incredibly naive (3). While it is undoubtedly true that practically all the assumptions made in the formulation of the computer world models produced so far are gross ones, and that undoubtedly some of them are invalid, one should be clear that this is not the basic reason for the storm of protest that the work has produced. The reason is that while the assumptions made by the computer modelers are in fact no more gross or unrealistic than those assumed by economists, they are, unfortunately, different assumptions.

Challenging the Implicit Assumptions

Models of technological innovation, substitution and mineral discovery that are used in economics bear roughly the same order of resemblance to reality that "economic man" bears to a real person. Their substantiation rests on no more than an argument of the sort "It stands to reason that. . . ." Such models have assumed axiomatic status in economics and any work which questions or ignores them is anathema to the traditional economist.

Nevertheless, because the majority of criticism directed at world-modeling exercises is misdirected does not mean that there are not serious defects in the models in question. There is always the danger that the authors, like the economists who are so opposed to them, may confuse their models with the real world. At the present stage of the work this would be most foolish. Indeed, it is very doubtful whether truly predictive models of world behavior could ever be developed. In the meantime it is best to view both traditional economic theory and world models as useful parables from which some insight as to possible future options may, with care, be gleaned.

Perhaps the true value of world models is that they call into question the implicit assumptions of traditional economics and that from this conflict some progress may ensue. It is probably only fair to let Dennis Meadows' colleague, Jay Forrester, have the last word:

> *A lot of people believe this [building of models] is impossible, because they feel that one cannot make a model of anything as complicated as a social system, and of course they are partially correct—a model is a great simplification. But we have no choice about the use of models. The mental image that we use for passing laws, for running cities, for operating a government—these mental images are models— because one does not have a city, or a country, or a world in one's head, one only has certain images—which are models—and so the question now is: Is the model adequate? Is it the* best *model which we can make?—and the answer is no! it is* not *the best model which we can make!* (Interview from Open University Technology Foundation Course (T100) television programme, *Limits to Growth.)*

And this is a model of reality. □

References

MAY, B. *Third World Calamity.* London: Routledge & Kegan Paul, 1981.

MEADOWS, D.H., D.L. MEADOWS, J. RANDERS, and W. BEHRENS. *The Limits to Growth.* New York: Universe Books, 1972, 1979, 2nd ed.

MESAROVIC, M. and E. PESTEL. *Mankind at the Turning Point.* Hutchinson, 1975.

PAVITT, K. "Some Consequences of Physics-based Research." *Physics Bulletin,* January 1973.

INDEX

All-Union Scientific Institute for Systems Research, 75, 80
  systems approach to modeling, 80-85
APT system, Mesarovic's, 79
Architecture. *See also* Form.
  Bauhaus, 51, 55, 59-60
  form in, 59, 60, 62
Artificial intelligence, 6

Behavior, bifurcal nature of, 311-313. *See also* Physics, reversible vs. irreversible change.
Bell Labs, 298
Bohm, David, 301
Bohr, Niels, 288, 290
Boltzmann, Ludwig, 307-309
Born, Max, 305
Brain
  computer model of, 277-281
  functions beyond computerized model, 282-284
  right and left hemispheres of, 13
  unlike a machine, 280
Bremer, Stuart, 123
Brendendieck, Hin, 12, 51-64
Brown, Phelps, 179-180
Bruckmann, Gerhart, 116, 118
Bureau for Systems Analysis of the State Office for Technical Development (Budapest), 11

CARPS, IBM Tokyo Center, 79
Catastrophe
  models, 93-94
  theory, 5
Catastrophe or a New Society, 120
Clayson, James, 247-263
Club of Rome, 9, 115, 120, 161
Cobb-Douglas production function, 173
Computer
  increasing speed of, 295-296
  modeling. *See also* Fiscal impact models.
    as enhancement to understanding, 164
    in operations research, 247-249
    politics vs. technical rationality, 135. *See also* Modeling implementation, politics in.
  simulation, 6

Data collection
  two philosophies of, 97-98
Delacote, Goery, 268
Demography
  definition of, 237-238
  measuring, 238-239
Descartes, René, 13
Design. *See also* Form.
  holistic approach, 64
  increasing influence of consumer on, 64
  non-operational aspect, 62-63
  visual clarity, 62-64
Developing countries
  cultural barriers, 319
  economies of, 47-48
  operations research in, 247-254. *See also* Operations research.
Dirac, Paul, 294, 301
Durkheim, Emile, 107
Dynamic programming
  definition of, 93
  mathematical and theoretical complications, 95

Earth
  change from an anaerobic to an aerobic atmosphere, 33-34
  depletion of resources, 40-43, 46
  food chain of, 36-37
  greenhouse effect on, 44-45
  pollution of, 43-46, 47-48
Ecological models
  applied to urban and regional planning, 87-88, 99
  global, 44-47
  inadequacy of data, 97
Ecological systems, 31-48
  variables in, 39-40
Ecology
  community in, 35-38
    ecological succession, 38-39
    matter-energy flow vs. information flow, 36-38, 40
  effect of man on, 40-48
  fundamental concern of, 34
Economics
  analysis, failure of traditional, 181-182
  definition of, 163-164
  econometrics, 168

growth
   importance of incremental improve-
      ments in, 251-252
   limits to, 48. *See also* Economies,
      upper limits of growth in.
   model, Leontief's, 46-48
   modeling
      effectiveness of, 168
      emergence of global, 124-125. *See also*
         Global models.
      international (global), 122-123
      of Indian economy, 235-237
Economies
   steady state vs. growth, 162
   upper limits of growth in, 162-163
Economist, The, Editors of, 285-302
Education
   interplay of teacher, pupil, and nature,
      270-272
   physics modeling exercises in, 268-275
   role of models in, 265, 267-268
Eighth Global Modeling Conference, 123,
   124
Einstein, Albert, 288, 292
   theory of relativity, 286, 294
Entropy, 21, 31, 43, 45, 305-307
Epimenides paradox, 72
Ergonomics, 7
European Economic Community, 23
European Organization for Nuclear Re-
   search (CERN), 23

Fiscal impact models
   defined, 131, 133
   Irvine example, 135-151. *See also* Model-
      ing implementation, Irvine example;
      Models, urban and regional plan-
      ning.
Flohn, H., 45
Food and Agriculture Organization (FAO),
   23
Forecasting in International Relations, 14
Form. *See also* Design.
   and structure, interplay of, 60-61
   bilateral approach, 62. *See also* Form,
      "outside-in approach," and "inside-
      out approach."
   effect of miniaturization on, 51, 61
   in modeling trends. *See* Modeling trends.
   in product design, 60, 62
   "inside-out" approach, 59-60. *See also*
      Form, bilateral approach.
   "outside-in approach," 55, 59, 61. *See
      also* Form, bilateral approach.
   structure and position, 51-52
   visual appearance in, role of, 62
Forrester, Jay W., 46, 120, 167-184, 321

Fractals, Benoit Mandelbrot. *See* Mandelbrot, Benoit.
French Institute of Informatics and Automation, MODULECO system of, 79
Future
   gloomy view of, 46
   in global modeling, 125-127, 321
   models as blueprint for the, 101-103. *See
      also* Social planning.
   role in planning the, 106-107
Future of the World Economy, 121
Fyfe, W. S., 40, 45

Games, theory of, 93, 96
Gelovani, Viktor A., 12, 75-86
Georgescu-Roegen, N., 43
Global modeling
   based on preferred future, 125-127
   distinguished from others, 117-118
   guidelines for non-modelers, 116-117
   interaction with economic modeling,
      124-125
   origin, 118
   role in 1980s, 115
   tenets of, 118-119
   three categories, 120
Global models
   differing world views in, 318, 319
   economists vs. modelers, 319-320
   international economic
      Dynamico, 122-123
      Project LINK, 122, 125
   IIASA Conference models, 115
      Bariloche (Latin American World
         Model), 120, 126
      Forrester/Meadows (World III), 46,
         94-95, 120
      FUGI (Future of Global Interdepend-
         ence Model), 121, 125
      Mesarovic-Pestel (World Integrated
         Model), 120
      MORIA (Model of International Rela-
         tions in Agriculture), 121, 125
      SARUM (Systems Analysis Research
         Unit Model), 121, 125
      United Nations World Model, 121
   politically oriented
      GLOBUS (Generating Long-term Op-
         tions by Using Simulation),
         123-124
      SIMPEST (Simulation of Political,
         Economic and Strategic Interac-
         tions), 124
   should be understood by non-modelers,
      116
Global 2000, 125

Gödel, Escher, Bach: An Eternal Golden Braid, 72-73
Gödel, Kurt, 71-73
Gödel's Theorem, defined, 71-72
Guetzkow, Harold, 123

Hansen, J., 44
Hayek, F., 103
Heisenberg, Werner, 289
Hofstadter, Douglas, 72
Holister, Geoffrey S., 12, 72, 317-321
   interviewing Dennis Meadows, 161-165
Holling, C.S., 11
Hooke's Law, 268, 272
Herrera, Amilcar, 120
Hickman, Bert, 122
Hungarian scientists and education, 209-230. *See also* Science, social study of.

Informatics, 11
Institute for Comparitive Social Research of the Science Center (Berlin), 123, 125
International Institute of Applied Systems Analysis (IIASA) (Laxenburg, Austria), 11, 14, 116, 118, 120, 121, 122, 125
IIASA Conference models (global), 120-121. *See also* Global models, IIASA.
International Union for Pure and Applied Physics, Conference of (Trieste, 1980), 268

Jankelevitch, V., 310
Jeffers, John, 87-99
Jacobsen, Edward, 12, 71-73
Josephson, Brian, 298

Kahn, Rahat Nabi, 12, 231-245
Karplus, Robert, 269
Kaya, Yoichi, 121, 125
Kepler, Johann, 68
Keyzer, Michiel, 125
Kiss, István, 11
Klein, Lawrence, 122
Koch curves, 6
Kraemer, Kenneth L., 131-160

Laws as a model, 10
Lenin, 127
Leontief, Wassily, 46, 47, 121
Levien, Roger, 122
Life, emergence of on Earth, 32-34
Limits to Growth, 9, 95, 115, 118, 120, 319, 320, 321

Little, Graham R., 101-111
Llinás, Rudolfo, 12, 277-284
Lovelock, J. E., 33

Malthus, Thomas Robert, 320
Mandelbrot, Benoit, 6
Mankind at the Turning Point, 120, 319
Marx, George, 265-275
Marx, Karl, 101-103, 107, 108, 127
Mathematical modeling, 163-164, 248-249
Mathematical models
   as physical "laws," 65, 68-69
   as related to experimentation, 69-70
   collection of data, 97
   definition, 67
   dependence on data, 96-98
   in ecological systems, 92
   in urban and regional planning. *See* Urban and regional planning.
   objectivity, 76
   stages of construction, 66, 77-78
   uniqueness of, 65, 67
   use of simpler, 96
McKim, R. H., 62
Matisoo, Jim, 298
May, Brian, 319
Meadows, Dennis, 46, 120, 319
   interviewed by Geoffrey S. Hollister, 161-165
   objections to his theories, 319-320
Meadows, Donella, 116, 118
Medium-Term Plan (Unesco), 14
Mesarovic, Mihalo, 120
Miller, James Grier, 19-50
Miller, Jessie L., 19-50
Modeling
   adequately structured problems in, 76
   appropriateness for developing countries, 247-248. *See also* Developing countries.
   as an art, 268
   compared to playing, 270
   critical role of computer in, 98-99, 251. *See also* Computer modeling.
   crucial element in education, 163
   data banks in. *See* Data collection.
   definition of, 163
   educational systems, 241-244
   global. *See* Global modeling.
   in education, 265-275
   micro-approach (heuristic), 247-251
      encouraging managerial creativity, 253-254
      managerial consistency in, 250

problem oriented rather than discipline oriented, 116
role of computer in, 98-99, 251
socio-economic systems, 75-86
subjectivity in, 76
systems approach. *See* Systems analysis.
two phases of, 131-132
trends, form in, 61
Modeling implementation
elements of success in, 133-134
Irvine example, 151-157
politics in, 133, 139, 146, 149, 150, 156, 157, 194-195
population change, 237-241
routinization in, 148-152
three stages, 132
Models
consistency in, 73
definition of, 3, 87, 235, 247
dynamic. *See* Systems, dynamic.
fiscal impact. *See* Fiscal impact models.
future
refinements in, 11
trends, 164-165
general equilibrium, 14
global. *See* Global modeling.
holistic approach to, 11-13
mathematical. *See* Mathematical models.
predictive element of, 8-9, 65-67, 88. *See also* Future.
problematique. See Problematique.
reasons for, foreword, 3, 14. *See also* Operations research.
relationship to reality, 78, 88, 91, 98, 99, 178-179, 195, 266-268, 317-318.
role in research, 267
topological, 93-94
types of, 4
analogy, 6
caricature, 11
computer 11. *See also* Computer.
design, 6-7
forecast, scenarios, 7, 10, 76. *See also* Future.
life model, 10-11
paradigm, 10
sample, 4
scale, 7
simplification, 5-6
symbolism, 4-5
use in urban and regional planning. *See* Urban and regional planning. *See also* Fiscal impact models.
Morowitz, H.J., 32-34

Newton, Sir Isaac, 313
his laws as mathematical models, 68, 69
his mechanics, 288, 289
New Zealand Planning Council, 104

OPEC, 162
Open society, struggle for, 102-103
Open Society and Its Enemies, The, 101
Operations (operational) research, 5
definition, 248
micro-approach, French case study, 254-261
purpose, 248
traditional approach, 248-249
Organisation for Economic Co-operation and Development (OECD), 121

Parikh, Kirit, 14
Pavitt, Keith, 320
Pellionisz, András, 277-282
Perception of objects, 63-64. *See also* Form.
Perkel, Donald, 277, 279
Pestel, Eduard, 120
Physics
as human science, 303, 310
classical stress on universality, 313-315
definition of modern, 315. *See also* Quantum mechanics.
mechanical determinism in, 303-305. *See also* Quantum mechanics, unpredictability in.
reversible vs. irreversible change, 305-308, 310. *See also* "Time's arrow," dimension of irreversibility.
Physics—Concepts and Models, 269
Planck, Max, 288
Plato's *Republic*, 8, 103
Policy studies
process models in, 231, 233-235
systems models in, 231-235
usefulness of models in, 245
Politically oriented models (global), 123-124
Popper, Karl, 101-103, 108, 307
Prigogine, Ilya, 12, 303-315
Problematique, 13
Product development
designer's role in, 53-54
engineer's role in, 52-53, 54, 59

Quantum mechanics
and the layman, 286
gravity problem in, 300-301
history of, 286-289, 294

mathematical difficulties, 301
propositions of, 289-290
unpredictability in, 292-294, 308-309

Regression analysis, 168
Research and development (R&D)
    discipline oriented vs. mission oriented,
        186, 200. See also Scientific and
        technological research, utilization
        of.
    effect of quantum mechanics on, 295
    institutional resistance to societal goals,
        197, 199-200
    non-use of scientific knowledge, three
        types, 201-203
    policy before and after World War II,
        190-191
    societal utilization
        definition of, 186
        models of, 187-190
Resource Policy Center, 161, 164
Ricardo, David, 320
Richardson, Jacques G., Foreword, 3-18
Richardson, Jr., John M., 12, 115-129, 319
Risk assessment, 10
Roberts, Nancy, 163
Roberts, Peter, 121
Robotics, 7
Rousseau, Jean Jacques, 108

Schrödinger, Erwin, 268, 289
Science, social study of
    center vs. periphery, 210-211, 228-229
    defined, 209-210
    Hungary, case study of, 211-228
    physics, 312-313, 314
Science and Future Choice, 14
Science and technology
    effect of quantum mechanics on,
        285-302
    utilization of research in
        components of, 192-195
        global problems, 203-205
        interactive model, 195-197
        national R&D vs. societal system, 187,
            189-190
        proposed focus, 191-192
        theory of finalization, 197-199
        three aspects of, 187
Science policy, international, 228-229
Scientific view, provisional nature of, 318.
    See also Physics, mechanical determin-
    ism in.
Scolnik, Hugo, 120
Sendov, Blagovest, 65-70
Set theory, 72

Shred-out, evolutionary process of, 22
Simplex algorithm, 5
Sloan School of Management, 181
Social planning
    causality in, 102
    decision making in, 104
    goal-setting in, 106, 192-195
    politics of, 105-106. See also Modeling
        implementation, politics in.
    problem-flow vs. blueprint for future,
        106-109. See also Societies, na-
        tional goal-setting.
    utopianism in, 103
Societies. See also Modeling, socio-economic
    systems.
    approaches to study of, 101
    bringing about change in, 107-108
    confusion between form and function of
        government, 105
    homeostasis in, 203-205
    national goal-setting in, 104-106
    socialism vs. capitalism, 102
Sperry, Roger, 13
Stengers, Isabelle, 12, 303-315
Stolte-Heiskanen, Veronica, 12, 185-207
Structure, operational, 52
Swerdloff, Alissa, 12, 277-284
System dynamics models, 175-181
    activities contributing to development of,
        175-177
    definition of, 175
    use in global modeling, 116
System Dynamics National Model, 79, 167,
    168, 174, 181-183
    definition of, 181
    principle data sources, 177-178
    strengths, 182-183
    types of data, 168-175
Systems
    analysis, 5, 77-85
    an essential condition of, 93-94
        definition of, 88-89
        steps in, 89-91
    definition of, 19-20
    dynamic, 12-13, 77, 80, 164
    Earth as multiple, 30-31
    general theory of, 20-22
    living, 22-29
        emergents, 23-24
        homeostasis in, 25-29
    nonliving systems, 29-31
    seven levels of, 22-23
    living compared to nonliving, 24-25

Tamás, Pál, 209-230
Technological forecasting, 10

Technology. *See also* Science and technology, utilization of research.
  role of tools in, 252-254
  transfer, 47. *See also* Science and technology, utilization of research in.
  problems in, 197, 201-203
  proposed process, 191-197
  usual process, 186-191
Tensor Network theory of brain function (hyperspace), 282
Theory of chaos, 5
Thermodynamics, laws of, 30, 43, 305-306
Third World Calamity, 319
Thom, René, 5
"Time's arrow," dimension of irreversibility, 307-308
Toffler, Alvin, 104-105
Tóth, Esther, 265-275
Tse-tung, Mao, 127
Two Cultures, 201

Unesco (United Nations Educational, Scientific and Cultural Organization), 88, 319

United Nations, 23, 46, 47, 204
  Centre for Development, Planning, Projections and Policies (CDPPP), 121
  Department of International Economic and Social Affairs, 122
  ESCAP (Economic and Social Commission of Asia and the Pacific) region, 121, 125
University of Geneva, 124
Urban and regional planning, 87-99
  a consultative process, 98
  purpose of, 96
  use of mathematical models in, 87-99
Universal models, attempts to create, 77-78

Warsaw Pact, 23
Weber, Max, 107
World Health Organization, 10

Zermelo-Frankel-Skolem (ZFS) axiomatic set, 72